TIN PAN ALLEY

A CHRONICLE OF THE AMERICAN
POPULAR MUSIC RACKET

BY

ISAAC GOLDBERG

NEW YORK · 1930
THE JOHN DAY COMPANY

PRINTED IN THE U. S. A.

FOR THE JOHN DAY COMPANY, INC.

BY THE QUINN & BODEN COMPANY, INC., RAHWAY, N. J.

TO GEORGE GERSHWIN

for the "Rhapsody in Blue,"
the "Concerto in F," "An
American in Paris," and
not least for . . . . .
his unaffected friendship

ABOUT THE AUTHOR

ISAAC GOLDBERG is a native of Boston. He was graduated from Harvard in 1910, *summa cum laude*, and in 1912 received his Doctorate in Romance Philology. While at Harvard he did intensive outside work in musical theory and composition.

He has been a magazine and newspaper editor and a lecturer on music and belles-lettres. He is addicted to radio, "talkies," musical comedies, puns, toys of every description and head-splitting volumes of esthetics. He was rocked to sleep with the melodies of Gilbert and Sullivan and is generally accepted in this country as the outstanding Savoyard authority.

Mr. Goldberg's published works include the following:

SIR WILLIAM S. GILBERT
STUDIES IN SPANISH-AMERICAN LITERATURE
THE DRAMA OF TRANSITION
BRAZILIAN LITERATURE
THE MAN MENCKEN
HAVELOCK ELLIS
THE THEATRE OF GEORGE JEAN NATHAN
THE STORY OF GILBERT AND SULLIVAN
THE FINE ART OF LIVING
TIN PAN ALLEY

Introduction

THIS is a book that needed to be written, and we are all grateful to Dr. Goldberg for having written it. American popular music has become a very important part of American life; it has reached, indeed, as appears from the chapters upon Ragtime and Jazz, into the hearts of many European countries. It is one of the most colorful aspects of the American scene and, as the American Society of Authors, Composers and Publishers attests, it is getting into the class of Big Business. Tin Pan Alley, in a word, is a unique phenomenon, and there is nothing in any other country of the world to compare with it. New York, being the musical and theatrical center of the nation, where most songs and stage acts are made, naturally gave rise to the Alley of the Tin Pans.

. . . .

With this enormous increase of interest we who engage in song writing are being asked more often than ever by laymen as well as by aspiring composers for our formula, if any: just how, where, why and when we write our music. In placing my experience on the record here, I wish not to stress my own work, but to correct a few of the many popular misconceptions about song writing.

Often one hears that composing a song is an easy affair. All a number needs for success, it seems, is thirty-two bars; a good phrase of eight bars used to start the refrain is repeated twice more with a new eight-bar added which is much less important.

INTRODUCTION

It sounds simple, of course, but personally I can think of no more nerve-racking, no more mentally arduous task than making music. There are times when a phrase of music will cost many hours of internal sweating. Rhythms romp through one's brain, but they're not easy to capture and keep; the chief difficulty is to avoid reminiscence.

Out of my entire annual output of songs, perhaps two—or at the most, three—come as a result of inspiration. We can never rely on inspiration. When we most want it, it does not come. Therefore the composer does not sit around and wait for an inspiration to walk up and introduce itself. What he substitutes for it is nothing more than talent plus his knowledge. If his endowment is great enough, the song is made to sound as if it were truly inspired.

Making music is actually little else than a matter of invention aided and abetted by emotion. In composing we combine what we know of music with what we feel. I see a piece of music in the form of a design. With a melody one can take in the whole design in one look; with a larger composition, like a concerto, it is necessary to take it piece by piece and then construct it so much longer. No matter what they say about "nothing new under the sun," it is always possible to invent something original. The song writer takes an idea and adds his own individuality to it; he uses his capacity for invention in arranging bars his own way.

Composing at the piano is not a good practice. But I started that way and it has become a habit. However, it is possible to give the mind free rein and use the piano only to try what you can hear mentally. The best method is one which will not permit anything to hold you down in any way, for it is always easier to think in

GEORGE GERSHWIN

a straight line without the distraction of sounds. The mind should be allowed to run loose, unhampered by the piano, which may be used now and then only to stimulate thought and set an idea aflame. The actual composition must be done in the brain. Too much, however, should not be left to the memory. Sometimes, after the phrase seems safe in the mind, it will be lost by the next day. When I get a phrase which I am not sure I will remember the following day I set it down on paper at once. Occasionally compositions come in dreams, but rarely can they be remembered when you wake. On one occasion I did get out of bed and write a song. That number, incidentally, is one of my recent compositions, "Strike Up the Band!"

Like the pugilist, the song writer must always keep in training. He must try to write something every day. I know that if I don't do any writing for several weeks I lose a great deal of time in catching my stride again. Hence I am always composing.

My work is done almost exclusively at night, and my best is achieved in the fall and winter months. A beautiful spring or summer day is least conducive to making music, for I always prefer the outdoors to the work. I don't write at all in the morning, for the obvious reason that I am not awake at the time. The afternoon I devote to physical labor—orchestrations, piano copies, etc. At night, when other people are asleep or out for a good time, I can get absolute quiet for my composing. Not that perfect peace is always necessary; often I have written my tunes with people in the same room or playing cards in the next. If I find myself in the desired mood I can hold it until I finish the song.

Many of us have learned to write music by studying the most successful songs published. But imitation can go only so far. The young song writer may start by imitating a successful composer he admires, but he must break away as soon as he has learned the maestro's strong points and technique. Then he must try to develop his own musical personality, to bring something of his own invention into his work.

For some song writers it is not even absolutely essential that they know anything about music. Many of the popular composers with the greatest number of successes to their credit can't read a line of music. What they have is an innate sense of melody and rhythm; all they seek is to write a simple tune that the public can easily remember. In order to write longer compositions, the study of musical technique is indispensable. Many people say that too much study kills spontaneity in music, but although study may kill a small talent, it must develop a big one. In other words, if study kills a musical endowment, that endowment deserves to be killed. I studied piano for four years, and then harmony. And I shall continue to study for a long time.

.   .   .   .

Most of what I have said, naturally, is drawn from my own experience, and may be quite different from the experiences of others. Dr. Goldberg gives a glimpse into the methods pursued by various authors and composers.

I agree with him that the popular song of to-day partakes of the nature of folk song. Foster's tunes, which we now venerate as folk songs, were in their own day just popular songs. I agree with him, too, in his conception of the waltz as a fundamental, undying dance. Willard Huntington Wright, in *The Creative Will* (that was before he became S. S. Van Dine and went in for a career of crime-fiction) pointed out the superiority of the 3/4 rhythm to all other dance rhythms,—a superiority that lay in its natural balance of accents. In a 3/4 dance, the feet alternate accents in the successive bars. In 2/4 or 4/4 time the same foot lands always on the same accent.

Dr. Goldberg suggests that perhaps the jazz habit of shifting the normal accented beat from the first and third to the second and fourth beats of the measure may be not only an attempt to shake off routine, but also an unconscious balancing of effects. The jazz situation, by the way, has for years been all jazzed up; among other things, the treatment of ragtime and jazz in *Tin Pan Alley* goes far to clear up the muddled situation.

There is, no doubt, increasing sophistication in Racket Row; yet I am sure that there will always be a market for sweet, sentimental songs, as there will always be a sweet, ingenuous public.

.   .   .   .

Tin Pan Alley is not only a valuable addition to our archives of Americana; it is a swell, a gorgeous story.

GEORGE GERSHWIN.

Table of Contents

List of Illustrations

TIN PAN ALLEY

1. «Vamp Till Ready . . .»

TIN PAN ALLEY. . . . The man who first coined this phrase was in his way a minor American poet. Into an amazingly graphic —and auditive!—metaphor he crowded a description that in each of its three terms is vividly suggestive. Tin . . . it is the one metal to suit the dull reverberations of the passing popular song. Pan . . . the one instrument to sound its flat repetitions, its tinny monotony. The raucous troubadours of the obvious, the minnesingers of beery and synthetic passions, wander well off the highways of song, far from fragrant meadow and field. They populate, and sometimes infest, the alleys of the modern city where, at times, a flower pushes its way up from beneath the pavement. Alley . . . not even street. The hinterland of song, where dwell the stepchildren of art. TIN PAN ALLEY. . . .

It is a phrase that comes evidently from the Alley itself—or from sympathetic Newspaper Row—bestowed not in top-lofty condescension but in a certain fondness that cannot be entirely concealed beneath the commercialism of Songsters' Avenue. These are hard-boiled ladies and gentlemen, not in business for their health, as they will assure you. Staff notes into bank notes might be their motto, and their heraldic device a loud-speaker rampant. Yet not infrequently, like Casanova playing the magician for a charmer, they fall a prey to their own incantations and by their own deceptions are taken in. They weep at their ballads, and laugh to the tune of their optimistic formulas, their smiles-through-tears. To repeat a lie endlessly is to establish its truth. And can it be really a lie if it sells a million copies?

If there is crassness in Tin Pan Alley, there is a trace of glamor, too. If it is an ideal breeding-place for sentimentality and cynicism, it is sometimes bathed in the glow of its tinsel dreams. At its height, it attracted a type of minstrel who cried in earnest over his humble ditties—who philosophized like a weeping Carpenter —who sang sermons to the Good Life and smiled at Fortune. To sing, even the lowest type of ribald song—to versify, even the most patent doggerel—is to take wing, if but for a moment, above the material concerns of earth. Between the god Pan, who is dead, and the great God Tin Pan—a tin god who lives down in Our Alley—is a bond of breath as insubstantial as the air that blew once from Pan's pipes over the landscape that was Greece—as insubstantial, but as inshatterable.

That sober roisterer, "Hank" Mencken, supposedly first among the New Inhumanists, ends his *American Language* with a most humane coda: "In all human beings, if only understanding be brought to the business, dignity will be found, and that dignity cannot fail to reveal itself, soon or late, in the words and phrases with which they make known their high hopes and aspirations and cry out against the intolerable meaninglessness of life."

Let us transpose this, into a simpler key, for the untrained voices that sing our popular songs. For song, in all likelihood, came before speech, and even in Tin Pan Alley it phrases, however blunderingly, however stereotypically, the fundamental hopes and disillusionments of this, our common living.

[2]

The professional parlors of Broadway . . . Hothouse of America's popular music.

From a hundred hives of melody rises, skyscraper-high, a mad drone of words and tunes, in a counterpoint of chaos. Out through the windows, on wings of song, fly these ephemerids to enjoy their life of a day and to pass on that life to their successors in a long line that produces the illusion of immortality. The song dies; the singing lives on.

Once, in the days when the popular song had not yet taken on airs of sophistication, these parlors were humble, unpretentious rooms, as comfortably dirty as a newspaper office. An eight-by-ten compartment . . . A lame hat-rack . . . A roll-top desk crammed with an indigestion of documents . . . A battered upright piano, pocked with cigarette stains . . . An un-self-conscious spittoon. In these dingy quarters first were heard the ditties that made their way around the world.

With increasing business came added accommodations for the singers who, in these cubicles, were trained in the art of putting over the song. A row of cells would be ranged along a narrow corridor; into these, at certain hours of the day, would retire the artists of vaudeville, there to consider the new lists and to select what most suited their needs and their precious personalities. If Caruso could not read a note, why should they be ashamed of pleading guilty to technical ignorance? In all likelihood, the composer himself was a musical illiterate. The paper on which the words and music are printed is, in any case, dead until the "artist" resurrects it from the mute symbols. And so, if need be, they learn their ditties by the honorable method of rote—by the sheer impact of repetition.

[3]

TIN PAN ALLEY

The old drilling ground is gone whither the hits of yesterday are gone. And what a Phœnix has risen from these ashes! There are professional departments suggestive of Spanish stuccos and Mediterranean languors. You could drive an automobile around the place in traffical comfort. (When the Babel of rehearsal is at its height, it sounds as if someone were doing this very thing.) Were it not for the heterogeneous sounds issuing from the rooms that run along two legs of the square, the air might be monastic. Other professional departments desert this simplicity for a riot of modernism. Pluggers' Den has become Pluggers' Paradise. It is the new scenery; but the play remains the same.

These temples of art have their presiding deities,—the staff singers and pianists who serve as the fuglemen of the trade. The compartments are their warerooms and they are the models, as it were, on which the big-time and small-time virtuosi try out the latest musical styles. The vaudevillians listen as the resident song-ster sings them the latest hit—we hope it will be one—roaring them gently as any sucking dove. Does it fit them? Is it their type? Can they panic their public with it? (*Can* they? Why, in Schenectady last week they simply stole the show with "If Hearts Were Flowers, I'd Be a Bouquet"!)

Why the compartments should be there at all is a puzzle. They shut out sight, perhaps, but not sound. Notes leak thickly through the porous walls and these various tributaries meet in a river of noise that inundates the central reception room.

The singers, the vaudevillians, the company pianists, parceled off into these music boxes, strain for tonal privacy. In vain. Tenors, altos, bassos, sopranos, merge in a communism of keys. Or a battle of music. The effect is unwittingly modernistic. The

song that you will be hearing over the radio next week, and singing unconsciously the week after, is in E flat, and it can hardly
help if the lady learning it has to compete with a file-voiced tenor
who is trying to wipe an accidental off her staff with his
whining ballad in B flat. It isn't the easiest thing in the world
for a male quartet, being initiated into the mysteries of a specially scored chorus, to manage an oily blue chord in A major
while an equally oily contralto, bottled up in the next cell with
a perspiring pianist, is wailing plaintively, if none too securely,
in G.

> "From Harmony, from heavenly Harmony
>   This universal frame began:
> When Nature underneath a heap
>   Of jarring atoms lay
> And could not heave her head."

By sheer coincidence there is a moment's rest in the cacophony.
A moment's, only. Before another measure the racket is loose
again. A rhythmic accompaniment being thumped into the prima
donna's ear, so that she'll be sure to find herself off beat at the
right spot . . . "—that I ask is love!" . . . A jazz "break" on
the unprotesting keys . . . The quartet goes suddenly silent, and
the place seems somehow strangely vacant. . . . "And You Broke
My Heart on Two-Time Old Times Square!" . . .

Oh, say, can't you see, through the very walls, in a sort of ecto-
plasmic radiance, these artists flinging their precious personalities
across the visioned footlights?

Yes. Dawn—a dawn that begins at high noon—has come up
like thunder over Tin Pan Alley Bay.

Wandering minstrels, these (wandering often away from the key) . . . Things of shreds and patches, of ballads, songs and snatches. A few hours later, when the June Moon has set upon their revels—say, at two or three in the afternoon—a transformation takes place. Out of all this disharmony the various strands unravel themselves, and each is woven into its own pattern of amusement. We have not heard the band rehearsals, as they take place in the morning—or on the roof—so as not to drown out altogether the human voices. Free rehearsal quarters in return for pushing one of the company's hits. . . . That night the band is seated before a microphone, ready to play, for the first time, by special permission of the copyright owners, a special arrangement of the latest song from the pen of one of our foremost composers. The singers, on stage and in cabaret, are crooning or pantomiming or reciting or enacting—at times they simply sing—the new hit.

The public be damned—and served.

Yonder, across invisible pathways of the air, beyond the illuminated motley of Broadway, before rosaries of variegated footlights, in movie houses that can hold the population of a large town, in unfragrant shacks little wider than the screen that catches the shadowy magic of the evening—yonder lies the Master and the Slave whose name is Public.

Master, because the songs of Tin Pan Alley are aimed at its heart and the dances at its feet. The denizens of the Alley have their sharp ears ever to the ground, listening to the vibrations of popular interest. They are, overwhelmingly, the journalists—sometimes the reporters—of music.

Slave, because the songs do entrance its heart, and the dances ensnare its feet. Because these ballads and snatches are made of its own vernacular and, at the same time, make it over in turn. Tin Pan Alley at once follows the taste of the crowd and creates that taste. The influence between Public and Alley is strangely reciprocal; it is a living circuit in which the interchange is constant. Each has re-made the other in its image, until something like complete fusion has been effected.

Poets, the wise saw tells us, are not made; they are born. Popular songs are not only born, still or loud; they must be made.

Only God can make a tree, but the songs of the street and of the lighter theater are made for—and by—fools like you and me. It is a fanciful folly that moves them, laughing at such luxuries as inspiration, yet often hewing its path through mild hysteria to just that inspiration which it denies. It is easy enough to account for a hit after it has happened. Poe did a clever job of it himself when he told, altogether too rationally, how he came to write "The Raven." It is doubtful whether even the unpretentious manufacturer of our song and dance successes can foresee a happy strike, can offer a recipe. Just why, for example, did A suddenly interpolate that couplet at the end of the first verse—it is known among lyrists as the "vest"—which caught the imagination of the public and made them eager for the chorus to follow? What was there in the lines that had everybody tagging them on to conversations the next day? What wrote their way into the daily wisecracks of newspaperdom? The lyrist himself could answer only, "Oh, I don't know. It just came to me." That, in its simple way, is a paraphrase of "inspiration." And could the composer explain, in cold blood, the source of that little rhythmic twist, that sudden turn of the melody, which spelled the difference between a hit and a miss

[7]

—between a "wow" and a "flop"? Yes; after the fact, but not before.

Inspiration is a capricious visitor; it comes to shanties as to symphony halls. Nor is it an unknown word among the routineers of Tin Pan Alley. Said a connoisseur of the Alley to me only the other day: "The old-time psychology of the hit songwriters only turning out hits because of 'hunger,' as they have it in Tin Pan Alley, is again proving itself. Berlin, Donaldson and the rest prove it. The average songsmith now is among the plutocrats of the Alley, according to old-time standards, getting $750 and $1000 weekly as drawing accounts, and yet not being sufficiently inspired to turn out a hit. Now they just fit a theme song to a situation and if it doesn't sell, well, it's just the same to them, as they have their annual guarantees of $40,000 to $50,000. Hitherto they've earned that amount only by delivering one or two sensational hits. Berlin's veering away from the mob through his society marriage explains him. Donaldson, when he was flat, wrote 'Blue Heaven,' 'At Dawning' and so on. Since he has taken his profits as a member of the firm of Donaldson, Douglas and Gumble, he hasn't delivered."

Like his more cultured brother the song racketeer can roll his eye in a fine frenzy, seeking for his machine-made product a habitation (not too local; indeed, as universal as the combined agencies of publicity can manage it) and a name. Especially a name. For he knows what's in a title. The trade, indeed, has developed a specialist who deals in titles alone. The company that produced the talkie *Burlesque* paid to Havelock Ellis no less than $10,000 for the four words, "The Dance of Life." (Havelock Ellis and the talkies! What hath God wrought!) Titlers in the song business hardly collect $2500 per word; yet the fact that such experts exist at all is eloquent tribute to the importance attached by the music industry to a catchy phrase.

The music industry . . . The poet and composer of our dreams works at the caprice of the sun, the moon and the stars. These are their leisurely calendar. The men who write our songs and dances know these cosmic beauties as so many stage props; they have seen them on the front covers of the music sheets; most important of all, they know that sun rhymes with *one* (the only one, naturally); that moon and June and spoon and tune are as inseparable as ham and eggs; if they don't come together, something is wrong with the normal order of things. To rhyme June with rune would be almost *lèse majesté*. Inspiration in Racket Row punches a time clock. Time, tide and mass production wait for no man. The mills of these gods grind rapidly and they grind exceeding well.

Recall, from that charming fantasy, *Beggar on Horseback,* the scene in which the composer-hero, forever wailing about his unfinished symphony—the masterpiece that a hostile world will not let him write—is thrust behind the bars of a cage and bidden to produce for the seething low-brows of the nation. By the waters of Babylon (Long Island, as Willie Howard would add), there he sat him down and wept when he remembered his symphony. . . . "For there they that carried us away captive required of us a song; and they that wasted us required of us mirth, saying, Sing us one of the songs of Zion . . ." He was only a songbird in a gilded cage: the symbol, supposedly, of high talent trapped in the snare of Broadway. Let him but write a hit, and what a transformation! The gilded bars turn to ingots of gold; they melt away into his pockets, and he is free.

[9]

Listen to him in his cage. You wish that the box were sound-proof. He has struck a phrase that is pregnant with possibilities, but oh! the obstetrics of it! Let us imagine that our composer in the metaphorical cage is one who can play with more than a single finger. He has got off to a good melodic start. Words? What need has he of words? Let the lyrist worry about them, later, when the tune is done. Beginnings, here, contrary to the proverb, are easy; it is the ends that are hard. He plays over some four or five bars. Shall he ascend now, or descend? Shall he change that dubious note in the harmony—we assume that he knows what a chord is— or shall he take a chance on a mild dissonance? Once, twice, thrice he plays over the progression. It simply will not sound right. He doesn't know why, although a student from an elementary class in harmony could tell him that some bad voice-leading in the inner parts is betraying him into the false chord that has him snagged.

Harmony? Musical grammar? What is harmony to him, or he to harmony? As much as the grammar of language is to his word-partner—namely, slightly more than nothing at all. A too close attention to correct diction would ruin chances by stamping the lines as high-brow. This music, these words, are refreshingly full of "ain't's," "between you and I's," "do like I do's."

So, let the troublesome spot pass. No matter. The arranger can help the composer out of that hole. What's an arranger for, any-how? He merely fills in the picture. The grand idea belongs to the fellow at the piano, torturing his thought into an appearance of sense. Broadway is over-populated with expert pianists—didn't Saint-Saëns, in his *Carnival of the Animals*, include them in his musical menagerie? Theorists swarm in every publishing firm. They can name all the chords; they can write down a song faster than you can sing it to them; they were fed on the classics. But they lack musical "it." They have all the knowledge, but none of the ideas that can be turned into cash. They're like the swell stenographers in Mr. Babbitt's office: they can spell all the hard words and turn out a snappy looking letter, but they must get all the ideas from the boss.

Doesn't Providence watch over babes and fools? What was the moral of *June Moon?* You mustn't aim over the heads of your public. In fact, if you're above that public, better hide it. If you're not an inch higher than their brows, so much the better for your chances. If the sap from Schenectady in this take-off by Lardner and Kauffman had been a trifle smarter, he would have missed out on both the song hit and the girl. As it happened, the reward for his golden mediocrity was gold and gold hair—the shekels and the blonde. Of such is the alchemy of Broadway.

No. The arranger, as the composer will assure you, is a handy man about the house. What would he do or be without the creative genius of the composer?

And what, as both performer and publisher will ask you, would the composer be without the publisher and the performer? The lyrist and the musician merely write the words and music. But who markets it? Who puts it over? Who "wows" it? Who brings it to life and sends the public to the department stores for the sheets, sometimes to the tramp, tramp, tramp of a million purchasers?

> Sing a song of Tin Pan,
> And Cock Robin, too.
> Who really scores the hit
> That magnetizes you?

[11]

TIN PAN ALLEY

"I," says the Lyrist,
"With *my* words and patter;
Take *my* lines away
And the rest doesn't matter."

"I," cries Composer,
"With *my* tune and tinkle.
Without them the song
Would be dead as Van Winkle!"

(Arranger looks on
With a cynical frown.
"He thinks up the tune,
But *I* set it down.")

"You?" sneers the Plugger.
"Go tell that to Grover.
You guys set it down,
But *I* put it *over!*"

Mr. Publisher smiles.
"And whose shekels stake it?
If it wasn't for *me*,
How could *you* fellows make it?"

From the wings speaks a ghost.
"How these kids run amuck!
Shall I tell them the truth,—
That it's me,—Lady Luck?"

2. Before the Flood

WHAT is American music? And what is American popular music? For there seems to be a difference. One of our most gifted and radical critics of music and the other arts, Paul Rosenfeld, begins his monograph on the music of the country with the categorical statements that American music is not jazz and that jazz is not music. One of our most conservative and academic spirits, Daniel Gregory Mason, shakes hands with Rosenfeld across the keys. Aren't these violent reactions to a violent stimulus? Nobody, to my knowledge, has ever said that American music is only jazz; to say that jazz is not music is to issue an ukase instead of exercising discrimination. The distinction between so-called art music and the music of the people is one of degree, not kind. Often the two musics overlap, not only in interest but in value. To say that popular music aims only at superficial entertainment, while art music seeks to establish values inherent in esthetic relationships is to indicate a difference of critical approach, a difference in temperament on the part of the special composer and the special public. To be sure, popular music of later days is a frankly commercial pursuit. It thus tends to establish formulas, to turn out a product of robots, by robots and for robots. In a word, in its own way, it becomes aridly intellectual, just as the cheapest melodrama, in its own way, becomes intellectual, formulized, and only pseudo-emotional. Yet the aim of the composer may be one thing and his result another. Music may hardly be judged by the conscious purposes of its practitioners. And it has happened, strangely enough, that a popular composer, ignorant of his craft, has achieved a music that stands on its own as an esthetic creation.

Is it really important that there should be a national music? Does not this interest belong as much to history as to art? Can a composer, by taking thought, add cubits to his national stature? If there is anything valid in nationalism as evidenced by art— even in a minor art—will this not appear in the work of a composer, or of a poet, without too conscious an effort? First let there be good music, and good poetry. The adjective of nationality can wait.

The matter, of course, is not altogether so simple as this. We have had popular music since whites first landed on this soil. Ours arrived from England, with the language. As it came into contact with each varying phase of life in the New World, it underwent a change, now obvious, now subtle, until in time the song of the people was no more pure English than was the language of the people. Song is a form of speech reserved chiefly for emotional utterance. A history of song, especially popular song, may contain, deeply imbedded, the history of a people. If it be light, frothy, superficial music—why, then, life is not all depth. . . . Dost thou think, because thou art virtuous, there shall be no more cakes and ale? . . . And since when have cakes—let us not speak of ale—been forbidden to the virtuous?

There was a time when talk of a possible great American opera led inevitably to the Indian. He was the aborigine of our continent; therefore, what more natural than that he should rear his head in our opera as on our coins? A theory such as this would find far greater justification in South America than in the America of the North. There has been, in the lands under the Southern Cross, a genuine intermingling of the Caucasian and the redman. Among us, from the early days of the Indian wars, the national policy has been one of segregation; we have smoked the pipe of peace . . . and the Indian has virtually disappeared. The Indian was never a vital part of our life; he was never real to us, even in the novels of Cooper. He was a creature of the circus; of the dime novel; of the carved wooden image that served as the protective deity of cigar stores. His powwows never became a social vogue, like the Harlem cabaret. He was never even a slave, exercising upon us that peculiar influence which the conquered, throughout history, have wrought upon the conqueror.

Lately, another attack upon the American popular song was launched in terms of nationalism. Mr. Henry Cowell, the persuasive and not altogether unconvincing advocate of new harshnesses in music, points out that the Anglo-Saxon has had nothing to do with the development of jazz. "We know that jazz is accepted by most Americans as something delectable and to be enjoyed, but that it comes to them just as much as something from the outside as it does to the European, who, it must be pointed out, has also accepted jazz in the same way. The Anglo-Saxon American has no more talent for writing or playing jazz than the European. Both of them are bungling at it."

The road to skill lies paved with treacherous cobblestones. There are American *musics*; need there be *an* American music? Deems Taylor has wisely reminded us [1] that we are not a homogeneous race, and that this has important consequences for our

[1] *Civilization in the United States.* An Inquiry by Thirty Americans. Edited by Harold Stearns. New York, 1922. See essay on "Music," pp. 199-214.

musical life. His own operas, *The King's Henchman* and *Peter Ibbetson*, certainly do not err upon the side of musical chauvinism, but, by that same token, neither do they interpret his country or his age. (Who said that they must?) The United States, a political and an economic experiment, is perforce an artistic experiment also. It need not aim at a unity of racial expression before—if ever—it achieves a racial unity. (And, again, who said it must? Is not race a disintegrating concept?) Its peculiar conditions produce peculiar, but not therefore insignificant, results.

Nicolas Slonimsky (his polyglot, cosmopolitan background, combined with a judicious eclecticism, provide for him an excellent vantage-point of observation) has pointed out an interesting distribution of our serious composers' interests. The New Englanders incline toward musical Indianism (Edgar Stillman Kelley, Henry Hadley, Paul Hastings Allen, Henry F. Gilbert, Charles Ives); the New Yorkers lean toward jazz.[2]

There are, of course, exceptions. Gilbert was, in his charmingly simple way, a pioneer of symphonic ragtime long before the days of Gershwin and Copland. Yet why need we look, in our more serious musicians, for a single style that shall be a blending of the Indian and the negro influences? Why may not these, in the richness of our national life, flow in parallels down to the sea? Gilbert, in his conscious Americanism, suggested an amalgamation. In the end, his music proved to be—Gilbert, and this was eminently as it should have been.

What has actually happened is the recession of the Indian influence. The Indian era in our music, as exemplified in the theories and the suites of MacDowell and Gilbert, is, for the

[2] *Modern Music.* February-March, 1930. "Composers of New England," pp. 24-27.

moment, over. Herbert's hybrid opera, *Natoma*, was still-born. Even for our popular songs the Indian vogue ("Hiawatha," "Navajo") may have vanished for good. But who dares prophesy about popular songs? . . .

It needs but a significant composer to establish the musical importance of our Jewish, our Irish, our Italian element. As for the Anglo-Saxon, he has *accepted* jazz; he has let it speak to him and for him. He may yet write it with a skill that crosses the bridge from imitation to creation. Yet, if he does not, what can this mean but that America has more than one music, and that the authenticity of its various musics lies beneath geographical divisions and racial quotas?

Meantime let us notice that the "Anglo-Saxon American" is himself not an unmixed breed. And if he has not been able to write or play the latest manifestations of our popular music, he has not been unvariably the straight-jacketed caricature that we have come to know as the Puritan.

Strangely enough, the first native son of American music was a lively forerunner of our own dancing day.

Our early "popular" music was naturally restricted to hymn and hurrah—to the religious and the patriotic. Historians are generally agreed that the first really popular song in the English world of the Atlantic shore was the "Liberty Song," first published in the *Boston Gazette* of July 18, 1768. The words were written by John Dickinson of Delaware and had been inspired by the refusal of the Massachusetts Legislature to rescind the Circular Letter of Feb. 11, 1768, relating to the imposition of duties and taxes upon the American colonies. Two lines from the song will suffice:

[17]

Come join hand in hand, brave Americans all,
And rouse your bold hearts at fair Liberty's call. . . .

However, if we fought England with our own words, we sang
them to her tunes. The "Liberty Song" took its music from a piece
composed by Dr. Boyce for Garrick's "Hearts of Oak"; the
original song had been sung at Drury Lane Theatre, London, at
Christmastide, 1759.

Words of like import would be set to sacred tunes. On July 22,
1774, there first appeared a patriotic exhortation attributed to
Meshech Weare, who was to become, two years later, president of
the State of New Hampshire. He made—in view of what since
has happened to American liberties—a strangely moderate
request:

Rouse every generous thoughtful mind,
The rising danger flee,
If you would lasting freedom find,
Now then, abandon tea! . . .

So, too, our first popular sentimental song to achieve print was
foreign in tune, adapted from the old Irish air, "Langolee." The
words appeared in the *Philadelphia Ledger,* in 1775, as "The
Banks of Dee." The hero was a Scotchman who had left to join
the British forces in America; the heroine, of course, was a girl
who had been left behind.

Our "Yankee Doodle," our "America," our "Star-Spangled
Banner" of the War of 1812—these beat and sing and wave to
music from Europe. We sang our own words before we wrote our
own tunes. Uncomprehending carpers look scornfully down upon
Tin Pan Alley because its practice is to write the music first—for

[18]

the music is the thing—and then fit the words to the music. Yet this is precisely what our own patriots, in the fervor of their advocacy, performed. . . . It was not long, however, before something like a completely native product appeared. It was a poor thing, but it was our own. The long trek to Tin Pan Alley had begun.

Puritan into Jazzer.

The gentlemen whose chief concern is with priority rather than with values seem undecided as to whether the first American composer was Frederick Hopkinson of Philadelphia or William Billings of Boston. Billings, to be sure, was born eleven years before the composer and poet of "My Days Have Been So Wondrous Free," but on the other hand, Hopkinson's famous song was published eleven years before Billings's horrisonous "New England Psalm-Singer." Knowing Billings as we do from his writings and from the impression that he left upon his contemporaries, it is not likely that he would have kept any of his compositions in manuscript for more than a decade. He was not one to hide his light under a bushel. Hopkinson, born a British subject, became an ardent patriot. He was a friend of Washington, to whom he dedicated eight songs, and of Franklin, Jefferson, and Joseph Bonaparte; he was a member of the Continental Congress and one of the signers of the Declaration of Independence. He was in the aristocratic tradition, a lawyer, a college man, a player upon the harpsichord and the organ, facile with the pen, and even an inventor. Billings was a commoner. But so far as we know, he was the first American to make of music a regular vocation, and therein

ll the rest his true claim
to historic significance.

Music, as its pioneers in America conceived it, must have been imported into New England with the heroes, the morality and the vermin of the *Mayflower*. It was not so much an art in itself as a means of giving discreet testimony unto the goodness and omnipotence of the Lord. Otherwise, it was suspect. A year before the *Mayflower* arrived, the first slaves had been landed in Virginia, and in the course of time they were to transform the English remembrances of their masters into haunting spirituals. The music of the New Englanders yearned back to ancestral England, though it did not cling so closely to the original pattern as the tunes of the Virginians who had preceded them to these shores. It was a cloistered, an inhibited art. The music of the enslaved Negro yearned back to darkest Africa, and derived from tribal, open-air exuberance. It was a release and a compensation. But while the blacks were thus fashioning a new folk music in the South, the New England whites were debating the very propriety of singing at all.

There was subtle mischief, they suspected, in the exercise. Some held that it was well for men but wicked for the ladies. Others thought that no good Christian would ever sing right out in meeting; he would only chant to himself and God—in the pious phrase, "make melody in his heart." Others found that while they could listen to singing, as it issued from the untrained, ill-practiced throats of the early settlers, they felt impelled to draw the line at singing the Psalms. Their opponents argued that *only* the Psalms, and not hymns or anthems, might be sung, since the Hebrews had plainly sung the Psalms. Singing, again, was held by one group to be the sole right of Christians; the heathen Indians might be vouchsafed only the privilege of saying "Amen." All believed that real skill in singing concealed a devil. Musical composition was vanity. "To sing man's melody," wrote the Rev. John Cotton in 1647, "is only a vain show of art. . . . God cannot take delight in praises where the man of sin has a hand in making the melody."

The early New Englanders knew little about reading notes; some five tunes, carried in the memory, at first sufficed for their purposes of worship. The introduction of musical instruction, sorely as it was needed in the raucous congregations, was at first resisted with pious debate. The Pilgrims at Plymouth, less prosperous than the Boston Puritans, had developed, out of their lack of books, the practice of lining out the Psalms and hymns—a barbarous method whereby the deacon or minister, as musical fugleman, would sing the hymn line by line, followed by the rest of the congregation. The Puritans, closer in touch with the homeland, were more progressive, and soon outgrew this crude method. Singing societies appeared among them in the first quarter of the Eighteenth Century. The original collections of music, of course, were English, even when called "The American Harmony" (1769). The congregation gradually developed, out of its better singers, a choir, and the members of this choir, not exempt from the vanity of the rest of us, developed secular ambitions and sought for chances to sing with the exhibitionistic avidity of opera principals. The music they sang was quick to feel this ungodly influence and was soon on the road to profanation. We read of "fleshly anthems," and of "fuguing choruses" (lively capers amongst the usual four parts), and as a final tribute to the mun-

[21]

danity of the choir there appear at last genuine solo passages.

Boston, the cradle of what was once American Liberty, is also the true home of American music. It was there that William Billings was born on October 7, 1746, and there he died, in indigent circumstances, on September 26, 1800. He was twice married; in 1764 to Mary Leonard, and in 1774 to Lucy Swan. He had six children—five girls and a boy. The family Bible, from which these records derive, is still extant. His funeral was held on September 29, 1800, from the house of Mrs. Amos Penniman, in Chambers street, West Boston, and he was buried in Boston Common.

Chambers street, in the days of the Spanish-American War, was my own childhood's favorite playground, although at that time it was no longer the wild spot of a hundred years before. The Boston Common Burial-Ground still sprawls—a peaceful anachronism—across the historic acreage of the inviolate park in the heart of the city, while a few feet away a ball-field is noisy with future champions of the diamond, and across the street the air is melodious with orthophonic phonographs, loud-speakers, piano-players and the impatient honks of a pestilential automobile jam. I have looked over these crumbling stones, these decaying vaults, in vain for the name of Billings. He sleeps, our first American musician, in an unknown grave, lulled by strident noises that would have been dear to his swelling heart. For he was an American, a Yankee Doodle Boy, as well as—indeed more than—a composer, and he fondly loved his racket.

The gods had not favored him at birth. They had jazzed him up to begin with. He was not good to look upon. He was blind in one eye, one of his arms seems to have been somewhat withered, his legs were of uneven length, and his voice had a rasp that, when he grew up and sang in the choir, became a bellow. To this neglect of Nature he added his own. He was a slovenly fellow, and there was little in his trade—that of a tanner—to encourage personal cleanliness. For his physical shortcomings, however, he was quick to make up in an ambitious aggressiveness. Beyond a doubt he was one of our earliest go-getters; he was full of pep and personality. He blew his own horn lustily and let the trumpets sound before him.

In music he was self-taught. It was pupils of Billings who founded the Stoughton Musical Society, the oldest musical association in the United States, on November 7, 1786. The man, uncouthly original, had ideas of his own; they were grounded upon his long practical experience among the singers he labored with all his life. He was the father of the American church choir; he was the founder of all our singing schools; he was one of our first concert managers. He it was who first introduced a violoncello into church music. He began the use of the pitch-pipe. His part-music discovers him, finally, in the rôle of our first musical realist.

Practice Makes Imperfect.

His earliest warblings, crude and ungainly as himself, were certainly more wild than native. He wrote them down on the walls —even the hides—of his tannery, with chalk. More or less consciously, he was in rebellion against the English Psalm-books that had been in use for almost a century and a half—the Ravenscrofts, the Ainsworths, the Tansurs, the Tubbs, and all that dreary company. Billings moved, or rather, in all senses of the word, limped with the times. His crude artistic vitality sought release from the musical inhibitions of the church. He addressed the readers of his printed works with gusto and bluster. When the time had arrived for separation from England he enlisted his pen in the revolutionary cause and put forth a series of tunes that blend, in almost equal measure, the religious and the patriotic. He was something of a rhymester, too; the Orpheus of congregational singing became readily the Tyrtæus of the Revolution. He paraphrased the Psalms for the use of soldiers; he wrote his own clarion calls. The hearth and the bivouac were equally familiar with his stirring compositions. For stirring they were, though they rode rough-shod over the rules of harmony. Billings was no theorist; he learned by doing, although practice never made him perfect. In himself, almost, he was New England's one-man conservatory of music. Best known among his friends was the rebel Samuel Adams, who, as singing companion of the leather-lunged William, must often have had his voice drowned out by the uproar of the composer.

Billings knew little or nothing about the rules of composition, and easily rationalized his impatient ignorance into a sort of musical Rousseauism. "Nature," he proclaimed, "is the best dictator." He was not, he declared, to be hedged in by rules, nor did he expect that others would follow his personal procedure. "Every composer for himself," he cried, as he set forth to take Music by assault and battery.

Billings, to be sure, was not the discoverer of faster tempo in the music of his day. Though he was soon denounced as an American iconoclast, it was from English psalmodists that he borrowed the style that brought him such dishonor.

Billings rushed in where angels feared to tread. "The New England Psalm-Singer" is a strange and fearful thing—one of the

curiosities of musical literature. It is full of music evolved out
of the tanner's inner consciousness. Yet it by no means lacks a
certain fascination, sprung from its very uncouthness. Billings
seems to have been fond of a rhythmic melody and a melodic
bass; often he had his bass run parallel to the melody in thirds
and sixths, in a manner that is still current among such of the
clergy as feel impelled to sing impromptu harmonies to a hymn.
His music offers a free field to the connoisseur who delights to
pounce upon angular melodic lines, bad doublings, consecutive
fifths, and all the other familiar bugaboos that the modernists
have raised from the gutter to the throne.

The composer himself was almost as quick to repent as to sin.
Eight years separate his firstling from his second, which has come
down to us by the name that it soon won among its contemporaries:
"Billings' Best." Billings had a sense of humor that he could turn
upon himself. "Kind reader," he says, in the preface to this second
collection, "no doubt you remember that about ten (*sic*) years
ago I published a book entitled 'The New England Psalm-Singer,'
and truly a most masterly performance I thought it then to be.
How lavish was I of encomiums on this, my infant production!
Said I, thou art my Reuben, my first-born, the beginning of my
strength; but to my great mortification I soon discovered it was
Reuben in the sequel and Reuben all over. I have discovered that
many of the pieces were never worth my printing or your inspec-
tion."

It was this second and the fourth of Billings's books that won
him his reputation. For many years, says an unknown authority
of the *Musical Reporter*, "no other music . . . was heard throughout New England. Many of the New England soldiers who, during

the Revolutionary War, were encamped in the Southern States, had his popular tunes by heart, and frequently amused themselves singing them in camp, to the delight of all who heard them." It was in 1778, in an attempt—very successful, as it proved—to give expression to the temper of the times, that Billings wrote the first American war song, "Chester." It was his "Over There." The tune is fairly familiar to students of early Americana; it is, in any case, accessible in more than one reference-book, so that I need not transcribe it here. The complete words, however—also by Billings—are rather rare:

> Let tyrants shake their iron rod,
> And Slav'ry clank her galling chains,
> We fear them not, we trust in God,
> New England's God forever reigns.
>
> Howe and Burgoyne and Clinton, too,
> With Prescott and Cornwallis join'd,
> Together plot our Overthrow,
> In one Infernal league combin'd.
>
> When God inspired us, for the fight,
> Their ranks were broke, their lines were forc'd,
> Their Ships were Shatter'd in our sight,
> Or swiftly driven from our Coast.
>
> The Foe comes on with haughty Stride,
> Our troops advance with martial noise,
> Their Vet'rans flee before our Youth,
> And Gen'rals yield to beardless boys.
>
> What grateful Off'ring shall we bring,
> What shall we render to the Lord?

BEFORE THE FLOOD

Loud Hallelujahs let us Sing,
And praise His name on ev'ry Chord.

The words and tune were very popular with the troops. Notice the rhyming of *join'd* with *combin'd*. Billings's other patriotic compositions—words and music—include "Retrospect," "Independence," "Columbia," and a biblical paraphrase, "Lamentation over Boston," the last written while Boston was occupied by the red-coats. By the river of Watertown he sat him down and wept; yea, he wept as he remembered Boston.

The craziest exploit of Billings was undoubtedly his practical answer to the critics of his "Reuben." This music, they asserted, was, among other things, too simple. The intervals employed were almost limited to the third, the fifth, the octave. Where were those appetizing dissonances, the seventh and the ninth? What did this presumptuous tanner know about the sacrosanct rules of preparation, progression, modulation, resolution? In reply, Billings composed a four-part Babel which, with malice prepense, he labeled "Jargon." To this he added a long manifesto, addressed to the Goddess of Discord.

I venture the assertion that "Jargon" is one of the most interesting documents in our musical history. Somewhere in the soul of this eccentric Bostonian was an imp of jazz. "Jargon" is a musical *jeu d'esprit*, with an array of discords that would put a Stravinski or a Honneger to rout. Here, for Billings's critics, was a dash of musical billingsgate. One can picture their horror over the climax with its unabashed descent of sevenths between tenor and bass. There is not a single consonance in the piece after the hollow harmony of its opening. Billings's more practical critics showed their opinion of his music in unmistakable deeds.

[27]

After he had left the tannery for the uncertain life of a musician, he set himself up near the White Horse Tavern and hung out his shingle: "Billings: Music." Tin Pan Alley had been blue-printed. . . . One night two cats were found hanging from the sign by their tails. They were observing no rests in their concert; the composer, releasing them, could draw his own conclusions.

It is as a humorist, conscious and unconscious, that Billings is most likely to interest the contemporary American musician. He was, distinctly, a forecast of a national type. He had the inchoate impulses of a colonial and post-colonial George M. Cohan and George Gershwin. He was a born realist and he strove to live music, to rouse it from its cataleptic, droning doldrums into something with a pulse, a stir, a relationship to daily living. For this, one may gladly pardon him his transgressions. When he set, in a hymn, the sentiment "Clap your hands," he added the direction that the singers suit the action to the words. Billings must always have been talking to his choir; he could not keep himself out of the picture, even in his written pieces. Should there occur the words, "They shall laugh and sing," he set his singers a laughing chorus that looks heartier on paper than it must have sounded in actual performance.

"Modern Music."

The crowning achievement in his secular music, however, is his choric entertainment entitled (and the adjective is significant) "Modern Music." There is, in place of the usual tempo-indication at the beginning of the score, this N.B.: "After the Audience are seated and the Performers have taken the pitch *slyly* from the leader, the Song begins." I underscore the word *slyly* because, in itself, it is a commentary upon the man's psychology. So, for that matter, are the words of "Modern Music" in their entirety:

> We are met for a Concert of modern invention;
> To tickle the Ear is our present intention.
>   The Audience are seated
>   Expecting to be treated
> With a piece of the Best,
> With a piece of the Best.
>   And since we all agree
>   To set the tune on E
>   The Author's darling Key
> He prefers to the rest,
>   Let the Bass take the Lead
>   And firmly proceed
>   Till the parts are agreed,
> To fugue away, then change
>   To a brisker time
>   And up the Ladder climb,
>   Then down again, then mount the second time
>   And end the strain, then change the key
>   To pen five tones and flow in treble time.
>   The Note exceeding low keep down a while
>   Then rise by slow degrees;
>   The process surely will not fail to please.
> Through Common and Treble we jointly have run,
> We'd give you their essence compounded in one;
> Although we are strongly attached to the rest,
> Six-four is the movement that pleases us best.
> And now we address you as Friends to the cause,
> Performers are modest and write their own laws.

Although we are sanguine and Clap at the Bar,
'Tis the part of the hearers to clap their Applause.

The words, "Let the Bass take the Lead," are followed in the original by the entry of the other parts, each with words appropriate to its specific action at the time.

Yes, Billings had the soul of a modernist-jazzer-realist. "He was as realistic," asserts one commentator, not without exaggeration, "as Richard Strauss in a symphonic poem; and Billings would have recognized in Strauss a kindred spirit." Certainly in this Boston original dwelt remote, remote possibilities of a *Sinfonia Domestica*. He felt dimly the opportunities of musical characterization. We should remember him gratefully if but for one great service: he made his music live in a day when, utterly out of touch with the wonders that were happening in Europe, it threatened to become a series of undifferentiated dirges. He woke up his native Boston; he flooded the church with a little fresh air and tonic sunlight. He enriched the music of his country with something of the energy that thrilled in his own misshapen body and cantankerous soul. The fellow was, in his generation, alive.

3. Pearls of Minstrelsy

THE influence of the Negro upon the psychology of the American has been tremendous, and often most potent where it is most vehemently denied. The Mason and Dixon's line is written into our statute books and into our geographies; it is inscribed in our social categories; yet it never made an impression below the surface of our minds. The white may have educated the black; but that education has been returned in a dozen subtle ways. We taught him things; he taught us feelings. We gave him knowledge; he has helped to give us passion, which is not the meaner of the gifts. From the first, the white has been under some psychologic compulsion to mimic the Negro, at first in ridicule and superiority, then in understanding and sympathy. The Negro, at almost every step, has participated in the making of our popular song.

He re-worded the biblical teachings, he re-sang the hymns of the white, touching the words with his African fervor and simplicity, re-shaping the music and its rhythms with his racial, ancestral dances and rituals. Sophistication has worked its spell on him as on his white brother. There are many Negroes to-day who regard the spirituals with shame; they resent the uncouthness of these primitive outpourings and would relegate them to the hinterlands. They are redolent of slavery days, of low social strata, of a past that one would fain forget. The very best of the Negro singers, especially such as have won the favor of the white in concerts and on the stage, display a curious, and perhaps but half conscious, discoloration. While so many whites are trying to sing black, these blacks attempt to sing white. It is a strange competition.

Nor is it merely a fad. The recent rise of Harlem, the vogue of the colored revue, the recrudescence of Negro influence in jazz band, street song and concert hall, is not a new thing or a passing fashion. It is a phenomenon that is almost as old as the nation itself.

Before the various types of jazz was the modern coon song; before the coon song was the minstrel show; before the minstrel show was the plantation melody and the spiritual. It is safe to say that without the Negro we should have had no Tin Pan Alley; or, if this sounds like exaggeration, certainly Tin Pan Alley would have been a far less picturesque Melody Lane than it is to-day.

Why has the coon song become so representative of our popular music? Why is it impossible to think of our street songs for long without encountering the influence—whether pseudo or real—of the black? Why, whether in the early days of the southland, or in the contemporary life of Gotham, is the rhythm, the lingo, the accent of the Negro so persistent?

The Negro is the symbol of our uninhibited expression, of our uninhibited action. He is our catharsis. He is the disguise behind which we may, for a releasing moment, rejoin that part of ourselves which we have sacrificed to civilization. He helps us to a double deliverance. What we dare not say, often we freely sing. Music, too, is an absolution. And what we would not dare to sing in our own plain speech we freely sing in the Negro dialect, or in terms of the black. The popular song, like an unseen Cyrano,

A MINSTREL POSTER OF 1867

The Origin of Jazz

provides love phrases for that speechless Christian, the Public. And the Negro, a black Cyrano, adds lust to passion.

Can this be one of the reasons why the American Anglo-Saxon has held aloof from the exploitation and particularly the creation of songs in the musical vernacular? Can it be only a coincidence that the three races who have contributed most to our popular song—the Negro, the Irish and the Jew—should be the familiar examples of oppressed nationalities, credited with a fine intensity of inner life and with passions less bridled than those of the more conventional—not necessarily the more frigid—American Anglo-Saxon?

Compare this with our national attitude toward grand opera. To Americans, grand opera in English is still something of an incongruity. Passionate utterance upon the operatic stage looks too much like an undignified surrender to the emotions—ergo, a lack of efficiency—an admission that one has an erotic life. It is more proper to "foreigners." Or it is very well for musical comedy where the matter is laughed off between one scabrous jest and another, or disguised in the rhythms of a jazz number, to words that rarely rise above the status of a moronic caterwaul. Here, the Negro is our "foreigner." . . . Americans singing seriously of passion are not convincing to their fellow Americans . . . or to themselves.

The Negro of our popular song comes alive in a way that the Indian never did. One reason, of course, is that he is often the entertainer who writes the song and who sings it. He is the performer—constantly present in the flesh as in the imagination. He is, in a word, part and parcel of our life, whether rural or urban; he sang for us on the plantation; he sings for us in the cabaret.

Between Negro and Irishman, between Irishman and Jew, between Jew and Negro, stretch subtle bonds of sympathy that unite them under the surface tension of racial—and often artificially stimulated—antipathies.

Certainly I am not unmindful of the purely commercial aspect of Tin Pan Alley. The Jew is a good business man; as we shall see, he paved the Alley; he established the first firms to appreciate the possibilities of large-scale production and of mass exploitation. Into the business, however, he could no more help bringing something of the racial poetry than could the Negro and the Irishman. A humble poetry, a lowly conception of words and music, yet tinged indelibly with the hue of folk feeling and folk thought.

Origins of Minstrelsy.

To the Negro we owe the first native form of stage entertainment, the Minstrel Show, which was originated by whites in the early forties. Indeed, not for a quarter century did the Negro, glorified in such organizations as Lew Johnson's Plantation Minstrel Company, tread the boards of the "nigger minstrel" show as a performer. The white began by imitating, by burlesquing him, and *he* ended by imitating the white so far as even to put on, over the swarthy face that Nature had given him, the art of black make-up. It is a symbol.

The prototype of the Minstrel show already existed on the Southern plantation, which boasted its black band of banjo and bones, and its entertainers of the master and his guests. Old King Cole called for his fiddlers three; Massa called for his slave

revelers. One such band, we are told, organized semi-profession-
ally and made a tour of the plantations.

One of the first Negroes on the English stage was, of course,
Othello. He had an early successor in Oroonoko, from the tragedy
of that name (1696) by Thomas Southerne. In 1768, at Drury
Lane, was first given the comic opera, *The Paddock*, by Isaac
Bickerstaffe and Charles Dibdin. Dibdin, the composer, created
the part of Mungo, black slave of a West Indian planter. In America the piece was produced on May 29, 1769, in New York, with
Lewis Hallam in the black rôle. Mungo's song could not have
sounded altogether strange to the ears of the Northerners:

> Dear heart, what a terrible life I am led!
> A dog has a better, that's sheltered and fed.
> >   Night and day 'tis the same;
> >   My pain is deir game:
> Me wish to de Lord me was dead!
> >   Whate'er's to be done,
> >   Poor black must run.
> >   Mungo here, Mungo dere,
> >   Mungo everywhere:
> >   Above and below,
> >   Sirrah, come; sirrah, go;
> >   Oh! Oh!
> Me wish to de Lord me was dead!

It is, in its blackened-white way, a "blues."

There were other blacks upon the English stage who found their
way early to the United States: Friday, from a pantomime entitled *Robinson Crusoe* (Drury Lane, 1781; Park Theatre, N. Y.,
January 11, 1786) and another Friday in *The Bold Buccaneers*,

or The Discovery of Robinson Crusoe. There is record, too, of a
company of negro amateurs resident in New York around 1822
and 1823.[1] More important, if authenticated, and more interesting,
is the claim of Gottlieb Graupner to be the first to sing, in character, a negro song upon the American stage. It was in Boston, on
the evening of December 30, 1799, in a performance of *Oroonoko,*
at the end of the second act. Graupner (according to a notice in
Russell's *Boston Gazette* of that date) was to appear that evening
at the Federal Theatre;[2] he sang, according to Charles White, an
old minstrel and manager, "The Gay Negro Boy." If this be so,
Graupner is doubly an American pioneer, for it was this same
Gottlieb Graupner—as none of the commentators seems to have
realized—who in Boston at the dawn of the XIXth century
founded the first American orchestra. He opened one of the
earliest music stores in the country, on Franklin street, where also
he printed music. Later, he was one of the founders of the Handel
and Haydn Society.

Who first sang "The Battle of Plattsburg," the next of the
popular negro songs? It came from a drama entitled *The Battle of
Lake Champlain,* produced in Albany, in 1815, at the Green Street
Theatre. Was it "Pig-Pie" (also called "Pot-Pie") Herbert, or
Andrew Jackson Allen? And was the tragedian Edward Forrest
the next in line? Forrest, in 1823, did play a negro part in a farce
by Sol Smith, given at the Globe Theatre, Cincinnati, and called
The Tailor in Distress. In 1824, James Roberts was singing "Massa

[1] See *Annals of the New York Stage,* George C. D. Odell. New York, 1928. P. 70 ff.
[2] This is a moot point which it is perhaps too late to settle. According to other
authorities the theater at this time was closed in mourning for George Washington.
See, for detail, *The Negro on the Stage,* by Lawrence Hutton, Harper's, June, 1889,
pp. 131-145. The article was later included as one of the chapters in Hutton's valuable
Curiosities of the American Stage, Harper, 1891.

George Washington and Massa Lafayette," in a Continental uniform and a black make-up. There was, too, George Washington Dixon, who as early as 1827 was singing John Clements's "Coal Black Rose" and "The Long-tailed Blue" in an Albany theater. In 1834 he sang "Old Zip Coon" in Philadelphia, and claimed the authorship of this, our first self-styled coon song. (The words are not remembered to-day; the tune we all know as "Turkey in the Straw.")

"Zip Coon," in an early pamphlet on Minstrelsy, is attributed to George Nichols, author also of "Roley Boley." Nichols himself first sang "Clare De Kitchen," which he had arranged after picking it up from the negro firemen on the Mississippi. As for "Zip Coon," it confesses to an even lowlier ancestry. The tune was taken from a rough jig dance called "Natchez Under the Hill"; here the boatmen, river pirates, gamblers and prostitutes were wont to foregather for the old-time hoe-downs.[3]

Stage negroes, then, were fairly common before Thomas D. Rice, in his epochal characterization of Jim Crow, dramatized and crystallized the negro-songster type, and thus laid the first solid foundation of Ethiopian minstrelsy. A host of imitators sprang up. Yet not for some fifteen years—Rice had copied the type from a negro nondescript in Louisville and was bringing down the house with it at the Columbia Street Theatre, Cincinnati, during 1828-9 —did it occur to anyone to organize a blackface troupe.

Rice's "Jim Crow" gave to our stage a type and to our language a striking phrase that ever after was to stigmatize our physical and psychic segregation of the Negro. The words of the tune, as

[3] *Fun in Black, or Sketches of Minstrel Life.* By Charles H. Day, with The Origin of Minstrelsy, by Col. T. Allston Brown. New York, 1874.

Rice appropriated them from the sadly deformed darky who is supposed to have been his inspiration, were simple enough:

> Wheel about, turn about,
> Do jis so,
> And every time I wheel about
> I jump Jim Crow.

The original words, we learn, were a set of rhymeless stanzas, sung as follows by the Negroes of Kentucky:

> I went down to creek, I went down a-fishing,
> I axed the old miller to gimmy chaw tobacker
> To treat old Aunt Hanner.

> **Chorus**
> First on de heel tap, den on de toe,
> Ebery time I wheel about I jump Jim Crow.

> I goes down to de branch to pester old miller,
> I wants a little light wood;
> I belongs to Capt. Hawkins, and don't care a damn.

Certainly the dancing directions in the original are more explicit than in the chorus as popularized by Rice.

Enter the "Ham."

Of like historical and etymological interest is the too-well-forgotten later personality of Andrew Jackson Leavitt, who also gave to our language a picturesque word—possibly two. His song, "The Hamfat Man," [4] was in its day as popular—for its words

[4] Grease paint was introduced into this country by Charles Meyer, who came to the United States in 1868. Before this, actors dabbing on color would coat their faces with ham fat. For a note on Meyer, see *The New Yorker*, July 26, 1930, p. 8.

and for its dance—as Daddy Rice's "Jim Crow" itself. Leavitt, writer of numerous burlesque negro sketches ("Deaf as a Post," "Ole Bull in a Tight Place," "The Coming Man") adapted the air from an old Scotch melody to his banjo. He had intended it for Johnnie Campbell, the song-and-dance artist of the day. Campbell liked the tune and Leavitt's words, but the orchestra leader would have none of it until pressure was brought to bear. The morning after its first performance found the minstrel world ringing with it. On both sides of the ocean the song was taken up by the lowliest troupes until, as a term for all third-rate actors, "hamfat men," later abbreviated to "ham," entered the dictionary. To-day, the once famous chorus needs translation into English:

> Hamfat, hamfat, zick, zal, zan.
> Hamfat, hamfat, frying in de pan.
> Git into de kitchen as quick as you can,
> A hootchy, cootchy, cootchy, the hamfat man.

This was long before the Oriental lasciviousness of a certain belly-dance at the World's Columbian Exposition of 1893. Where did Andy Leavitt find the "hootchy cootchy"? What did he mean by it? And how did it reach the Midway Plaisance?

It was with Daddy Rice that Joseph Jefferson, the third, made one of the most precocious and most original entrances into the theatrical profession. In 1833, at the age of four, he was carried on to the stage by the original Jim Crow, in a bag on his shoulder. Rice dumped the tot on to the boards, whereupon Joe, a miniature edition of his sponsor in every detail, broke into the now famous dance.

[39]

In 1838 S. S. Sanford was singing in New York as the negro doorkeeper in *The Masquerade, or Tickets on Tick*. The following year, likewise in New York, he was featuring "Jim Along Josey." "Old Darkey Sweeney," on the bill of Feb. 4, 1840, at the Bowery Amphitheatre, rival house to the Bowery Circus, was, with the assistance of a pupil, doing a variety of airs on the banjo. Two weeks later, the same house offered "Jim Crow's visit, in which John Smith, Thomas Coleman and all the talented Ethiopians will appear." At Vauxhall Gardens, in June of 1840, under the redoubtable Barnum, we find the pioneer Sanford again. Next month Whitlock is billed as "King of banjo players."

The Minstrel show, then, is found in embryo long before it takes definite shape in 1843 under the inspiration of Whitlock. Indeed, negro acts were an important part of every circus; according to contemporary report, negro songs, in the early days of the circus, were sung from horseback in the sawdust ring. It is not impossible that the ring formation of the minstrels derived from the shape of the sawdust arena, and certainly, between the baiting of the ringmaster by the clown and the regulation victory of endmen over the interlocutor there is a family relationship.

Accounts of the origin of negro minstrelsy vary with the numerous tellers. Essentially, the accredited version runs something after the following fashion:

One day Whitlock asked Dan Emmet, who happened to be in New York, to practice the violin and the banjo with him at his boarding house. As they were practicing, in walked Frank Brower, unexpectedly. He was fascinated by the music; Whitlock asked him to join in with the bones. Now, as *they* were at it, who should come in but Dick Pelham, who listened with amazement. Whitlock asked him to procure a tambourine and join the band. They named themselves the Virginia Minstrels and gave their first performance in Bartlett's billiard room. Their first formal appearance was at the Chatham Theatre, on February 17, 1843, at a benefit for Pelham. They sang, they played, they danced, they did The Essence of Old Virginia and The Lucy Long Walk Around. The evening, artistically and financially, was a huge success.

The new idea in minstrelsy spread like wildfire. Imitations, expansions, grew up overnight.

The great name in black minstrelsy is Edwin P. Christy, who followed hard upon the Virginia Minstrels, in 1844. So popular did the Christy group later become in England that the name Christy became synonymous with minstrelsy in general. It was Edwin who fixed the minstrel-show pattern, who gave to the entertainment a definite form, which was afterward copied in many details by the burlesque show in its first glory. The pattern was hardly complicated; it boasted, indeed, an Aristotelean beginning, middle, and end. The First Part consisted of the show proper— the gambolings of Interlocutor, Tambo and Bones, with choric support. It ended with a grand review of the performers, called the Walk Around. The middle provided the "olio"—an excellent English word, by the way, with definite relationship to the Spanish *olla,* and signifying, originally, a hodge-podge, or a dish of many ingredients, not to say a hash or potpourri. As the potpourri was a medley of airs, so the "olio" was a medley of talents. In the "olio" of the minstrel show we have already the birth of the rival who, in time, would supersede minstrelsy. The olio was, to all intents and purposes, variety, vaudeville. As for the afterpiece, it was the embryo of yet other rivals to minstrelsy, who in turn would supersede vaudeville itself: Burlesque, the Cinderella of the musical stage, and her loftier sister, Musical Comedy.

The pattern of the minstrel show was at once simple and logical. As background to the outstanding performers sat a semi-circle of flashy "coons," in their gaudy frock coats and equally fancy trousers. In the center, against this melodious assembly, sat Mr. Interlocutor, whose aristocratic descendant, in this day of night-clubs and refined intimate entertainment, is known as the master of ceremonies. Mr. Interlocutor was so named because he served as the telephone exchange, as it were, between the end men, Mr. Tambo and Mr. Bones. In later years it became a custom that the bone end man be fat and the tambo lean. The tradition—an ancient and obvious device, old when Don Quixote and Sancho Panza were young—persists down through Weber & Fields. Tambo was at the right end of the audience; Bones, at the left. Tambo was expert on the tambourine—hence his name—and generally strummed a banjo; Bones, as his name suggests, was an expert in manipulating the clappers. What a variety of rhythms he could conjure out of these little ebony strips! As children, we know another type of bones; the tin layer of wood with metal clappers attached. It required no skill to drum out rhythms on these degenerate instruments; the ebony clapper required art, and was not, like our playthings, a cheating contrivance.

Mr. Interlocutor wore a dress suit, perhaps as compensation for the false prominence of his rôle. He was a queen bee; he did little but look handsome—and ask leading questions. He was a high-class "feeder" to Tambo and Bones. The swell gang behind him were the chorus; their instrument was the tambourine. Between the gags of the end men and the oily interspersions of Mr.

Interlocutor, there would be songs and dances, with choruses and tambourine effects from the gentlemen of the ensemble.

Ring and Parker . . . The Congo Melodists, who first introduced vocal harmony . . . Buckley's New Orleans Serenaders, earliest burlesquers of grand opera. (Burlesque and travesty were inherent in blackface minstrelsy.) The Ethiopian Serenaders started the 3-a-day show. In 1850 the Ordway Minstrels originated the street parade of the entertainers as a ballyhoo for the production.

The Vagrom Foster.

Stephen Collins Foster (1826-1864) belongs by self-dedication to the history of negroid minstrelsy. Born on the Fourth of July, he, too, is one of our Yankee Doodle Boys. Again, like the vast majority of our plantation singers, he was a Northerner. His parents had come from Virginia, but Stephen was born in Pittsburgh. His father was an amateur fiddler; the son, who had shown musical aptitude at the age of six, taught himself the flageolet and made his début as a composer in his fourteenth year with a Tioga Waltz for flute ensemble. He was a restless spirit; his education was sporadic. At sixteen he first showed genuine promise with the song, "Open Thy Lattice, Love." Even as a boy he was fascinated by amateur minstrelsy. For a group that met at his house twice a week to sing under his leadership he wrote during 1845-46 a number of songs, among them "Oh, Susanna" and "Old Uncle Ned." A minstrel troupe, passing through Pittsburgh, made the first of these so popular that Foster sensed his vocation and its destined specialty.

It was not in his vagrom nature to make a serious study of music; he never achieved a sound technique. He was content to sing for a simple age and for simple people. It was in 1852, when organized minstrelsy was not yet a decade old, that he announced to E. P. Christy his intention of pursuing "the Ethiopian business (*i.e.*, minstrelsy) without fear or favor," and "to establish my name as the best Ethiopian writer." Certainly his ambition was early fulfilled, and largely through the troupe that bore the famous Christy name throughout the United States and Europe. "The Old Folks at Home" (could Tin Pan Alley have hit upon a more appealing title?) or, as it is equally well known, "Swanee River," was originally presented, with the consent of Foster, as the composition of the selfsame Christy.

Foster attempted the so-called drawing-room ballad, but he is best remembered for such negroid products as "Uncle Ned" (1848), "De Camptown Races" (1850), "Swanee River" (1851), "Massa's in the Cold, Cold Ground" (1852), "My Old Kentucky Home" (1853), "Old Dog Tray" (1853) and "Old Black Joe" (1860). His career was short, ended not only by the accident that carried him off in 1864, after he had written his last song, "Beautiful Dreamer." He rode in, with a fine intuitive gift, upon the crest of Minstrelsy. Before his twenty-fifth year he was supporting himself upon his writings. New York proved good neither for his body nor his soul; drink and homesickness did the rest. Though "Swanee River" had sold over a million copies, Foster was the easy prey of unscrupulous dealers. In his declining days he would sell songs outright, for a pittance. The well-known manager, Sanford, in an interview given out in 1882, recalled the minstrel days of his friend Foster, and claimed to have been the first to present to the public "My Old Kentucky Home," "Hard Times Will Come Again No More" and "Come Where My Love Lies Dreaming." "I paid him $50 for the three songs, and they were all sung for the first time on the same night . . . at Library Hall, Pittsburgh, and we had Jenny Lind as opposition."

Foster, indeed, toward the end, became as much a hack as any lowly scribbler of Tin Pan Alley to-day. "Swanee River," which inaugurated a whole school of melodic pseudo-nostalgia, owes its title to a mere accident of euphony. Foster had never seen the muddy stream in Georgia and Florida whose name he was to glorify. He knew no more about the S(u)wanee than a mammy-singer knows (or cares) about Dixie. As a matter of fact, the original draft of the verses showed the name Pedee. Foster felt dubious about Pedee river, and asked his brother to discover a more euphonious Southern river whose name had but two syllables. Brother Foster was unesthetic enough to suggest, in all seriousness, the Yazoo. ('Way down upon the Yazoo river!) Stephen vetoed it. Brother then navigated—through an atlas—until he struck the Swanee. The Swanee flowed right into the title, and there it has remained as our perennial symbol of the scenes whither, in our longing, we would return. What, after all, need it matter if Jolson would die of boredom in the land of cotton? Or if Dan Emmet, dashing off the words and music of "Dixie," in New York of 1859, as a routine job for a Walk Around, chose the name with as little concern as Foster chose Swanee? The song lives in the heart of the listener. Swanee and Dixie cease to be names; the magic of Minstrelsy transforms them into the Lands of Heart's Desire.

J. P. McEvoy, inquiring once of that master-lyrist, Gus Kahn, why the song-boys all wrote of the South, received the reply that it was because Southern place-and-State names lent themselves to rhyming. There is, I believe, a deeper reason. The South is the romantic home of our Negro; the Negro made it a symbol of longing that we, half in profiteering cold blood, but half in surrender to the poetry of the black, carried over into our song. Our song boys are of the North. Paradise is never where we are. The South has become our Never-never Land—the symbol of the Land where the lotus blooms and dreams come true.

The followers of Foster, like him, are children of the North. George F. Root (1820-1895) was born in Sheffield, Mass. Henry Clay Work (1832-1884) was born in Middletown, Conn. Root is regarded as one of the first American composers to discover the possibilities of the popular market. His "Battle Cry of Freedom," "Tramp, Tramp, Tramp, the Boys Are Marching," and "Just Before the Battle, Mother," are all good tunes, easy to sing, simple in harmonic arrangement and well set to their words. They will outlast most of the hits of Tin Pan Alley. So, too, Work's "Marching Through Georgia" will be marching on long after the majority of our contemporary best-sellers will have been buried without taps. His "Kingdom Comin'" is, unjustly, half-forgotten.

Also from Connecticut, where he was born in New Haven on April 6, 1834, came Hart Pease Danks, composer of "Silver Threads Among the Gold." Eben Eugene Rexford, who wrote the words while a student at Lawrence College, Appleton, Wisconsin, was born in Johnsbury, New York, 1848. As Root and Work illustrate the association between war and popular music, Danks blends the religious with the widespread secular. From 1854 to 1864 he was in Chicago; from the end of the Civil War he was in New York as a bass singer and a musical director. He died in Philadelphia on November 20, 1903. "Silver Threads Among the Gold," originally published in 1873, was one of the greatest "hits" of its time. It has sold upward of 2,000,000 copies. In the same year Danks had written "Not Ashamed of Christ"; the year before he had signed his operetta, *Pauline*. His first composition was a hymn entitled "Lake Street"; first of his printed pieces, however, were the sentimental songs, "The Old Lane" and "Anna Lee," which go back to 1856.

For more than three decades the minstrel companies fascinated the country until, in the late 70's, with the advent of Haverly's Mastodons they had grown to the "40—Count 'Em—40" that was painted on the bass-drum of the band. Twenty years later, though Dockstader came valiantly to their defense, they had really become a troupe of blackface vaudevillians. Merely to name all the famous troupes would make an almost interminable minstrel parade. They fast became, among other things, one of the chief means of popularizing the current songs. Ah, yes! There were "spots" and "plugs" in the olden, blackface days. In 1876, the year of the Centennial Exposition at Philadelphia, Rice & Hooley's, minstrels then newly formed, still used the old-style one-circle formation, with the singers on one side and the orchestra on the other, while the bass drum and the bass fiddle filled in the rear.

Who remembers their songs to-day? "It's Nice to Be a Father," "Baby's Got a Tooth," "Wither and Decay," "They All Belonged to the Hardware Line." For ballads: "Little Robin," "Tell Kittie I'm Coming," "By the Blue Alsatian Mountains," "Rocked in the Cradle of the Deep," "She Gave Me a Pretty Red Rose," "One

Hundred Fathoms Deep," "When the Corn Is Waving, Annie Dear."

Haverly's Mastodon Minstrels, "40—Count 'Em—40," soon won Rice away. It was this organization that, with more members to display, abolished the old style first part and introduced, to replace the original minstrel circle, the pyramided tiers of song-sters. More songs: "Empty Is the Cradle—Baby's Gone," "See That My Grave's Kept Green," "Stick to Your Mother, Tom," "We Never Speak as We Pass By," "A Curl From Baby's Head," "The Letter in the Candle." Already the colored composer had begun to take his place among the whites not only as an anonymous folk influence but as an individual. Sam Lucas's "Carve Dat 'Possum" was a favorite of the Seventies. And who hasn't heard, times beyond counting, James Bland's "Carry Me Back to Old Vir-ginny," "Oh, Dem Golden Slippers," "In the Evening by the Moonlight"?

This is the era of the statue clog dance and the military drill, as well as the pedestal clog. Upon twenty square inches of space atop a pedestal some eight or ten feet high the dancer would turn back-somersaults and land in time to the music. Barney Fagan, who was to be in at the beginning of the ragtime craze with the words and music of "My Gal Is a High Born Lady," was at this stage of the game one of the fanciest clog dancers in the blackface aggregation; he originated many of the steps that were later used in vaudeville.

With the craze for size in minstrel shows there developed the custom of having two sets of end men. Even third sets were known. This was done, explains Arthur Gillespie, himself an old-timer, for several reasons. "First, because it made the array of talent seem greater, and, secondly, to keep peace in the family. . . . With men like Emerson ('Sunflower' Emerson), Rice,[5] Johnny Cushman, Johnson, Armstrong, Richardson, Maxwell, Mack, Sadler, what could a manager do but show them *all* in the first part. Each had his following and each got a reception—the principals an 'ovation.' "

Harry Kennedy, a phenomenal ventriloquist, was then at his height. He wrote the words and music to such hits as "My Grandfather's Clock," "You'll Never Miss the Water Till the Well Runs Dry," "I Owe Ten Dollars to O'Grady," "Mister McNulty." . . . At the Casino on Wabash Avenue, Chicago, Frank Hall was soon managing an assembly of burnt-cork songsters recruited largely from the mastodontic Haverlys. "Honey" Evans, in those days, was a simple balladist. Here, too, were the Dillon brothers, who one day would be plugging their own songs, "Put Me Off at Buffalo" and "Do, Do, My Huckleberry, Do."

The Barlow, Wilson, Primrose and West show brought to prominence another of the minstrel composers. In these simpler days it was commoner than now for a popular songster to write both words and music. Howard, possessed of an admirable tenor voice, was the natural plugger of his own compositions. Two hundred thousand dollars was at this time a vast figure for royalties on sheet music; this is what Howard is reputed to have made collectively on such favorites as "When the Robins Nest Again," "Only a Pansy Blossom," "I'll Await My Love," "A Mother's Watch by the Sea," "Two Little Ragged Urchins," "Only a Blue Bell," "Sweet Alpine Roses," "Sweet Heather Bells." . . . It was

[5] The reader should distinguish between "Daddy" Rice (Thomas D.) and Billy Rice, the noted "stump speaker." Gillespie's reference is to Billy, who became Hooley's partner in the middle Seventies. There was also William Henry Rice.

with this minstrel company that Banks Winter made his début. His song, "White Wings," which has recently been revived by the radio, but never really died in the old homes of the nation, made him famous and rich.

Royalties in the minstrel days, strangely enough, were higher than they are now. Men such as Howard, Winter, Harley and Kennedy received from five to eight cents on a copy. Howard, on "Only a Pansy Blossom," received thirteen. The rate to-day is from one cent to three; modern sales, however, are much greater than in the blackface days.

Whiteface teams appeared in minstrelsy as early as 1882, when Ferguson and Mack brought down the house in the Standard Theatre, San Francisco, with an Irish low-comedy act. The tocsin of the minstrel-show was faintly audible in the distance.

Rewards and Fairies.

There were big money-makers before the era of Follywood's fabulous philanthropy. Hooley and Haverly paid Emerson and Rice as high as five hundred dollars per week. In the early eighties the large companies had a weekly expense of from $250 to $1200. The "40—Count 'Em—40" payroll was $1550, having shrunk as a result of the release of certain headliners. The lesser fry had to be content with diminutive figures. Song-and-dance men were getting $8 to $25 per week; clog-dancers, $12 to $30; musicians, $12 to $25; vocalists, $15 to $35. All this was net, as traveling expenses were met by the management. Performers who could play a musical instrument received $5 per week extra.

As for principals, in 1882 they were being almost as well paid as in the palmy days of the Civil War. A contemporary document is interesting for its names—major and minor—as well as for its figures:

"Joe Emmet, to whom a week of work is now worth several thousand dollars, was formerly very glad to get $40 or $50 when he blacked his face, and he got even less at the old Broadway Bowery in this city. When he went with Dan Bryant's minstrels his salary was what the boys call 'away up.'

"Gus Williams, who played one week with the Mastodons in Chicago four years ago, was paid $175. Haverly paid Billy Emerson $250 a week for ten years, and this comedian can still get the same salary any time he desires to take it. He is now in California with a troupe of his own.

"Billy Rice, the fat moke, who enlivened the bone end of the Mastodons for several seasons, was paid $100 a week. He and Richard Hooley are now running a company that is playing in the smaller towns. Primrose and West, for several years in business for themselves, formerly received $75 a week each. J. W. McAndrews, the 'watermelon man,' got $75 a week from Haverly. He is now in London getting $125 at the Panlion Music Hall. George Thatcher, the stuttering comedian, whom George Wilson imitates, received $125 a week before he became proprietor and manager. Sam Devere, the banjoist, got $100 a week when he was with the Mastodons, but Hyde & Behman are now paying him $150. Billy Carroll, playing the banjo with the Tony Pastor combination this year, is paid $75 a week. He was formerly a partner of Billy Harris, with whom he did a quick change act from white to black face. Barry Maxwell, an excellent 'old man,' was paid $25 a week by Haverly a year ago and is getting much more now.

Milt Barlow, in the same line with Maxwell, was paid $75 a week before he formed a co-partnership with George Wilson, who refused $200 a week to travel with the Mastodons. E. M. Kayne, the well-known stage manager and interlocutor, has a salary of $70 a week. Frank Cushman, who is to take Billy Emerson's place on the minstrel stage when Billy retires, got $50 a week last season, is getting $75 now, and will soon have $100. Pete Mack, the comedian, gets $50 a week. C. S. Shattuck, the basso, whose song, 'One Hundred Fathoms Deep,' was such a success, is paid $40 a week for his singing and the direction of all the vocal music of the San Francisco Minstrels. George W. Harley, the soprano voiced gentleman, has $20 a week. Paul Vernon, who impersonates females, formerly with the Mastodons, gets $35 a week. William Welch and John Rice, song and dance men, were each paid $30 a week by Haverly, but now get $75 each as directors of amusement for the two Callender troupes. Daniel F. Thompson, song and dance, gets $30 a week; Thomas Sadler, song and dance, $35; James R. Walsh and Billy King, song and dance, $20 each; Robert Hooley, song and dance, $25, and among the vocalists, Chauncey Olcott, $25; O. H. Carter, $20; William Willis, $20, and Alfred Holland, $20. The three German brothers, song and dance and general utility, receive a joint salary of $75 a week.

"Charles Queen, who leads the clog-dancers with Thatcher, Primrose & West, and dances on a pedestal, is paid $75 a week. George W. McAuley, pedestal clog-dancer, gets $25 a week. Alexander Zanfretta, the clown who appeared with the Mastodons last season, got $200 a week while in England and during three months in this country. He made a second contract running to the end of the season at $100 a week. The only Leon, female impersonator, receives $160 and expenses for a week's work. Harry Kennedy, the ventriloquist, who is with the San Francisco Minstrels, receives $85 a week. Manchester and Jennings, who are now on the road with a variety company of their own, got $40 a week each when they played at the old Comique in this city. Hugh Dougherty, the comedian, now with Thatcher, Primrose & West's company, is paid $125 a week.

"Even the genuine darkies on the minstrel stage command pretty good salaries. The list for Callender's consolidated companies is equal to that of any first-class white company on the road."

The band of the early minstrel troupes was virtually a precursor of our modern jazz band—in spirit, if not in roster of instruments. The orchestra—let us call it such—was essentially percussive, as were the early jazz orchestras. Violin, bones (so called because originally they derived from the shortened and flattened ribs of a favorite quadruped), tambourine, triangle (a horseshoe held by a piece of string and struck with a ten-penny nail), the jawbone of a calf played upon by a dried shin-bone . . . these were among the music-producers of an era now departed forever.

The minstrel show displays certain affinities with the *commedia dell' arte*; it was a patter of types, with much of the impromptu about it. There were no women, although a long line of impersonators became famous for their "wench" rôles. This, in time, was to prove its undoing. This, and perhaps the stereotyped monotony of its pattern.

No female minstrels at all? So run the records. We shall have to revise them to read, almost none. Constance Rourke [6] has left

[6] See her admirable *Troupers of the Gold Coast*, New York, 1928.

us a picture of the juvenile Lotta Crabtree, on the way up from San Francisco to Sacramento, being taught the complications of soft-shoe dancing by a negro breakdown virtuoso. Taylor's troupe, with whom the child was traveling, had for a night or two joined forces with Backus's minstrels, and Lotta was easily induced to blacken up and do her darkey stuff.

> I can play the banjo, yes, indeed I can!
> I can play a tune upon the frying pan,
> I hollo like a steamboat 'fore she's gwine to stop,
> I can sweep a chimney and sing out at the top . . .

Lotta added to her repertory such minstrel stand-bys as Joe Blackburn's "Sich a Gittin' Upstairs" and "The Long Tail Blue," "Jim Along Josie" and the mining-camp variations upon "Oh, Susanna!" She had learned the banjo from a minstrel named Jake Wallace; it was not long before the redoubtable Thomas Maguire was billing her with his mixed minstrels at his Opera House, and at the Eureka, in San Francisco.

> Before I left we danc'd two reels,
> (De holler ob her foot war back of her heels!)
> I played on de banjo till dey all began to sweat,
> Knock'd on de jaw-bone and bust de clarinet.
>
> .   .   .   .   .
>
> Loud de banjo talked away,
> And beat Ole Bull from de Norway,
> We'll take de shine from Paganini,
> We're de boys from ole Virginny.

No lady blackface troupers? On the program of Forrest's Melodeon, San Francisco, Friday evening, April 12, 1861, Miss

Lotta, who had now reached the responsible age of sixteen, is down for a song and dance with the Female Minstrels. There were a few women in the burnt-cork business, after all.

There was something of relief in the very name of the new entertainment that was rising up to replace these black revels: Variety. Variety, graduating into the refinements of Vaudeville, and the dawning splendors of the musical comedy, were not long in ousting the simplicities of the minstrel show. They were more varied. And, more to the point, they had girls. Choruses were not a permanent background, as in the case of the minstrels; once Interlocutor had pronounced his ritual invitation-and-command, "Gentlemen, Be Seated!" followed by a flourish from the band, the gentlemen were too much in evidence for the rest of the entertainment. Choruses of females were more colorful, more exciting. The trio of banjo, bones and tambourine, too, yielded to a more civilized group of instruments that could languish as well as beat time. Besides, entertainment in terms of the Negro, without any element of racial prejudice, was bound to end in monotony and lead to a welcome change of color as well as of type.

The old minstrel show, truth to tell, for all the sentimental memories that are linked to it, must have been a pretty dull affair. Its wheezes were old when Cleopatra was a child. Read them, if you have the courage, in the sere chapbooks. Its tunes were undistinguished, for the greater part, though they had the country by the ears. The words of its ditties chiefly served to fill space. And yet, it is from the minstrel show that we get our patterns of modern popular song. And if, even to-day, an Al Jolson or an Eddie Cantor seems somehow not himself without the blackface make-up, it is because he got his start in these troupes of pseudo-Negroes. Almost every song-and-dance man of note, from the times of Harrigan and Hart down to our own sophisticated day, began behind the burnt cork.

The influence of the minstrel show in giving our popular entertainment a dark hue was at once subtle and potent. Let us imagine, if we can, a minstrel troupe composed of Irishmen, or Germans, or Jews. The very suggestion sounds incongruous. It is out of tune with the traditions of our early history. The Negroes on the plantations, with their inborn spirit of song, provided a scene that needed but to be taken in hand by the exploiting white and set upon the stage.

In our own day the Negro, as the result of white influence, has assumed his proper place in the roster of our amusements. Sissle and Blake, Miller and Lyles, carry on the tradition of Williams and Walker. Only when the pseudo-Negro minstrels were dying out did the finer exponents of black artistry appear.

Elegy.

Philip Hale, the learned annotator of the program books of the Boston Symphony Orchestra, waxing reminiscent of the songs that were sung by the Christys at the height of their fame and fortune, once wrote a note on American popular songs that may serve as an elegy for the minstrels.

"The pleasure in looking over the songs of years ago is a melancholy one and not solely by reason of associations. The sentimental ditties that once had the semblance of pathos now provoke sneers and laughter. The comic songs that formerly provoked laughter are now foolish and depressing." There follows a composite photograph of the *dramatis personæ* of the ditties:

"The poet, leaving Annie in sorrow, begged her not to weep; he asked, heartsick and alone, the whereabouts of his schoolmates, the shy, the dull, and the gay; with weeping eyes, he wandered by the riverside all day, mourning over the stolen Nellie Gray; he tolled the bell for gentle Lilly Dale; he welcomed back missed Willy; he could not forget the smile of faithless Rosa; he sighed as he thought he should never hear again the winning voice of gentle Annie, not even when the springtime came and the wild flowers were scattered on the plain; he invited generously and in a silvery voice his tried and trusty companions to come where his love lay dreaming. Rosalie, the prairie flower, was nipped in the bud, borne away by softly whispering angels. The banjo was hushed—not a plunkety-plunk; for gentle Jenny Gray, the golden-haired maiden, slept under the willow; 'vanished scenes smiled' on sweet Ellen Bayne; the gentle fingers of Jenny with the light brown hair will cull no more the nodding wild flowers. Lieutenant Colonel Addison had the courage to ask in two verses: Where Are the Friends of My Youth? A lady passed the coffin of a stranger lad, pressed her lips to his forehead, and exclaimed: 'Let me kiss him for his mother.' Ella Leene wished sweet flowers planted o'er the grave where she 'takes repose.' A weary and friendless man haunted the hazel dell in which Nelly was sleeping. The 'silent language' of bluebirds was: ' 'Tis the grave of Eulalie'; Marion Lee went the way of all flesh in spite of the snow-white plume her bonnet bore; Death stopped at Nelly's door: was this the celebrated and 'lubly Nell' who was 'a lady'? She, too, died. Blue-eyed Minnie joined the procession led by the lean old fellow with a scythe. There was Hally, associated with thoughts of the mild September and the mocking-bird; [7] sweet Lilla Brown, with voice of silver, had been for some years in the happy land; sweet Anne Page lay 'neath the 'daisied track.' Brother fainted at the door, and Massa was in the cold, cold ground; earthly music could not waken lovely Annie Lisle; Angelina Baker left her lover to weep and 'beat on the old jawbone.' There were scores of songs about m-m-m-uther.''

There were topical songs, "colored ball" songs, and the familiar rest, but never with the touch of a later cynicism and sensuality. We were still in the age of purity, which Edward Harrigan, when the Irish were to become prominent in the eighties, would defend upon the stage of his immigrant farces. It is a curious fact that the taboo upon the theater did not, in the minds of over-scrupulous folk, extend to the minstrel show. Even the Quakers of Pennsylvania patronized them.

"What," asks the omniscient Hale, "was more characteristic of both American sentimentalism and indifference than the songs heard in the old minstrel shows—Wood's, Christy's, Bryant's, Buckley's, Morris, Pell and Trowbridge, Kelley and Leon, Carncross and Dixey, the San Francisco Minstrels? But these songs are dead, along with the dry unctuous humor of Unsworth, the dry wit of Nelse Seymour, Wambold's singing, so full of simple pathos, the animal spirits of Charley Backus. Gone, too, is the dancing of the old days. Where now can be seen the frenzy of Cool Burgess

[7] James Weldon Johnson, in his *Black Manhattan*, points out that Septimus Winner, long accepted as the composer of "Listen to the Mocking Bird" (which was published under the name of his mother, Alice Hawthorne) was merely the arranger of this famous song. The composer of the piece was a Philadelphia barber, Richard Milburn, a Negro. "He was a guitar-player and a marvelous whistler, and it was he who originated the melody and at least the title." (*Op. cit.* p. 112.)

in 'Nicodemus Johnson'? Where is the double shuffle, the pigeon wing? Gone are the orators who entered hurriedly with umbrella and carpet-bag. Gone are such sketches as Harry Bloodgood's 'He's got to come'; the delightful 'Watermelon Man' of McAndrews.

"The very popularity of a vaudeville song brings death the sooner. There was 'Jasper.' It was an excellent song. The story of the Negro, whose love of bed rivaled that of Solomon's and Dr. Watt's sluggard, of the Seven Sleepers, or even that of Mr. George Thompson, of Lurgan, Ireland, who was in bed for twenty-nine years out of sheer laziness, was told with genuine humor, and the tune itself was in its way a masterpiece. Who sings 'Jasper' to-day outside of a graphophone? Where now is 'Abraham'? There was 'Bill Simmons,' a composition of which any poet and composer might be proud. It had ethnological, sociological, anthropological, esthetic value. It was a supreme tribute to the power of music. But 'Bill Simmons' is sliding into Time's dust-bin. The intensity of modernity brings the quicker forgetfulness. Nothing could have been more realistic and modern than Edward Harrigan's plays with Braham's music. These dramas would to-day be as unintelligible in the matter of local allusions as a comedy of Aristophanes is now to us, yet at the time they were full of 'the blab of the pave, tires of carts, sluff of bootsoles, talk of the promenaders.'

"The man remembering Dan Bryant and his companions, Birch, Wambold, and Backus, Harrigan and Hart and Johnny Wild, remembering their shows and still seeing and hearing the laughter of the roaring audience, feels chilly and old."

[59]

4. Blackface into White

THE minstrel show, as we have seen, contained in its "olio" the germ of its successor. Theatrical forms, like others, do not represent a steady, clear-cut evolution from lower to higher. They may be visualized rather as a series of parallel lines of uneven length. The older forms get the earlier start, but even after they have been superseded by fresher appeals to public patronage, they run along beside their rivals. The minstrel show did not die out as soon as Variety came in; nor did Variety die out when, in time, Musical Comedy put on satin gowns, silk stockings, flashy scenery, and grew away from its mother, Burlesque.

It is to Tony Pastor that the development of the variety show owes an unforgettable debt. He had come to it, not too inappropriately, from minstrelsy and from the circus ring. Born in New York, on Greenwich street, in 1840, of a father who for many years was a musician in the orchestra of the Park Theatre, he early absorbed the atmosphere of the playhouse. As a mere tot, Antonio had seen and heard the quartet of the original Virginia Serenaders at the theater where his father played. Here, indeed, must have been born his histrionic ambitions. At eight he had already made his début as a singer of comic duets with Christian B. Woodruff, later State Senator, in a Temperance Meeting at the old Dey Street Church. A few years later we discover him buying a tambourine, a wig and a box of burnt-cork. Minstrelsy was in its prime.

He gave performances in the family cellar, nervously eluding the paternal eye. On the steamer *Raritan,* plying its way between New York and Staten Island under Capt. Fisher, he engaged, for the experience, with a minstrel show that gave concerts to the passengers. At Croton Hall, just to be with showmen, he carried water for the comedian, and appeared occasionally as a talented child.

Papa Pastor, none too pleased to find Tony so fascinated by the stage, packed him off to the country to purify his hot blood. Here, however, Tony's further successes as an amateur at socials and church gatherings merely confirmed the child in his aspirations. Before long he was billed at Barnum's Museum as the Boy Prodigy. Here Col. Alvan Mann, one of the proprietors of Raymond and Waring's Menagerie, saw him and engaged him as banjoist and vocalist. An end man—or, as Pastor has written, an end boy—at fourteen! While thus employed, he organized numerous side shows; the future manager was breaking through the shell. From the Menagerie Tony was graduated into the Welch, Delavan and Nathan Circus, where his brothers William and Frank were employed as acrobats and equestrians. They taught him the tricks of their trade and he worked his way up to the position of chief clown. He was engaged in one circus or another until the outbreak of the Civil War. He appeared also in comedy rôles.

Pastor, during the four years' conflict, had conceived the notion that with a theater cleaned of smoking and drinking a manager might attract feminine custom and thus tap a vast new reservoir of patronage. Accordingly, on March 21, 1865, in partnership

[61]

with Sam Sharpley, an experienced minstrel manager, he made the first bid in history for women customers in the variety theater —a master stroke for a youth on the very threshold of his 21st year. That was at Paterson, New Jersey, and though Tony was profuse in his assurances that nothing of offensive nature would be permitted on his stage, the ladies at first proved uncertain, coy and hard to please. . . . They knew, from hearsay, that variety theaters were little better than low dives. Nothing daunted, however, the new impresario moved on to Tony Pastor's Opera House, at 201 Broadway, New York. Sharpley soon left Tony with the house on his hands. The women began to come, for prizes if not for performance. The Opera House offered rewards of half-barrels of flour, half-tons of coal and dress patterns. "I am quite serious in saying," writes James L. Ford in his delightful *Forty Odd Years in the Literary Shop*, "that the most important moment in the history of the development of the theater in this country was that in which Tony Pastor first gave away his coal, flour and dress patterns to secure the patronage of respectable women."

The rest is record. For ten years Tony was at 201; then he pushed up to 585 Broadway. In six years he was established at 14th Street, which, during his hey-day, he transformed into the song-and-dance center of the amusement world.

Tony Pastor and the Topical Song.

It is Pastor who developed to a high degree the topical song. "Most of these songs," he told an interviewer in 1895, "deal with some topic of the times which is capable of being looked at from a comical point of view. Now, the inquiry has often been put to

me, 'How did you get the idea of such and such a song?' In the
first place I am a great reader of the newspapers. I believe not
only in the power of the press, but in its utility. It is the most
valuable agent that the vocalist has ever had for securing subjects
for popular songs. The comic vocalist must be quick to perceive
the peculiar topic or phase of human life which is liable to interest the amusement-going public, and must be a little ahead of
the time. Having selected my subject for a song I jot down a few
ideas about it as they come to me, and afterward put them into
shape. Then again, I will use a good song coming from a professional writer. The ultimate success of these songs depends very
largely on the person who sings them."

For thirty years, from 1865 to 1895, Tony Pastor introduced
one or two songs nearly every Monday night of the season. During
the Civil War, two of the most popular ditties were "Root, Hog,
or Die" and "Hunkey Dorey." Did electricity come in? A song
greeted it. Did the ladies adopt the Grecian bend? It would be
set to words and music. Was a Charley Ross kidnapped, never to
be found? The tragedy was duly chronicled by the popular bards.
Tony recalled, out of this vast repertory, such salient bits as
"Things I Didn't Like to See," "I Am One of the Boys," "I
Wouldn't Be Anything Else," and "It's Wonderful How We Do
It, But We Do." At the last testimonial given to the grand old man
of Variety in the March before his death, in celebration of his
forty-third anniversary as a manager, Tony put on his old regalia
and sang again the hits of former years: "Down in the Coal Mine,"
"Sarah's Young Man," "The Girl All Dressed in Blue," "Walking
on the Balcony," "Smoking a Cig-aw," "Fl'ahting with Pretty
Girls," and "Heedless of Ma-maw."

Songs to-day are not so powerful politically as they used to be. In Tony's day they exercised a marked editorial influence, and even aided in bringing about social reforms. They ridiculed fads and fancies and laughed evil away.

Tony was a natural gag-man. Perhaps his greatest contribution to popular phraseology dates back to a political contest of 1884. The circumstance is long forgotten; the phrase lives on. Hewitt was running for Mayor, and his opponents had raised the cry that he was too radical to head a city like New York. Pastor rushed into the fray with a song that carried the refrain, "What's the Matter with Hewitt?" As the question recurred at the end of each chorus the members of the orchestra would bellow, in reply, "He's all right!" Hewitt was elected, though something beside the song must have done it. The rowdy phrase, however, was too good to pass into the history of the campaign. It lent itself so easily to daily conversation; moreover, a simple change of name made it pat for use in any political contest. In 1888, the Republicans adopted it for the Presidential fight, and it became, "What's the matter with Harrison? He's all right!" And ever since, whatever has been wrong with conditions political, somebody has been all right.

It is interesting, in this connection, to recall that the "blues," as we know them to-day, had their birth likewise in a mayoralty contest, and that—as we shall see when we come to discuss the importance of William C. Handy in the evolution of our jazz— what we know to-day as the "Memphis Blues" was originally the theme song for a politician by the name of Crump. Crump, by the way, was elected; jazzed into office, one might say, by his Handy man.

To-day, even the scene of Tony Pastor's triumphs is a memory. The old structure on 14th Street, which had been taken over by him in 1881, when the march had begun from lower Broadway, was demolished in 1928 together with Tammany Hall. Side by side they had flourished; side by side they went down. Tony had prided himself on his clean entertainments; he had dissociated it, he said, from the cigar-smoking and beer-drinking accompaniment of such amusements. Yet many a naughty evening made Tony's auditorium mirthful.

Pastor exemplified his name; he was a veritable shepherd to the whole histrionic flock. To be booked at Tony's was to achieve the pinnacle of vaudevillian ambition. His stage was the last stepping-stone to success on the "boards" of the legitimate. Gus Williams got his start here, with "Kaiser, Don't You Want to Buy a Dog?" Vesta Victoria, too, along in 1896, had likewise won the public with a canine classic, "Daddy Wouldn't Buy Me a Bow-Wow." Maggie Cline floored them with "Throw Him Down, McClosky!" Kelly and Ryan, the bards of Tara, sang "Good-by, Jack, Till You Get Back." Vesta Tilley, Francis Wilson, Lillian Russell, Eddie Foy, Nat Goodwin, Weber and Fields, Anne Yeamans, George M. Cohan . . . it is a noble roster.

Pastor died in 1908. He had accomplished his aims and had played his rôle in the history of popular entertainment. He had seen the farce-comedy and the light opera win away from variety its finer audiences, but could feel the satisfaction of a spent warrior who had done his share in the deed. It is said that he knew some 1500 songs. For years, indeed, before Tin Pan Alley had reared its own pleasures and palaces, Tony's was the song focus of Gotham.

TIN PAN ALLEY

Harrigan and Hart—and Braham.

The era of Gilbert and Sullivan in London town was contemporaneous with an institution that served, for New York and secondarily for the entire United States, a purpose similar to that which for two decades animated the series that was the Savoy. But in spirit, as in fact, an ocean of difference lay between the polite animadversions of Gilbert and Sullivan and the melodious rowdyism of Harrigan and Hart. The Englishmen dwelt in a fantastic realm of their own creation. In their work, which still has an undeniable vigor, there was also a suggestion of effeteness that derived not so much from an inherent quality of the collaborators as from the type of civilization that they portrayed.

Not so with Harrigan and Hart. They were, at their height, of New York newyorky; no delicate fantasy here, but a crude realism that was of the soil, for all its staginess; no effeteness, but rather a rawness garbed in authentic outfit. If Harrigan and Hart and Dave Braham were too much of their own day to remain for any other day; if Braham's music and Harrigan's librettos—let us call them such—lack the vitality that has preserved the operettas of their English contemporaries, they represent none the less an important epoch of the national humor, and even a document upon the national growth. They are among the treasured memories of a slowly rising American theater, as notable for what they helped lead to as for what they were. The Harrigan plays were plays in only a secondary sense. An outgrowth of the vaudeville sketch, they were built around the actor rather than shaped by the dramatist. They lived on the stage; the library would be fatal to

[66]

HARRIGAN AND HART, THE ANCESTORS OF GEORGE M. COHAN

It's a Great Day To-night for the Irish

them. And so they have had the jaunty, strutting career of the actor, whose sole immortality is remembrance.

Doubtless the later Gilbert, who had conveniently forgotten the operatic travesties of his 'prentice days, would have been appropriately shocked to behold the female impersonations of Tony Hart. Yet, at bottom, the chastity of Gilbert and Sullivan was paralleled by the fundamental purity of the typical Harrigan and Hart production. Just as the Comedy Opera Company, founded by D'Oyly Carte, was "how English and how pure!" so was the enterprise of Edward Harrigan pure and American. Over both the establishments hovered, after all, the spirit of a Queen who took her pleasures soberly.

"The moral standpoint," wrote Harrigan some forty years ago, in a short article upon his stage pieces, "is, if not falling into abeyance, at least changing to a very remarkable extent. Within the memory of theatergoers, the nude was almost unknown, and anything savoring of immorality was tabooed. At present no light opera nor spectacular performance can be a success without a superabundant display of corporeal charms, and the number of . . . plays . . . whose corner-stories are unchastity and vice is constantly on the increase." To-day, it might be Fred Stone or George M. Cohan speaking; Cohan, indeed, reckons Harrigan in his genealogy as surely as Harrigan reckoned Dion Boucicault.

It is the actor-tradition, not the play-tradition, with which we have chiefly to do. That is why Harrigan's depictions ran to types, and why he was quick to follow the lead of his public. "This, in all probability, is what gave me a decided bent, and has confined all my work to certain fields. It began with the New York 'boy,' the Irish-American, and our African brother. As these grew in

[67]

popularity I added the other prominent types which go to make up life in the metropolis and in every other large city of the Union and Canada. These are the Irishman, Englishman, German, Low German, Chinese, Italian, Russian and Southern darky. I suppose ere long"—Harrigan wrote these words in 1889—"I shall add the Bohemian, Hungarian, Roumanian, Polak and Scandinavian. As yet, however, their time has not come. This system has given my pieces their peculiar polyglot character."

Harrigan's sense of realism, again, was quite as acute as Gilbert's. If the famous librettist could draw, for his scenery, upon the English courts, the English navy, and the English army, Harrigan, with equal fidelity to his milieu, could pattern the bar-room of one of the Mulligan series after a saloon in Roosevelt street; the opium den in *Investigation* after a joint on Pell street; the dive in *Waddy Googan* after a den in the neighborhood of the Bowery. In fact, whether of types or of scenes, it may be said with equal truth that Harrigan had but to look upon them and enclose them in the proscenium of his theater.

He had little respect for the upper class as material for his international fair. "Polite society, wealth, and culture possess little or no color and picturesqueness. The chief use I make of them is as a foil to the poor, the workers, the great middle class. The average gentleman is so stereotyped that he has no value except in those plays where he is a pawn on the chessboard of melodramatic vice or tragic sin. He does very well in *Camille* and *Forget-me-not*, but I can't imagine him at home in a happy tenement-house or enjoying himself at a colored ball." That was written before this average gentleman went home to Harlem and rose to Nigger Heaven.

[68]

Harrigan, for his purposes and his talents, saw true. More: his work, though not in print, still lives. It forms part of the tradition of burlesque and vaudeville. As sharply as any Goldoni cutting out the patterns of the Venetian pantaloon and his confrères, Harrigan helped to fix the figure of the stage Irishman and the stage coon. As playwright, as producer, as predecessor of Irving Berlin in the rôle of New York's troubadour—the folk lore in Harrigan's songs has been forgotten together with the tunes—and as actor, Edward Harrigan marks an important epoch in the development of the American song-and-dance show. His day was a great day for the Irish.

He was born to wandering; the sea was in his blood. Harrigan's Cove, Nova Scotia, and Cape Harrigan, Labrador, bear witness to the renown of his ancestors as seamen. The Harrigans had come to Canada in the Eighteenth Century. Edward's father, born in Newfoundland, was William Harrigan, a sea-captain and shipbuilder; Edward was born, on October 26, 1845, at 31 Scammel street, New York, in what was then the center of the local shipbuilding trade. His mother, Ellen Rogers, had been born in the shadow of Bunker Hill, at Charlestown, Mass., but had received her early rearing in Norfolk, Va. It was there that William Harrigan had met her on one of his voyages, and married her. She, too, could boast an ancestry of the sea; what was more, she had acquired, from Southern residence, a repertory of Negro songs, dances and dialectal skill that her talented boy was quick to absorb. He must early have learned to play the banjo, which in later years, at work upon a negro novelty like *Pete*, he would meditatively strum in search of darky words for his composer. The typical Harrigan productions, which are pivoted upon the clash of the Irish and the Negroes in New York, were thus determined virtually at his mother's knee.

New York itself he learned in truancy. He had left school in his fourteenth year and was slapping about as an errand boy, as a printer's devil; by sixteen he was apprentice in a shipyard of the city. He must have frequented the theaters of the cheaper sort, for at about this time he is discovered delivering, in association with Campbell's Minstrels at the Bowery Theatre, a burlesque stump speech of his own composition. Meantime, his mother had died and his father had married a second time; as a result of dissension in the family, Harrigan went off to New Orleans as an able seaman. It wouldn't have been Ned if, during his later labors as a calker, he hadn't wandered about the levees, listening to the negro songs and taking down notes, without realizing it, for plays that were to come.

About California, more than a decade after the Gold Rush, there was still the halo of adventure. When New Orleans had ceased to interest him, the youngster set sail for the Golden Gate. His vessel was wrecked; he was cast ashore at Chagres, sick and penniless, and was—in the manner of a Cooper romance—nursed back to health by a compassionate Indian.

It was natural that, reaching San Francisco at last, he should hire out as a laborer on the docks; his real school had been the wharves of New York. It was natural, too, that he should hunt out the theaters of the city and shortly be inaugurating his stage career on the boards of the Olympic. In all likelihood he appeared as a one-man show; maybe his stump speech was the nucleus around which was built a song or two of topical interest; the entire output of Harrigan, indeed, possessed this topical nature. He rapidly became a town favorite, and before long was appearing at the Bella Union and the New Pacific Theatre. He remained in the city from 1867 to 1869. At the Bella Union he learned a few tricks from Alec O'Brien, with whom he often played. He sang and he danced; he impersonated darkies and chin-whiskered Dutchmen; he was acquiring the routine of production.

His association with Sam Rickey was even more valuable than that with O'Brien. Prospectively, Rickey was the model for Tony Hart. After two years of success in 'Frisco, Harrigan and Rickey began to look eastward; a series of one-night stands, including many a dive of the raw West, landed them at last in Chicago, where "the noted Californian comedians"—by grace of type and a showbill—opened some time in 1870. Harrigan was the Irishman, Rickey the coon. As success in 'Frisco had sent them to Chicago, so now success in the Windy City sent their eyes New Yorkward. On November 21 of the same year they made their début at the Globe Theatre, 514 Broadway, in a sketch entitled *The Little Fraud*. It was simply a take-off on a popular tune, and was followed the next week by *The Mulcahey Twins*. The entertainment was funny and tuneful; it took the town. Also, it swelled Mr. Rickey's head, and before many months Harrigan, now definitely dedicated to the stage, was going it on his own. He switched back to Negro impersonation, signed up with Manning's Minstrels, and went on tour with them.

It was in Chicago, where he had scored his first great success with Rickey, that he was to meet Anthony Cannon, *alias* Tony Hart. Hart, at the time but a handsome lad, was born in Worcester, Mass., on July 25, 1855; he was thus ten years the junior of his

[71]

future partner. Something too pretty in his person must have suggested, originally, his adoption of comic female rôles.

When Harrigan first met him, Hart was singing with Arlington's Minstrels. Here was a fellow to take Rickey's place, he thought; in a trice, as it were, they had come to terms and soon *The Little Fraud* was running at the Chicago Winter Garden, as merrily as if it had never been discontinued. As Boston claims the honor of having first discovered to America the genius of Gilbert and Sullivan, so may it with equal justice lay claim to having been the true discoverer of Harrigan and Hart. Seven years before Manager Field of the Boston Museum imported *Pinafore* into the United States, Manager John Stetson of the Howard Athenæum—it is still the Old Howard, in Howard street, dedicated as aforetime to the immortal themes of burlesque, with its churchly exterior, and its gallery seats thickly stained with tobacco juice—had spotted them and engaged them for his theater; here, as "The Nonpareils," they warmed the hearts of the city for more than one hundred nights in the self-same *Little Fraud*. Here, then, their career may be said to have begun.

They did not reach New York until October 16, 1871, where, at the Globe, likewise under the management of John Stetson, they made their metropolitan bow. They played then at the Union Square; for a time they went on the road under Tony Pastor, returning to his theater on the Bowery in the perennial *Little Fraud*, *The Big and Little of It*, and *Sweet Summer*. Only by December of the next year do they strike their true stride, at the Globe, now renamed the Theatre Comique. Here, under the benefits of a generous contract for two years, they grow wealthy and famous; here they study the contemporary nature of the variety show and decide

—that is, Harrigan decides—upon changes in the direction of a more natural type and more realistic background. Here, before the contract has expired, will be conceived the Mulligan series. And here, finally, is discovered the third partner in an entertainment that is to charm America for the next fifteen years.

David Braham was born in London, in 1838; he was thus seven years the senior of Harrigan, and by seventeen the senior of Hart. He was originally a fiddler, and it was as violinist that he engaged with Pony Moore's Minstrels when, at the age of eighteen, he first landed in this country. He knew the orchestra pit of almost every theater that served up dances and ditties to Broadway—Canterbury Hall, Wood's Minstrel Hall, the New Idea, Butler's Theatre, Mechanics Hall, and later, the Olympic, the Eagle, the Union Square and the Theatre Comique. He was, in fact, of a musico-theatrical family; his brother Joseph led the band at Tony Pastor's; another brother, under the régime of Rudolph Aronson, led the orchestra at the Casino; his son Harry, who conducted the musicians at the Madison Square Theatre and at Wallack's was later the first husband of Lillian Russell; to complete the picture, his daughter eventually became the wife of Edward Harrigan, and his son, when Dave became ill, wrote music for the Harrigan shows.

Here, then, at the Theatre Comique, was the man that Harrigan needed; he knew the sort of tune that Broadway of that day whistled. He knew it so well, in fact, that the famous melody of the Mulligan Guards was soon to find its way to Kipling's India, where it would become, for the soldiery, what "Tipperary"—an inferior tune—became in the World War. Braham was hardly a highbrow. But he was the very fellow to play Sullivan to Harrigan's Gilbert.

He set the themes of New York to the music of New York, with natural overtones of the English popular song. At the core of Harrigan's doggerel burns a vitalizing sincerity; these verses, whether in single example or as a historical collection, depict an era; Harrigan, in his unpretentious way, was the folksinger of an epoch, remembering its days and ways and setting them down in simple language.

What his songs were, his plays were: reminiscence, commentary, parody. The knight of his particular epos was a man whom everyone could recognize instanter: Dan Mulligan, who mixed his groceries with liquor, and spiced both with politics. Food, drink and warfare: epitome of life itself. Dan, however, was to become something more than a symbol of Irish ascendancy in the seventies and eighties; he grew into the hero of a minor American saga. Harrigan had conceived him in 1872, but he did not come to life until July 15, 1873, at the Chicago Academy of Music, whither the Josh Hart Combination had arrived on its travels.

Mulliganiana.

The Mulligan cycle—it is no less—had its true origins, not in the Chicago skit, but in *The Mulligan Guards Ball*, which was first presented, in New York, on January 13, 1879. It was not long before the town was agog, between this admirable burletta on the target companies that infested the States after the Civil War, and the good ship *Pinafore*. A long line of sketches had signalized the union of Harrigan and Hart, and in the summer of 1875 they had gone on tour with Martin W. Henley, who was thenceforth to act as their business manager. Next year they leased the Theatre

Comique, made Braham their official composer (he was now Harrigan's father-in-law), and a famous institution had been inaugurated.

It was here that Anne Yeamans, John Wild and William Gray founded more than one tradition of the vaudeville stage. The mingled top-loftiness and humility of a Moran and Mack or an Amos 'n Andy derive, if indirectly, from the patterns established by Wild and Gray. It was these gentlemen who, in the early days of the Comique, started off the bill with a comic skit; there would be a sentimental song to eke out the olio, whereupon would follow the regulation afterpiece. Harrigan was still feeling his way; Boucicault suggested such old-country excursions as *Iascaire* and *The Lorgaire*. Harrigan's forte, however, was to be, not the Irishman of overseas, but the Paddy that drank and fought right under his nose. It was a happy thought that sent him back to his old sketch on *The Mulligan Guards*. Out of the success of the first elaboration grew the series that followed the Mulligans through chowder parties, Christmas celebrations, picnics, ward politics, mudscows and mud-slinging, down to the silver wedding of the garrulous, bellicose, but loving Irish couple, Dan Mulligan and Cordelia of the frustrated social aspirations.

Essentially, the Mulligan cycle chronicles the racial antipathies that divided the Irish, the German and the Negro; but the antipathies are not so deeply rooted that they may not blossom into understanding and coöperation. Salient among the knights of this round table are Dan and his wife Cordelia; Tommy, their son; Rebecca Allup, their colored cook, maid and Lord Low Everything Else; Sampson Primrose, owner of the alley barbershop and "policy" resort; Palestine Puter, captain of the Skidmore Guards, the black rivals of the Mulligans; Gustavus Lochmuller, butcher and political opponent of Dan; Bridget, the Irish wife of this German he-devil. A merry chase they led their public during the five years at the Comique.

And the critics, too. Harrigan had definite notions as to what he was about, but propitiating the high-brows was not one of them. Yet they came and listened and were conquered. As early as *The Mulligans' Chowder* the *Times* spoke of Balzac and Zola as undisgraced prototypes of the humble Harrigan; the *Herald*, in *The Mulligan Guards Nominee*, saw *The Pickwick Papers* of the Bowery Dickens. Another lustrum, and William Dean Howells was invoking the names of Shakespeare and Molière as stage-manager ancestors of this gifted Irish actor-producer, while the *Times* spoke of a theatrical Hogarth.

Harrigan, certainly, did not suffer from lack of contemporary appreciation; a day came when Brander Matthews brought the great Coquelin to see him, and was surprised to discover that Harrigan managed French with passable skill; (he had taken private lessons); Matthew Arnold, apostle of Swift's sweetness and light, also caught the popular contagion.

When the original home of the Mulligan series proved too small to accommodate the surge of loyal New Yorkers, the New Theatre Comique was opened on August 29, 1881, at 728 Broadway, with *The Major*. Rivalry still held the scene; for the nonce, the Mulligans had disappeared; there was little change, however, in the character of Harrigan's verses. *Cordelia's Aspirations*, evolved out of *The Mulligans' Surprise*, brought back, on November 5, 1883, the indispensable family. This time it was La Mulligan, as a climber, seeking to leap out the frame of the picture. She did, only

[76]

to fall back with a resounding plump; the series ends on a pathetic note in *Dan's Tribulations,* produced on April 7, 1884. Back to the grocery goes the wiser and sadder Dan, his wealth squandered by the aspiring Cordelia. His adventures among the shanties, the mudscows, the target companies, the politicians of New York, the blacks and whites and yellows of dive and waterfront, the secret societies of the Full Moons and the *Turnvereine* of his German cadets, the clothes stalls of his Jews—these are all as a tale that is told.

Perhaps there is a relation of one sort or another between the end of the Mulligan cycle and the end of the partnership between Harrigan and Hart. *Investigation* had followed the chronicle of Dan and his regression; again Kipling found, in a Harrigan piece, in the person of "the solid Muldoon," a figure for his Indian tales. On December 23 of the same year the New Theatre Comique was destroyed by fire; the building was not covered by insurance and the loss to the partners was $100,000. Temperamental differences between them were growing into barriers; Hart, fond of the lighter aspects of theatrical life, tugged in a different direction from Harrigan. Their parting was amicable enough; they appeared for the last time together at Colonel Simm's Theatre in Brooklyn, on June 13, 1885. Hart's place was effectively taken by Dan Collyer, and an institution had come to an end.

Harrigan and Hart, after the fire, had leased the New Park Theatre. It was here that Harrigan continued for almost five years, undaunted by the loss of a fortune and of an associate even more precious. His pieces took a more serious turn. *Old Lavender,* reverted to an early sketch, which he enlarged into a portrait not without pathos; *Pete* likewise reverted, in part, to a still earlier sketch, *Darby and Lanty*, that had already been subjected to a number of transformations; *Waddy Googan*, named after its hackman hero, descended into the night life of a growing metropolis, and prompted the *Times* to mention Zola's name again, while *Town Topics* played up Cruikshank.

Harrigan had recouped himself in both finances and spirit. He was riding at the top of his bent. This troubadour of *hoi polloi* was being hailed as America's representative dramatist. He celebrated the Christmas of 1890 by opening, on December 29, his own Harrigan's Theatre, with *Reilly and the 400*. The play was to become famous as establishing yet another theatrical tradition, that of Ada Lewis's tough girl, her gum playing a *perpetuo moto* between her jaws. How many recall from it now the spirited waltz of "Maggie Murphy's Home"—a Gotham tune that can dance with the best Victor Herbert ever wrote, swimming in his favorite lager?

> Behind a grammar schoolhouse,
> In a double tenement,
> I live with my old mother
> And always pay the rent.
> A bedroom and a parlor
> Is all we call our own,
> And you're welcome, every evening,
> At Maggie Murphy's home.
>
> Chorus
> On Sunday night, 'tis my delight
> And pleasure, don't you see,
> Meeting all the girls and boys
> That work down town with me.
> There's an organ in the parlor

To give the house a tone,
And you're welcome every evening
At Maggie Murphy's home.

Such dancing in the parlor,
There's a waltz for you and I;
Such mashing in the corner,
And kisses on the sly.
O, bless the leisure hours
That working-people know,
And they're welcome every evening
At Maggie Murphy's home.

On Sun - day night, 'tis my   de - light And pleas - ure don't you see

Braham, for one reason or another, had balked at setting these words; the tune, played to this day, became one of his greatest hits.

He was a fellow of melodic simplicities; his music was no more sophisticated—it did not have to be—than Harrigan's catalogue of words. Yet I believe that anything like a full account of Victor Herbert's musical comedies should consider, as one forerunner, the humble Boweryism of David Braham. In little touches such as the mincing notes of the chorus to "Maggie Murphy's Home," and the jocund octave on the word "pleasure," Braham achieved expert musical delineation.

For three and a half years Harrigan was to carry on (in both senses of the phrase) at the theater named after him. On November 4, 1891, Hart died in the city of his birth, Worcester, Mass. Perhaps another signal of the end came with the death of Harrigan's eldest son, Edward, in February, 1895. The loss took the heart out of him; the theater was leased, in April of the same year, to Richard Mansfield, and renamed the Garrick. The Garrick it is to this day, under the auspices of the Theatre Guild.

There were a few more flashes from the guttering candle, but the Harrigan public was passing just as inevitably as was the public of Gilbert and Sullivan in London town. Rivalry of the races in New York City was giving way to a harmony which the Harrigan pieces had foreseen. For, after all, though you couldn't get his Irish and Negroes and Germans together, you couldn't keep them apart. Hadn't Harrigan himself married the daughter of his part-German composer, thus duplicating a classic situation in his own *Mulligan Guard Ball?* And, in *The Mulligan Guards' Christmas* doesn't Bridget Lochmuller's brother, Planxty McFudd, marry Diana, the sister of Dan Mulligan's wife, Cordelia,—thus adding to the interfamilial complications? When Mulligan runs for alderman (*The Mulligan Guards Nominee*) isn't it the colored vote that he seeks, and don't the Skidmores—that phalanx of dark Apollos—parade in honor of his election?

On August 31, 1896, at the Bijou Theatre, Harrigan attempted to reëstablish himself in the popular favor with *Marty Malone*. A revival of *Old Lavender* at the Murray Hill Theatre was equally unsuccessful. As late as September, 1903, loath to believe that his public had forsaken him, he produced, at the Murray Hill, his last piece, *Under Cover*, with music by George Braham, son of David. Coincidentally, Anne Yeamans, herself in the show, was represented in the cast also by her daughter, Jennie. In the last, as in the beginning, the contentions of Irish versus Negro form the theme, and the quarrel this time raged over the question whether a certain parcel of land was an Irish race track or a darky cemetery. The play ran for a few weeks, and went on a road tour. Another revival or two kept Harrigan occupied on the road, and then came the sunset.

On April 11, 1905, Dave Braham died after a long siege of kidney disease, leaving a widow, two sons and four daughters.

Harrigan missed the old gang. To a friend he observed that the new generation didn't know, and therefore couldn't appreciate, the Mulligan types. He missed, too, his gallery gods. "I'd hate to play," he once confessed in an interview, "in a theater without a gallery." He had one ear cocked to the verdict of what he called his twenty-five cent critics. In fact, it was a habit of his to sit incognito among his audiences, the better to gauge the effect of lines and situations.

There were several farewell appearances, one at Wallack's, on October 6, 1908, another at a Lambs' Gambol in the Metropolitan Opera House, in 1909. He ended his days amid deep depression, in his home at 249 West 102nd street, where he died on June 6, 1911.

Out of songs his pieces had grown; to-day, only the songs remain—the songs, and a reputation for stage-production and an ensemble unequaled in its day. The very supernumeraries in a Harrigan production were, both by instinct and by training, artists. They were regarded as such not only by the producer but by the foremost stage critics of the era. Harrigan had a conscientious eye for apparently insignificant detail. He did not make the mistake of thinking that the importance of an actor varied in direct ratio to the length of time he appeared on the stage. The reputation of Ada Lewis, for example, was made in a rôle that allowed her but one spoken line in the performance.

What pleased William Dean Howells in the Harrigan productions was almost precisely what later pleased Brander Matthews. Howells, in 1886, recognized in the Irishman "the spring of a true American comedy, the beginnings of things which may be great things." Harrigan, indeed, was more decent than Shakespeare, maintained the ruling spirit of the "Editor's Study" in *Harper's*.

Harrigan did not pass into literature, however; he was, as an influence, absorbed into the history of the American theater. His songs, as a part of New York's folklore, receded long ago into that distance which is happily veiled by pathos. Hart, of course, can be truly remembered only by those who saw him in the yielding flesh. Braham's music, once the admiration of the continent, gathers dust in the libraries and is heard occasionally in a medley of old-time numbers. It is, on the whole, as old-fashioned, but as quaint, as the daguerreotype. *Sic transit gloria theatri!*

There are few to-day, outside the ranks of the specialists, who know the songs of Harrigan and Braham. Truth to tell, like most ditties of a vanished day, they have faded into an irrecoverable past . . . "The Mulligan Guard" . . . "The Pitcher of Beer" . . . "The Babies in Our Block" (parent of "The Sidewalks of New York"), with the catalogue of names that Harrigan was so fond of, and the interpolations of old Irish tunes.

The late Seventies and the Eighties were especially melodious with Irish tunes. The Irish had preceded the Jews as immigrants

on a large scale. Parnell was a living inspiration. Irish singers
filled the variety theaters and sang "Remember, Boy, You're
Irish," "Give an Honest Irish Boy a Chance," "The Land of the
Shamrock," "Why Paddy's Always Poor." McGinty, dressed in
his best suit of clothes, was going down to the bottom of the well.
Drill, ye tarriers, drill! And drill they did on every stage of the
metropolis. Harry Kernell, at Pastor's, was teaching Clarence
McFadden the most famous of all dances:

> One—two—three—balance like me
> You're quite a fairy, but you have your faults;
> While your left foot is lazy, your right foot is crazy
> But don't be uneasy, I'll learn you to waltz.

Harrigan and Braham, though not neglecting the Negro, were
naturally part of this Irish era . . . "The Widow Nolan's Goat"
. . . The not-quite-to-be-forgotten "Paddy Duffy's Cart," with its
central line, "Oh, I love to talk of old New York, and of my boyish
days" . . . "The Gallant 69th" . . . "The Beauty of Limerick"
. . . "The Knights of St. Patrick" . . . "No Irish Wanted Here"
. . . "Our Front Stoop" . . . "The Little Widow Dunn" . . .
"The Last of the Hogans" . . . "Down in Gossipy Row" . . .
"My Little Side Door" . . . "Johnny Reilly's Always Dry." . . .

The spirit of these songs, however, and especially of their music,
was not to be lost. A greater musician than Braham had already
arisen to carry on the tradition of Irish melody. Long before the
end of the Harrigan-Braham era, Victor Herbert and Tin Pan
Alley alike had struck their stride.

[83]

5. The Rise of Tin Pan Alley

Hearts and Flowers.

THE songs of a people are rarely written by great poets and great composers. They are sourced, usually, in simplicity and flow down the hills of mediocrity into the vast sea of the undying—if not the immortal—commonplace. In musical illiteracy they are born; in the hearts and on the lips of the musically illiterate or semi-literate they live their brief lives and die. Or, to be more exact, are forever reborn, with a slight change of word, a deft twist in tune. Popular music is nothing new. It is older, by centuries, than the music of the masters. By that very token it carries an appeal that reaches— if we are quite honest with ourselves—below the stratum of our cultivated taste to the levels on which the best of us, so little different from the worst, live in an unacknowledged harmony with earth's simplest creatures.

Popular song, musically, means in essence melody. Harmony, a late arrival in the evolution of music, is a correspondingly late arrival in the history of personal taste. There is music of the heels, music of the heart, music of the head. That, of course, is an oversimplified scheme, but it expresses vividly the respective predominance of rhythm, melody and harmony. The songs and dances made popular by the long era of the minstrel show reveal, in their exceedingly simple structure, a marked predominance of the rhythmic and the melodic elements. This is exactly what we might have expected. Such harmonies as occur are the simplest combinations and progressions known to musical grammar. The music, in other words, is a perfect counterpart to the words. It suggests, as it doubtless was suggested by, the characteristic instruments of the day. In the strains of "The Arkansaw Traveler," for example, or of "Pop Goes the Weasel," one hears plainly the scraping of the country fiddler; Foster's songs suggest the guitar or the melodeon; Emmet's "Dixie" is clearly the backwoods fiddle or the strumming banjo.

Music of the heels and music of the heart . . . This almost sums up the musical repertory of the minstrel show and its more gaudy successors. There will be little head in our home-and-street music until Ragtime suddenly flashes into being.

The *London Musical Times*, in 1880, when the Christy and the Haverly minstrels still had London by the ears, was speculating in much this strain upon the musical backgrounds of minstrelsy. "We have," it editorialized, "a convenient mirror of ourselves, if we choose to make use of it, in our kinsmen in the United States. In spite of a continuous dribble of emigration from all quarters of Europe, the Americans jealously preserve the laws, habits and domestic institutions of Englishmen. They rival us in commerce and the industrial arts, and outstrip us in small ingenuities; but with all their cleverness and greatness, they return to us our tunes, slightly modernized and banjoized, or dexterously set in the form of German part-songs, but in many essential respects precisely as they went.

"Our antiquarian knowledge is not equal to tracing the origin of prehistoric specimens of negro minstrelsy. We know that in former times there were songs called 'Jump Jim Crow' and 'Such a Getting Up Stairs,' which may or may not have been French, or even Pelagic remains wafted from Peru to the Mississippi. But coming nearer to authentic records, and meeting with the name of Christy, we alight on ground not only familiar, but hallowed. Some of the popular melodies of the class and period we are referring to, lend themselves easily to a particular kind of simple harmonization, and flow back naturally into old English forms which, in the youthful reminiscences of a few of us who still survive, are associated with drowsy, unreformed mumblings, lazily pealing organs, shadowy elms and cawing rooks, sundry flagellations, and other innocent joys of thirty or forty years ago.

"The basis of the more pathetic songs of the Christy Minstrels order is derived from good, sound Episcopalian chants which have crossed the ocean, and, following the pioneer's ax into the far West, penetrated the hovels of what was till lately the modern bond in the plantations of the South. They come back to us in one changed rhythm or another, but their spirit and origin no twang of the banjo can overcome, no soot and tallow can disguise.

"Again, in the Northern States there is a strong infusion of the British jig and hornpipe. In the conventional negro comic song, the Yankee drawl, the Scotch snivel, the Hibernian whoop, and the English guffaw amalgamate almost kindly with the yells and grimaces and other external manifestations of free and independent negro sentiment in the meeting house, dancing ring, or liquor shanty of New York or Pennsylvania.

"Traveling southwards, along the banks of the great river and its tributaries, we encounter a decidedly new and a more melancholy and refined musical element. Its sadness is blended with the strains of the English ballads of fifty or sixty years ago, and reproduced with a certain indescribable charm in one or two of the more ancient Christy Minstrels' ditties. The element we speak of proceeds doubtless from the Creole stock in Louisiana; and is, perhaps, mixed with the tango of the Cuban negro.

"It was in Louisiana that the pianist Gottschalk commenced to compose in a tone-painting vein, at the age of thirteen, when his senses were freshly impregnated with the luxuriant surroundings of a semi-tropical climate, when still a stranger to Parisian life, and before he became acquainted with Schumann and the apostles of musical progress in Leipzig. To the end of a prematurely closed and wandering existence, he never quite got rid of the banjo in his music, of the mournful cries of the banana seller, or of the melancholy impressions of the savannah."

Popular music, in its steady progression toward the Tin Tower of Babble, left the hinterlands far behind. Like the sturdy backwoodsman who had heard the call of the City, it was making its way inevitably to the Metropolis. The song that had soothed or enlivened our agricultural age could not be the song to accompany the excitements of our industrial civilization. Yet it is astonishing to what a degree, even to-day, the observations of the anonymous writer on the *London Musical Times* hold good. The more purely English influences remain, though they are confined largely to what we call our peasantry—to our folk of the mountain fastnesses and the prairie. The negro influence dominates the city. Between these two, always in disguises that take their protective coloration from the contemporary environment, subtle conflict is forever being waged.

TIN PAN ALLEY

Twin Masks of Popular Song.

Thus, two schools of popular song contend, in the late Eighties and the Nineties, for supremacy. Neither was as new as superficial investigators have considered it to be. Both the Ballad of heaving sobs and the nascent Coon Song trace their ancestry to the tear-drainer and the gay negroid tunes, respectively, of blackface minstrelsy. The minstrel show, too, had a passion for burlesque and travesty; it parodied not only life but its vocal stock-in-trade. Its ballads, as its black tunes, rapidly degenerated into denatured products, until at times it was difficult to distinguish between the sober song and its parody. The negro song, which once had the true ring of the plantation, became blackface music—music with a smearing of burnt-cork over its face, like the performers themselves. It was ready for Tin Pan Alley, and needed but the stimulation of the ragtime craze to leap from the stage of minstrelsy into the new market of mass production.

There was something honest about the doleful tales and the raggy-gayety of the old-fashioned entertainments, even when they became caricatures. Their naïveté, like their high spirits, was almost untouched by the sophistication that we find in a later day, though parody always implies criticism. The sobbing Ballad never died; it lives on, the eternal Sick Man of Tin Pan Alley, never so ready to stage a come-back as when it has been prepared, with mocking rites, for burial. It returns always in a new disguise, but always its tearful self beneath the raiment of the new fashion in song. So, too, the livelier ditty of the black is in its way immortal. Call it Ragtime yesterday, call it Jazz to-day—and what, to-morrow?—it is part of a universal pattern. The sad song and the gay song, ballad and rag, heart song and jazz—these are the twin masks of Tragedy and Comedy behind which the mummer of Melody Lane megaphones his infinite (and too often his infinitesimal) variations upon the eternal themes.

In the early Eighties Vaudeville is born out of Variety.[1] The enterprising Benjamin Franklin Keith, in association with George H. Batchelder, opens up, in a three-story building, Washington Street, Boston, a dime show composed of freaks. Keith and Batchelder were circus men, and their original purpose had been to make a few dollars during the idle season. Business proved so good that they abandoned the circus forever. Weber and Fields, among the first acts billed by the fathers of vaudeville, have left a graphic record of these humble beginnings of a venture that, on one great day, would rear a million-dollar playhouse close to the site of their original shop. In 1883 Weber and Fields were mere kids. They went on eight times per day, alternating a Dutch act with a song-and-dance performance. They received $40 per week. Eleven years later, Keith was paying them $400. And eleven years after that, $4000.

Keith, like Pastor before him, keenly sensed the importance of the distaff side to the new type of entertainment. He set out to capture not only the women but the children. Perhaps, between such business acumen as this and the growing importance of women in public life there may have been some connection.

---

[1] The successors to the Keith-Albee interests have decided (1930) to restore the name variety, or, rather—perhaps because the singular noun is identified with a leading theatrical journal—to call vaudeville henceforth by the name "Varieties." The change is for the better. Let us hope that the institution will improve with the name.

Perhaps, too, the great vogue of children's songs in the later Eighties is tethered, by some tenuous bond, to the same enterprise.

Between song and playhouse is an eternal companionship. It is the public singer who introduces a song, who stamps upon it his interpretation, who attaches to it his personality. It is not to be wondered at, then, that so much of our popular music, in the days before it became a factory product, should have been written by actors, by song-and-dance men. They were in constant touch with the public, able to gauge its taste, to feel on the instant the quality of its response. Songs were a staple of all productions, even of the legitimate theater, being often thrust into the action if for no better reason than that the audiences were fond of a little concert on the side. This is the story of our early theme song long before that sometimes melodious intruder burst from the horns of Hollywood, not too faintly blowing.

Harris Hangs Out a Sign.

It was Charles K. Harris who, first among the children that were to found Tin Pin Alley—and many of the pioneers were just that: children—shrewdly hit upon the scheme of building his songs around and into stage productions. Songs with a story . . . Songs for situations, and not dumped irrelevantly into the action . . . These were the principles upon which he began to work, from the moment when, as a stage-struck lad in Milwaukee, he had taught himself the banjo and began to pick airs from the strings and words from the air.

Harris haunted the theaters; he was soon giving private concerts at clubs and, though he had not the slightest technical knowl-edge of music, was offering instruction on the banjo. He pecked away at the piano, too, until he could give a fair account of him-self at the keys. His repertory was the old minstrel collection, and it seemed to him that folks were getting weary of the unvaried fare. When he first offered to remedy this deficiency himself, he was laughed off the scene; obstinately he toiled away in silence, meantime warming the seats where the gods of the gallery con-vened. It was at a performance of Nat Goodwin in a play named *The Skating Rink* that he was suddenly struck by the unfitness of Goodwin's songs. Then and there, together with his companion, Charles Horowitz, he decided to write a song for the play. It was an important moment in the history of our popular music. Good-win, after a little demurring, placed the song in the show: it was a sorry affair, in all conscience, named "Since Maggie Learned to Skate." But it was with that doggerel of words and music that Charlie Harris skated on to the rink of a career that was to revo-lutionize the popular song.

He followed up this technique of song placing, pestering actors and managers with an unceasing show of ideas. Thus were written "Creep, Baby, Creep"; "Let's Kiss and Make Up"; "Thou Art Ever in My Thoughts." Harris was impatient. All work and no royalties keep Jack a poor boy. His relations with local publishers had not proved satisfactory; there was one thing left: go into business for himself. Harris was now eighteen. Moving into a little office, at 207 Grand Avenue, Milwaukee, that had been vacated by the music firm of A. A. Fisher after a year's tenancy, Charlie entered upon his professional career with an overhead of $7.50 per month—the rent. Mark well the shingle that he hung out, for in its ambitious lettering you may read the first conscious proclamation of Tin Pan Alley:

CHARLES K. HARRIS
BANJOIST AND SONG WRITER
SONGS WRITTEN TO ORDER

Songs Written to Order . . . Tin Pan Alley, hitherto a wandering potentiality, is suddenly focussed upon that sign in four stigmatic words. To Order . . . words, music, emotions, notions, heart-beats, gutter-philosophies, elementary wish-fulfillments, pathos, bathos . . . You pays your money—that's important—and you takes your choice . . .

Is the popular tune a phase of the American folk-song? Academic hands flutter high in deprecation. The folk-song is redolent of simple hearth and countryside; the popular ditty is a synthetic product bespattered by the mire of city thoroughfares. The folk-song belongs to the healthy, wholesome youth of the world; the popular song is the street-walker of music, end-product of a civilization advancing with accelerated tempo to its doom. . . . The folk-song is genuine; the song of cabaret and cinema is false, conceived in concupiscence and dedicated to commerce. The one is a prairie flower; the other a hothouse breed. Say no word of a folk-song of the Melting-Pot. These are but the noxious fumes that rise from the ungodly stew. And so on, far into the night.

Names are unimportant. So are adjectives. There are true folk-songs—whatever the definition of a folk-song may be—that are as ribald and racy as any prurient patter of the café chantant. Born of earth, they are earthy. Purity of the village: impurity of the town—it is a blasted antithesis. What millions of the folk sing

[92]

MAUDE NUGENT
"Sweet Rosie O'Grady"

JAMES THORNTON
"When You Were Sweet Sixteen"

Albert Davis Collection

CHARLES K. HARRIS
"After the Ball"

PAUL DRESSER
"On the Banks of the Wabash"

GLORIES OF THE NINETIES

daily and nightly together is—while it endures—by that same token a folk-song, tonal and verbal image of the singer. The supposed beauty of folk melodies is frequently a non-musical phenomenon, reposing in association. As music alone, where is the beauty of "Home, Sweet Home"? Of "My Country, 'Tis of Thee"? Of "The Star-Spangled Banner," which began as the wettest of tavern tunes—

> . . . to entwine
> The myrtle of Venus with Bacchus's vine

—and has ended as the dryest of national anthems? *As music alone,* how inferior to these consecrated melodies are—to pick at random—such unpretending tunes as "A Hot Time in the Old Town To-night," "Ta-Ra-Ra-Boom-De-Ré," "Alexander's Ragtime Band," "The Man I Love," "Strike Up the Band"? Harmonically, the ordinary folk-song readily yields in interest to its step-brother. As for words, most of our early patriotic jingles couldn't have been worse if they had been penned in a White Way Café.

If to write for money and to write in the city is to disqualify that which is written, then we must throw out almost the entire canon of Stephen C. Foster. If popular songs die the death overnight, so did most of the tunes that our accepted folk-songs survived. This applies as forcibly to the so-called art-song. We know only the survivors. Perhaps the world—at least, our world—is too old for folk-songs of the ancient type. In any case, not the intention of the composer and the poet determines the category; that alone is folk-song which the folk ratifies.

And the folk ratified Harris. Blunderingly, inexpertly, he was raising his voice to sing a song they had been waiting for.

TIN PAN ALLEY

Virtue Triumphant.

The commercial insight of Harris—and there must, in some dim way, have been a modicum of that intuition through which all artists labor beneath the crust of acquired technique—entitles him to the honor of an adjective. Let us, then, christen his day and generation as the Harrisian age of our popular song. In the sign that he hung out on Grand Avenue, he concentrated in a flashing phrase the ground motif of the business that he was to adorn. In "After the Ball," he was shortly to provide the detonating hit that would match this theory with the proof of practice. So now Milwaukee basked in the double fame of its flowing Schlitz and its flowing melodies.

The Harrisian age . . . Age of songs that unfolded endless tales of woe; in triple-decker verses centering ever about the recurrent refrain . . . Condensed melodramas, tight-stuffed with villainies—with women wronged, with children abandoned, with lovers severed, reunited, with Vice reproved and conquered, with Virtue at last restored to her glittering throne. The motion pictures, during their protracted period of early adolescence, knowing—like early Tin Pan Alley—that their chief clientèle was composed of the women and children about whom Tony Pastor and B. F. Keith were so strenuously solicitous, filled the scene with babies. Babies on the screen and George M. Cohan waving the American flag . . . sure-fire stuff. Here, again, Harris anticipated the films. He wrote an entire nursery of juveniles . . . "Always in the Way" . . . "For Sale a Baby" . . . "Hello, Central, Give Me Heaven" . . . "There's Another Picture in My Mamma's Frame"

[94]

. . . "Baby's Eyes" . . . "Mud-Pie Days" . . . "Baby Hands"
. . . "Creep, Baby, Creep" . . . "My Mamma Lives Up in the
Sky" . . . "My Mother's Kiss" . . . It was the diaperhood of
the Alley—a Society for the Prevention of Cruelty to Children
set to children's music.

Love is the theme-song of the universe. It is Love that makes
the songs—and the profits—go 'round.

> But though I have an infinite variety
> Of themes that I might sing about to you,
> There is only one thing
> Though an overdone thing,
> Love, the olden theme that's always new.

So sang O. Henry and Franklin P. Adams in *Lo*, their ill-fated
musical comedy of 1909. The Alley knows, as Harris early knew,
the commercial value of love and tears. Tears, idle tears . . . The
tears of things . . . Crocodile tears . . . Synthetic tears . . .
Our popular song, in its industrial phase, begins largely under
the influence of women. It is women who sing songs in the home.
It is women who play them on the piano. The men, as it were,
serve only as the page-turners, unless it be to chant a sour note or
two in the amateur quartet of club or street-corner. Women, in the
Harrisian age, were women—still ingenuous, still untainted by
sophistication and adulterated modernism. They rocked the cradle
instead of the boat, and ruled the world. Thus it happens that, to
the songs that our parents sang before ragtime came to rescue us
from the musical doldrums, there was, in words and melody, a
distinctly feminine flavor. Yet Charles Hoyt, before the decade

[95]

was over, would be making his famous ironic toast: "Here's to woman—once our superior, now our equal."

A wise-cracker of Broadway exploded the other day with the report that the "waltz is coming back." One hadn't noticed that the waltz had ever gone out. It is one of those dances that live beyond the vogue of a night because they embody, somehow, the spirit of dance itself rather than the figures of a passing pattern. The innocent waltz! And yet a gay, not too innocent Goethe could write, in his even simpler day, of a "chaste and dignified polo-naise," after which "a waltz is played and whirls the whole company of young people away in a bacchic frenzy"(!)

There was no bacchic frenzy to our waltz-songs of the Nineties and early Nineteen-Hundreds. If the verses were frequently maudlin, the sentiments were as moral as the maxims in a copy-book. Often they read—and sound—like the sentimental admonitions of a drunkard in his self-pitying, weepy stage. There is the faint aroma of alcoholic hysteria about them. It is difficult, indeed, to dissociate the popular song from a hovering suggestion of *globulus hystericus*. Its tears are often as false as its laughter. And, as for its laughter, the relief of ragtime, welcome as it was, had more than a little of hysteria about it, as jazz still has.

The innocent waltz might become even an unwitting power for social reform. Hoyt's *A Temperance Town,* in which "After the Ball" had been given its first push to fame by the robust singing of J. Aldrich Libbey, carried in its diversified score that unforgettable tune, "The Bowery," by Percy Gaunt, composer for the Hoyt farces. It was not a flattering picture that was painted of that once so dangerous thoroughfare. Back in the hinterlands our peasantry heard the words and believed them. "Con" men, loquacious bar-

bers, predatory dives, unsympathetic policemen—it was no place
for tourists. "Big Tim" Sullivan, the New York political leader,
who ought to know his lots, said that the Bowery song reduced
the value of real estate by more than twenty-five per cent and had
killed the street.

Everybody was soon whistling Palmer and Ward's "And the
Band Played On." For the first time in history a newspaper—*The
New York World*—had put a song across. Newspapers would soon
be printing sheet music as supplements, or as part of their swollen
Sunday issues. Yet their potency as stimulators of sales would
never be very great. Some thirteen or fourteen years ago Shapiro,
Bernstein and Company—they were not founded until the turn of
the century—entered for a year into a publicity arrangement with
William Hearst that called for hundreds of full-page plugs for
current songs. It did not pan out well. "Songs," is Mr. Bernstein's
comment to-day, "must be heard by people who pay to hear them."

The waltz of the giddy Nineties . . . Bonnie and Jimmie
Thornton, singing his "She May Have Seen Better Days," "My
Sweetheart's the Man in the Moon," "When Summer Comes
Again," and that romantic assurance, "When You Were Sweet
Sixteen" . . . In the mid-Nineties Thornton was "The Napoleon
of Song Writers,—the man who has set the world a-singing" . . .
"On the Benches in the Park" . . . "Don't Give Up the Old Love
for the New" . . . "Let Me Call You Sweetheart Again" . . .
"Going for a Pardon."

Thornton had the true melodic gift. He was a born troubadour,
friend of the cup that inebriates even when it does not cheer. He
lived his active life two decades before his time, squandering his
talents in the tap-house. A hundred-dollar advance—at one time

[97]

Thornton was drawing $600 per week from Frank Harding—and off he was to the Hoffman House bar, there to drink up his song and to find another song in the drinks. Bonnie knew where to find him, and when she did, the "gang" scattered. Later, you might have found her and her melody man patching it up in a hotel-room over a dish of lobsters. Thornton, still on deck, was lately in the cast of Kern's *Sweet Adeline*. He had gone Neal Dow and was considering a vaudeville act with the suggestive title "Saloonatics."

Women in Tin Pan Alley.

The waltz of the early Nineties . . . Graham's "Two Little Girls in Blue" . . . Maude Nugent and her "Sweet Rosie O'Grady" . . . "Little Annie Rooney" . . . Sweet, innocuous tunes—no guile in them, and none of the effrontery that winks from their sophisticated offspring at "Three O'Clock in the Morning." Tunes that haunt the memory and linger patiently, unashamedly, in company of the inspired and inspiring symphonic repertory that does not, cannot somehow, oust them from their security . . . Maude Nugent, Anita Owen ("Sweet Bunch of Daisies," "Sweet Marie"). The women—an armful of them—were in at the beginning of Tin Pan Alley. Why were there not more? Why, even to-day, are there but a baker's dozen still?

Woman has always been the inspiration of song rather than the writer of it. By nature, by convention, even in these days of toppling social values, she is the passive, rather than the active, voice of love. Or so, in her elemental strategy, she would have us believe. Whatever the cause of this relative silence, it can have no specific relation to Tin Pan Alley as such, for the place of

woman in the music of the world, as in the more consciously artistic music of America, is small. She is the executant, not the creator.

Yet, from the days of Maude Nugent's "Sweet Rosie O'Grady"
to the new musical comedy by Kay Swift, there have been hits
by the ladies. Clare Kummer began her career with "Dearie."
Carrie Jacobs-Bond has sold 5,000,000 copies of that imperfect
song entitled "The End of a Perfect Day." Hattie Starr was widely
known, thirty years ago, for her "Little Alabama Coon," "Somebody Loves Me," and other ballads. Miss Starr, indeed, who wrote
her own words and music, found the field of composition so profitable that she abandoned the stage for it.

Mabel McKinley . . . Mary Earl ("Beautiful Ohio") . . .
Dolly Morse (widow of the tuneful Theodore) . . . Marion Gillespie . . . Mabel Wayne, whom Rudy Vallée calls "perhaps the
only really successful woman writer" . . . Dorothy Fields . . .
Kate Vaughan . . . Grace LeBoy . . .

There was once a theory that the innate refinement of woman
(a mystic quality in which I cannot believe) rendered them un-
able to cope with the vulgarities of popular music. Since much of
our most salacious fiction is being written by the ladies, it would
seem that the theory has collapsed. Certainly here is a tempting
field for the clever female of the species, and it may well be that
we are but at the beginning of her contribution to the National
Noise.

Tin Pan Alley deals in musical journalism—in emotional tab-
loids of the passing phase. It is preëminently opportunistic. For
this very reason its history is one of the truest indices of the
changes that have come over popular taste. A graph of the thematic
content of our street songs over the past thirty years would read

[99]

like a miniature history of our national morals. Once upon a time transgressions of the current sexual code were taken seriously. To-day, sophistication has washed away the humorless purity of the Nineties. *Nous avons changé tout cela!* Laura Jean Libbey and Bertha M. Clay yield to Elinor Glyn and Viña Delmar. Our early self-pity school was, if stupid, sincere; to-day it is semi-automatic. We are "wised-up," even in our commercial ditties. Emotion—unless the behaviorists should unexpectedly succeed in mechanizing every one of our reactions—will never go out of date. Certainly, however, the popular song, so far as concerns its words, has brought upon itself a peculiar crisis. To go back to the simplicities of the Nineties is out of the question. To go forward to refinements upon the present sophistication is to court smaller audiences—better ones, perhaps, but smaller—and Tin Pan Alley is not interested in diminishing returns.

The song of to-day is machine-made, machine-played, machine-heard. It is a formula, as surely as is the short story of the magazine, the crime fiction, the mystery tale. It obeys every rule laid down by editors in search of speed, pep and punch. It builds up a musical literature of escape, of wish fulfillment, of vicarious sex experience, of whoopee. It is in itself a tonal aphrodisiac, providing a limited but effective vocabulary of love for a vast audience whose conceptions—and executions—of love are, if limited, effective. It is impossible to have several millions of people simultaneously listening to or singing a song—however good or bad—without that song doing something to them, and for them. It is all the more astounding, in view of this psychological fact, that the censors so long have allowed Tin Pan Alley to flourish.

The Alley of the Nineties, however, needed censorship of a different variety. When it was not morbid it was moronic. As kids built up the Alley, so kids—or childish mentalities—first provided it with tunes and themes.

It was a world of clear-cut divisions in which the Alley moved. Motherhood had not yet evolved into Mammyhood. Childhood was, like life itself, drenched in tears. Lost children . . . dying children . . . precocious children . . . pathetic children, re-uniting severed fathers and mothers and going up to heaven in a halo of sacred fire. Where were the father songs? Father, dear father, come home with me now. . . . The relative absence of the father song can hardly be an accident. When father does appear, it is either as a reprobate—now repentant, now unrepentant—or as a good-natured scalawag. The Mother song, the Home Song . . . these are among the staples of balladry the world over. Tin Pan Alley is as sentimental over Mother as a florist on Mother's Day. But Father? Father is an unromantic figure. Motherhood is holy; fatherhood, in some dim way, is a joke. There is no money in it. . . . When there is profit in fathers, Tin Pan Alley will sing them.

The ". . ." Nineties.

The Nineties . . . In England they were Yellow, almost effete; in America, they were Gay, Naughty, Roisterous, Electric, Romantic, Moulting and, for color, a thomasbeery Mauve. The sauce of adjectives in which the decade floated betokens the variety of its appeal and the general liveliness of its progress. The Nineties had an air; they stood out alike from the decade that preceded and the one that followed. They were the growing pains of a nation taking its first decisive step from insularity to a place in the larger world. To-day, as we look back upon its styles in dress and thought, we smile indulgently at trailing skirts, pancake hats, bustles, mutton sleeves—all the stuffy apparatus of raiment that was thrown over its body and its mind. We sniff superiorly at its upholstered morality, and congratulate ourselves, publican-like, that we are not as they. The pathos of distance intervenes to soften our judgment, and, if we truly have a sense of humor, we know that some day—all too soon, at the accelerated speed with which the modern world moves on—our own vaunted day will provide like mirth and pathos to those who ride hard at our heels. A joke is often something that happened just before we arrived. . . .

The Nineties, nationally, opened with a Fair in Chicago and ended with a war—shots were fired—in Cuba. A World's Fair and an entrance into world-diplomacy . . . International commerce and Imperialism . . . The World's Columbian Exposition captured the imaginations of the people. It disclosed to them a pageant of international wonders, widening their horizons. Sousa was there; it was his constant playing of "After the Ball" that reverberated throughout the nation and set up loud echoes in the purlieus of Broadway. More: out of the store of exotic attractions one feature spread fast across the nation. The Hoochy Koochy dance . . . its music . . . and the parodies upon the tune, centering chiefly about Jim Thornton's "Streets of Cairo" . . .

> Oh, the funny feeling
> Through my system stealing!
> What is that?
> What am I at?

What the dance itself may have been, with its abdominal rotations and its slithering insinuations, was left to the day-dreams of the millions who could not hope to visit the Midway Plaisance. The music of it, however, with its insistent tom-tom and lascivious twists, worked its spell wherever it could penetrate, and the parodies left no doubt that the Nineties, if they ever got the chance, could be most orientally naughty.

That was in 1893, the year that George M. Cohan, at the age of fifteen, as the junior member of the Four Cohans advanced in mass formation against the citadels of Gotham. In two or three amazing years this cocksure, hot-tempered gamin—another kid for the Alley—would have May Irwin singing his "Hot Tamale Alley" before she discovered her "New Bully," and would be writing coon songs well in advance of the ragtime craze. Irving Berlin (née Izzy Baline) was eight years old, roaming the sidewalks of New York. George Gershwin was minus three. Popular music publishing, up to this time, had been more or less a sporadic affair. There had been, of course, numerous songs that had won a large public, but this had been the will of God rather than the will of the publisher. The trade had acquired no status largely because it had acquired no technique. It was largely passive. The public came to the song. Shortly there would be a reversal of rôles; the song would be sent out to pursue the public. Much of the lighter music had to be imported from England, since native providers were few. Harry Von Tilzer had begun his professional career as an actor; he was finding it difficult to procure home-made songs for his turns. There was but one way out: to manufacture the tunes for his own acts. Paul Dresser, like Von Tilzer a Hoosier son, gained his experience in the popular musical taste likewise upon the stage. Made in America was beginning to mean something for the lighter forms of entertainment.

The World's Fair was as a call to arms. The international spectacle, for a few pioneer spirits in the business, crystallized and dramatized a golden opportunity. It created, for the first time, a central market for their wares. What was a Fair without music? The budding firms of the East, especially, pricked up their ears and entered the lists with an outburst of melody.

The Columbian Exposition was something new under our sun. The music that, directly or indirectly, it engendered, was equally something new, even when the hand of the Eighties weighed heavily upon it. Perhaps it was not altogether the Fair. Perhaps the new popular music of the Nineties—how hopelessly old it sounds to us now, yet with what sly, if slow, persistence it is returning over the radio and the phonograph, and in the talkies—was imbued with something of the same spirit that had conceived and executed the Fair. There, in any case, it was. The era of large-scale production was in its lusty infancy. Soon we should be hearing, through the campaign for Woman's Suffrage, the threat of Trusts, the booming of Protective Tariffs and the other new themes in the national symphony.

Certainly the new spirit in music publishing had appeared well before the World's Fair, and in the selfsame city of Chicago. Here, in 1890, the enterprising Will Rossiter, whose name is so familiar on sheets and song-books, had founded the firm that still adds color to the agitated city. He had been inspired by Billy Scanlon's singing of "Peek-a-boo" and "Nelly's Blue Eyes." In those days, nom-de-plumes were the vogue for ballad writers, and Rossiter rechristened himself W. R. Williams. Williams is still his favorite composer. Rossiter has been a veritable patron saint to the beginner; the list of those whom he was the first to introduce makes a formidable roster of names that have since acquired fame and fortune.

It was under Rossiter's ægis that Charles K. Harris made his bow. "After the Ball" was still a few years in the future, and Harris, a disappointed youngster, had come to Rossiter from Milwaukee for some practical advice. The Chicagoan instructed him in the vagaries of copyright—a simple process that so awes the tyro—and introduced him to Bigelow, the plate-maker and Hack & Anderson, music printers . . . Harry S. Miller ("The Cat Came Back"), Harold Attridge, Anna Caldwell, Van and Schenck, Billy Jerome ("He Never Came Back," "I'm Old Enough to Know"), Fred Fisher ("If the Man in the Moon Were a Coon"), Jimmie Monaco ("Oh, You Circus Days"), Gus Kahn and Grace LeBoy, Egbert van Alstyne, Jack Yellen, Percy Wenrich, L. Wolfe Gilbert, Bobby Crawford, Al Piantadosi, George White (before he became Scandalous), Francis X. Bushman, Zez Confrey, Victor Arden, George Whiting . . . this is an incomplete roll call of Rossiter's débutants.

Rossiter was the first to sing his own songs in the retail stores. He was the first to issue cheap song books, having conceived the plan during the year of the Fair. During the next twenty years he was to sell millions of these. He began the practice of adorning orchestra music with fancy covers. He inaugurated the idea of advertising his songs in a theatrical paper; in the early days this meant *The New York Clipper*. What he did for song writers he did also for vaudeville acts; many a one he piloted and advertised into national popularity.

[105]

The distribution of song bills is one of our earliest traditions, dating back to the war of separation. It was begun, on a large scale, as early as 1878, when Henry J. Wehman, who had just reached his majority, broke away from his employers, The John Polhemus Printing Company, and set up shop in the hall bedroom of a five-room flat on De Kalb Avenue, New York. Wehman, who had been setting the little flyers at Polhemus's, in his spare time, and peddling them from shop to shop, naturally did his own typesetting; one ballad appeared on a sheet, and sold for a penny. With business increasing, the size of the sheets grew too, until the "song sheets" contained as many as thirty songs. Decrepit Bowreyites hawked them on the streets; orders began to pour in from circuses, theaters and other places of amusement. When Wehman moved to 130 Park Row he added to his line a list of Dream Books, Letter Writers, Recitation Books, Books of Magic,—indeed, the entire encyclopedia of proletarian curios.

The publishers of that day, unlike the music firms of the present, raised no objection to the reprinting of their song-words. In point of fact, the song sheets served as pluggers for the tunes and increased the sale of the sheet music. Wehman printed the Tony Pastor repertory and many of the Harrigan and Hart successes. By the year 1892 he was able to buy out the R. H. Russell Publishing Company, of Rose Street, thus acquiring the largest catalogue of paper-bound books in the market. Orders for "After the Ball" were coming in so fast that nobody stopped to count sheets; they were measured off by a ruler.

Wehman was not knowingly violating the copyrights of other publishers. In his innocence, he believed—and the conditions corroborated his belief—that his sheets were helping his neighbors. In 1893, flushed with prosperity, he opened up a Chicago branch. Treachery, and the end, were near.

A representative of a prominent New York publisher called upon him one day and with malice aforethought ordered a printing of 30,000 song-sheets containing words to which the New York publisher controlled the copyrights. The order duly run off, in walked the representative accompanied by a United States Marshal, who seized the 30,000 sheets. There was a lawsuit, and the innocent Wehman was mulcted in $30,000,—one dollar per sheet. It was a terrible blow; worse still was the newspaper talk of "song piracy," which added something like $100,000 damage to the firm. Wehman was stricken with apoplexy; other strokes followed and he died on March 27, 1900, at the age of forty-three. His widow carried on the business until her death, February 11, 1930, at the age of seventy-three.

Mrs. Backer, eldest daughter of the Wehman's, maintains the traditions of the firm. A card-shop, begun as a side issue in the days of the original enterprise, now flourishes under her direction. The song-sheet and booklet business was always largely transacted by mail; it still is. Though there is no advertising other than that which appears upon the back pages of the booklets, orders come in from Australia, South Africa, China, the Philippines, the Danish West Indies.

The song-book and song-sheet business faded from the picture with the establishment of the American Society of Composers, Authors and Publishers. Delaney, dean of the song-books that used to delight our youth, gave up the ghost and sold out his interests when, in 1914, the Society appeared above the horizon.

TIN PAN ALLEY

A new land was being set to new music. And the musical capital of that nation, after a hesitating residency in San Francisco and an uncertain stay in the Middle West, was definitely established in New York. All roads lead to Gotham.

An Alleyful of Kids.

Tin Pan Alley—it was not named until the turn of the twentieth century—was built by kids, by veritable gamins. Fourteenth Street, the amusement center of New York's early Nineties, was the magnet that lured them from their native hills and meadows, their metropolitan slums. The Alley would follow the Theater in its procession from Fourteenth to Twenty-eighth to Thirtieth to Forty-second. It still follows the Theater in its present advance upon the Fifties. From Indiana came Paul Dresser and Harry Von Tilzer. From Milwaukee, Charles K. Harris, already made by "After the Ball." From the East Side marched the three musketeers, Isidore, Julius and Jay Witmark. Firms were founded upon a shoestring. . . . A chance hit, and a couple of hundred dollars was sufficient to open an office. Success bred, as always it breeds, imitation. Stern and Marks, with their doleful ditty of "The Little Lost Child" and the passing policeman, would inspire the emulation of Shapiro and Bernstein. Of a sudden, it seemed, the business took on a Jewish complexion. The names before the Nineties are almost exclusively Gentile: Harding; Firth, Son & Co.; White, Smith & Co.; Wm. A. Pond & Co.; T. B. Harms & Co.; R. A. Saalfield; B. W. Hitchcock; A. J. Fisher (father of "Bud" Fisher, the cartoonist); Willis, Woodward & Co.; Chas. D. Blake & Co.; Will H. Kennedy; Sydney Rosenfeld; Howley and Havi-

[108]

land (later with Dresser); Sherman and Clay. A historic moment and there is a racial revolution: M. Witmark & Sons, Chas. K. Harris, Marks & Stern, Shapiro, Bernstein and Von Tilzer. These, then, are the true pioneers of popular music making and popular music publishing in the United States—a trade that has no parallel in the rest of the world.

The youth of the industry is best attested by the fact that many of the pioneers are still in business. Chas. K. Harris sits in his office, in the Astor Theatre Building, gazing back fondly at days that will never return, expectorating through the smoke of a thick cigar and damning the industry to hell. "What's ahead, Mr. Harris, for the sheet music trades?" Harris makes a grimace and spits out, "Ruin! That's what's ahead! Ruin!" Then, recovering his composure he proceeds to an antediluvian upright, playing by ear his own accompaniment and singing his latest song. It harks back to the immortal Nineties. . . . "Those," asseverates Harris, "were the days of the *geniuses* in Tin Pan Alley . . . Fellows who wrote both their words and music. Nowadays you see two names for the words, two for the music. It's a family affair! No, sir! The era of the geniuses is gone!" . . . Von Tilzer, tall, vigorous, dark-eyed, gray-haired, sucks likewise at a fat cigar as he grows reminiscent in his cubby-hole on the third-floor of 1587 Broadway. Tin Pan Alley? Where is it? Sheet music? Who hears of it now? Songs— the real songs—were written in the old days, when pluggers were pluggers. A team gets excited now when it turns out a song that sells a few hundred thousand copies. "Why, I've had 118 songs that sold over half a million copies apiece. Under that number I wouldn't dream of calling a piece a hit!" . . . Marks, Isidore Witmark, Bernstein, Haviland, and even Harding, whose father

[109]

founded the firm a year before Lincoln became president, are still
at their daily tasks.

Harding . . . He is sturdy, in his sixty-third year; brown,
faintly graying hair; neatly-trimmed mustache, but no beard; a
slight stoop, from constant bending over his music presses. The
Harding shop, in the flourishing days of the concern, was a ren-
dezvous for the actors and song-writers in the vogue. Nobody ever
plugged a Harding song, he will tell you; the songs were good
and, accordingly, were bought. What's more, rather than pay for
photographic publicity, the firm of Harding was itself paid for
printing a singer's picture upon the cover of a song. . . . He
recalls their frequent guests when he was a young man in the early
Nineties: What a fine wit was J. W. Kelley, whose "Slide, Kelly,
Slide," "When Hogan Paid His Rent," "Come Down, Mrs. Flynn,"
and especially "Throw Him Down, McClosky," kept the boys singing to the pace of Maggie Cline. And there was "It Used to Be
Proper but It Don't Go Now," sung by Lottie Gilson. The melodies
were adapted from old Irish and English airs. They were big stage
hits, but never reached great sales. Harrigan and Hart, on Sunday
mornings, at the old office on 229 Bowery . . . Jimmie and Bonnie Thornton . . . "The music business has always been, and
always will be, one of the meanest in the world. Nobody pays
his bill unless he is forced to. . . . In time, there will be but two
or three music publishers left. As for the boys now in Hollywood,
they'll soon be back on Broadway—if they can raise the price
of a return ticket." The future of Tin Pan Alley? "Fortunes have
been made in it, but I don't know many who ever managed to get
out of it and live comfortably." As for the present slump in the
trade: too much copyright fuss. The composers and publishers,

with their hawk-eyed society, have thrown a boomerang. "Taxing music is like taxing a man for wearing an overcoat. Once a man buys a piece of music, it should be his to do with as he pleases.

"Radio music is abominable. . . . Years ago songs appealed to the heart. They had some dignity then. To-day they are made to be howled and yowled. . . . Classical music is really a good tune dolled up with fancy trimmings. . . . No matter what happens to the song business, the amateurs will always be with us."

They have seen the rise of Tin Pan Alley from its first humble days to its transformation into a major industry of the nation. Firms have leaped into existence over night before their eyes, as if at the rubbing of Aladdin's lamp; and have fallen into obscurity at the behest of some sinister djinn. Fortunes have piled up on the breath of a single song, and have, like that selfsame breath, evaporated. Yet, not even the avowed commercialism of the traffic has robbed it quite of the glamor that has bathed it throughout the years. What lives on song, however sordid, must catch the spirit of song.

The New Firms.

There were hustlers in those days—the end of the Eighties and the stride of the Nineties across national history. No vast buildings had arisen on foundations of printed sheets. No army of office help . . . no intricate network of exploiting methods . . . no syndicates. . . . The head of the firm was a Pooh Bah; all the offices were rolled into one, under his hat. He accepted the music; he published it; he plugged it; he sold it. He haunted the burlesque and vaudeville houses, visiting as many as six or seven of them in a single night. He collared the star performers, whether of the first or fourth magnitude, and cajoled them into singing the precious song. Rossiter, Von Tilzer, Witmark, Stern and Marks, Bernstein—the story in each instance is the same. These enterprising gentlemen, some of them hardly out of short trousers, would haunt the green rooms, their pockets stuffed with the new tunes. They would sing the songs to the actors in their dressing rooms, in restaurants, under the lamp-posts of the thoroughfare . . . anywhere at all, to get a hearing.

Competition was keen. Singers were hardly safe along the Song Market, where the publishers lay in ambush for strolling performers.

There were, in the first days, not enough singers to go around. Every effort was made to switch the allegiance of a headliner from this firm to that. The successful actor's hotel or boarding house was unceremoniously invaded by the publisher or his representative; he had about as much privacy as, to-day, a radio-orchestra leader. Pay his board bill . . . Buy him a suit of clothes . . . Promise her a glittering stone . . . Present him with a trunk . . . Subsidize his act with a weekly pourboire. The performer heard but one refrain: "Sing our song!"

A Dresser Song?

Paul Dresser . . . as an actor the most jovial of good fellows; and as a songster, the weepiest willow of them all! Dresser, who had established his reputation in the late Eighties, had gone into music publishing just before the magical rise of the Alley. Howley and Haviland was the original name of the firm, and its establishment is a pretty example of how the new order was hatched in the nest of the old. F. B. Haviland—he is still in business, a radiant, well-preserved fellow who lives gladly through the days when sheet music was sheet music—had served his apprenticeship with D. S. Holmes of Brooklyn, a stationer who added music publishing to his troubles, and who had won a reputation for having issued "The Gypsy's Warning." A child of sixteen, Haviland slaved fourteen hours daily. It was too much; he switched to Ditson's as an order clerk, from which position he soon rose to that of City Department head.

This was in 1884. There were no music jobbers in those days, and the so-called City Trade catered to the stores in Greater New York and the surrounding territory, as well as to the out-of-town dealers who came to New York to do their purchasing. It was while at Ditson's that Haviland, an enterprising youth, became friendly with the firm of Willis Woodward, then situated in the Star Theatre Building at Broadway and Thirteenth Street. Woodward had an excellent selling catalogue that contained among other songs such perennials as "White Wings," by Banks Winter, Julian Jordan's "The Song That Reached My Heart," and Henry Sayer's much-disputed "Ta-Ra-Ra-Boom-De-Ré."

"Ta-Ra-Ra-Boom-De—?"

Let's pause for a few minutes over this noble tune. There is a tide in the affairs of songs, as in the affairs of men. If a song comes too soon, it is as bad as if it comes too late. "Ta-Ra-Ra-Boom-De-Ré" arrived at the precise moment when it was needed to herald the new spirit of popular music. Where did it come from? Who wrote it? George M. Cohan recently offered to settle its origin once and for all. The song, frequently heard "in the late-hour hide-aways on Sixth Avenue" during the season of eventful 1893, came from the Middle West. "Troupers resting from the West had heard the tune in Babe Connor's all-colored resort in St. Louis. In fact, Miss Connor, a colored beauty of arresting charm and in a zouave coat—the latest cut—was among those present in Union Square, laying claim to authorship, but making no legal fuss over the matter. More than one person was hoping she would bring her talented colored organization to New York, but after a week of loud protesting she fled to her native city—and stayed there." [2]

Another story—one of many—goes that Theodore Metz, the composer of "A Hot Time in the Old Town To-night," heard the tune in a Negro cabaret and got Henry Sayers to work it into a song for the "Tuxedo Girls," who, in 1891, were appearing in a minstrel farce comedy, *Tuxedo.* According to Spaeth, Sayers himself, press agent for the show, had heard it in Babe Connors resort. "Outside of the gibberish, the words were"—one is relieved to hear—"unspeakable. He substituted polite verses and eventually the song reached Lottie Collins, who made it a riot in England by singing the first part ultra-demurely and then going into a kicking chorus with what was undoubtedly the jazziest effect of 1891." [3]

The Morley-Throckmorton revival of *The Black Crook* in 1929-30 resuscitated the tune and the dance. Even in our day the number was able to carry the show. It must have been the fond associations.

[2] *The Evening World* (New York), in a series of articles as told to Charles Washburn. June 24, 1930, page B,1.
[3] *Read 'Em and Weep.* By Sigmund Spaeth. New York, 1927. P. 164.

There are more witnesses, however, to be heard from. Here is an unidentified clipping from a newspaper of the day: [4]

"The latest street song, Ta-ra-ra-boom-de-ay, is said to be of negro origin in the South, away back befo' de wah. Who was responsible for its revival no one seems to know. It quickly traveled across the ocean, and Miss Lottie Collins is understood to be responsible for its first infliction on an English audience. She has declared that, after catching the refrain in this country, she had Richard Morton arrange the words, and Mr. Asher of the Tivoli, London, put the music in shape. The song took at once. The stuff has lately been made the subject of a lawsuit in London. A motion had been made to restrain a certain firm from publishing the song. The plaintiffs sought to show that Lottie Collins secured the song in America, and they bought it of her, had it rewritten and produced it from the new words and score. Affidavits in support of their claims were read from Clement Scott, Macfarren, the composer, and others. The defendants produced an affidavit from Flora Moore, who says she sang the song in the United States as far back as 1884. The fun came in when counsel read the words of the original song, with allusions to Tuxedo and other local American hits. The text and its solemn delivery by the lawyer were irresistibly comic, and the spectators roared, and there was an attempt to join in the chorus, which was sternly repressed by the court. Affidavits taken in New York were presented, in which deponents declare that the song was sung in the United States as early as 1878. The literature of this important subject has lately been augmented by another account of the origin of the tune re-

[4] This, and the excerpt that follows, I found in a scrap-book of clippings, one of several score such bound volumes left to the Boston Public Library by Allen A. Brown and to be consulted only in the room in that institution named after him.

ported from London, and which makes the question one of international importance. It is said that Mr. Gilbert, father of the sculptor, Alfred Gilbert, composed an opera in which the refrain occurred, in 1854. An American gentleman saw the score and said he should like to have it. The composer consented, and it was only the other day, when on a visit to the Grand Theatre, he recognized his own composition. Still another claim is that the melody is a paraphrase in 2-4 time of a waltz, which is used by the Scotch Presbyterians for a hymn tune."

And another, from *Dunlop's Stage News:*

"The stories about the origin of Ta-ra-ra-boom-de-ay are amusing, and so many have claimed to be the discoverer or composer of it, that the mystery is almost as deep as the authorship of 'Beautiful Snow.' I have watched the paragraphs floating on the waves of journalism and for six months have waited for one, of many that could tell, to come forward. Not being myself so old as to remember the advent of the song in America, I can only tell what I heard about its importation, which was neither from France nor England, but from Africa, for the song is negro in every detail. There lives upon the west coast of Africa a tribe of hardy seafaring black men, known all over the South, West Indies and South America as Krumen. They were unlike the other slaves brought over in many particulars. Their noses were not flat, no 'nigger driver' ever drove them to any great extent; they did not as a rule mix with the other slaves, and could be implicitly trusted both on land and at sea. They were magnificent sailors, and as sailors were 'worth more,' hence they were mostly employed on the water. One of their conditions, if free, was that they should be allowed to see their home once a year, and they kept tally of the time to a day. When pulling at a rope, hoisting a sail or an anchor, one Kruman would shout, Ta-ra-ra-boom-de-ay, and with the *boom* all would give a mighty pull, just as any other sailor to-day pulls when singing. The Negroes at the docks in New Orleans caught the refrain and fifty years ago it had reached far into Louisiana, where a Ta-ra-ra-boom-de-ay was shouted when anything was to be hoisted at the sugar mills. People that knew New Orleans even twenty years ago, and 'looked over' Mahogany Hall, on Basin street, must remember the song, and many thousand people must have heard it, at least a dozen years ago, as sung by a Negress in St. Louis. Ta-ra-ra-boom-de-ay means Easy, easy, up she goes— and there you are, all reports to the contrary notwithstanding."

Well, in any event, however uncertain the birth—and the spell- ing—of Ta-Ra-Ra-Boom-De-Ray, De-Ré, or De-Ay, it has a long life before it.

To return to Haviland's account: "While at Ditson's, I met a young woman, Ida Benedict, who, I thought, was talented as a pianist and composer. I prevailed upon her to compose a waltz, which I dedicated to William H. Crane, then appearing in a play called *The Senator*. I saw Crane's manager, Mr. Joseph H. Brooks, and asked his permission to dedicate the waltz to Mr. Crane and print his picture upon the title page. The permission was granted, and after the waltz was published by me, and handled for me by Woodward, I secured permission to sell it in the theater during the run of the play, which lasted a year or more. I had several boys going through the aisles of the theater between the acts, selling the waltz; it sold splendidly. It was played by the orchestra, and featured by the leader, who was none other than

Harry Braham, one time husband of the famous Lillian Russell. Through this plugging the waltz became a hit of fair dimensions. It was my first venture as a publisher of music. I published several other songs, all of which were handled by Woodward & Co.

"Now, on the Woodward staff of writers was a chap, Paul Dresser, who had already written several good songs: 'The Pardon Came Too Late,' 'The Letter That Never Came,' 'My Mother Told Me So.' . . . As I was the buyer for all the New York publications used by the various Ditson houses in Boston, Philadelphia and Gotham, I had become quite intimate with Patrick J. (Pat) Howley. Genial, lovable and affable, although deformed from birth, he had a marvelous brain and a wonderful personality. It was in 1894 that he conceived the notion of going into the publishing business, approaching Dresser and myself on the subject. It was a go, and, accordingly, the firm of George T. Worth set up their offices at 4 East 20th Street, New York. Who was George T. Worth? He was nobody, and he was the three of us. The name was a blind. Pat kept his job with Woodward, and I kept mine with Ditson. Dresser was on the road with a show, playing one of the Johns in *The Two Johns*. Pat and I, after a hard day's work, would meet at 4 East 20th at night, toiling away to place the little company on its feet." [5]

The business was founded on less than two hundred dollars, and for the first two years it was tough sledding. A few songs were issued, but they fell upon deaf ears—"dead flops." However, things began to pick up sufficiently to warrant Howley's departure from Woodward so that he might devote all his time to the mythi-

[5] The quotations are from a statement prepared expressly for this book, dated May 28, 1930, and supplemented by letters dated June 5 and June 10, 1930.

cal Worth. Haviland remained at Ditson's; eighteen dollars per week was too munificent to abandon. Ditson, however, was not long in discovering Haviland's connection with Worth, and he was given his choice between the new firm and the old. He chose the new, and was promptly discharged. Homeless, without parents, penniless, he banged about on odd journalistic jobs until he could join his comrades on full time.

The firm of Howley, Haviland and Dresser employed as its staff pianist and general utility man a youngster by the name of Max Dreyfus. He was an inside plugger, playing the company's music for performers and teaching them how to sing it. He had not yet begun to compose. That would come shortly, when he would join the firm of Tom and Alec Harms and inaugurate a brief authorial career under the pseudonym, Max Eugene.

In the office of the old T. B. Harms company he was a modest youth who had been brought up on the classics and was working for anything that the trade brought in. When John Golden was at the beginning of his career, cheerfully swiping melodies from Arthur Sullivan and lilts from William Gilbert, Dreyfus served him, as he served numerous others, as arranger. For two dollars Dreyfus would listen to Golden pick out tunes on the piano and make a harmonized arrangement. "He was never very strong," recalls Golden, "and the rest of us used to feel a little protective toward him, thinking he was too frail to make the grade."

Dreyfus stands preëminent among the "pickers" of the Alley. As he rose in power in the firm of Harms, so he rose in his judgment of the youngsters who came to him for positions and for advice. He has been of uncanny percipiency in selecting talents for advancement. A man might have chosen Rudolf Friml or Jerome

Kern by happy accident. When he followed this up by advancing, in turn, such later successes as George Gershwin, Vincent Youmans and Richard Rodgers—the very names constitute almost a synthetic history of our musical comedy—he silently eliminated the element of accidental felicity.

In time, Dreyfus was to absorb the house of Harms and place it in the front rank of the musical comedy publishers. To-day his is a magic name in the higher reaches of Tin Pan Alley. He is the executive head of the Warner Brothers combination of publishing houses, which includes Harms, Witmark & Sons, Remick's and other strategic concerns. And if you should start humming the strains of "Cupid's Garden"—a composition by Max Eugene that was played in every show house some thirty years ago—he executes a hurried, if metaphorical, exit and leaves you as your own audience.

"Things began to brighten for us." (Mr. Haviland again has the floor.) "A boy in his 'teens brought in a song entitled 'I Can't Tell Why I Love You but I Do, Do, Do.' That kid's name was Gus Edwards. In came Charlie Lawler and Jim Blake—an actor and a hat salesman—with 'The Sidewalks of New York.' Luck had come our way at last. After that, Paul gave us 'The Blue and the Gray,' 'On the Banks of the Wabash,' 'Just Tell Them That You Saw Me,' and many others.

"Business was too flourishing for our crowded quarters. We removed to Thirty-second and Broadway, over the clothing store of Rogers, Peet & Co. Our success here was phenomenal. George Evans, the Honey Boy, brought us 'In the Good Old Summer Time,' which was introduced by Blanche Ring, then a girl in her 'teens, in *The Defender*. The song was an over-night sensation.

Clifton Crawford gave us 'Nancy.' Then followed, in rapid succession, 'Just Because She Made Them Goo Goo Eyes,' 'Ain't Dat a Shame,' 'Bill Bailey Won't You Please Come Home,' 'Keep the Golden Gates Wide Open,' 'Good-by, Dolly Gray,' 'Mandy Lee,' 'In the Baggage Coach Ahead.' Things were· tremendous."

Theodore Dreiser.

It was Paul who had been instrumental in luring his brother, Theodore Dreiser, out of the West. It is now an old story that Theodore penned the chorus of "On the Banks of the Wabash." "I know absolutely whereof I speak," wrote Dreiser some thirty-two years ago, "when I say that the words of 'On the Banks of the Wabash' were written in less than an hour of an April Sunday afternoon, and that the music did not require a much longer period. The whole deed was pleasurable and easy, while the reward was proportionately great. Yet there is not more than one good popular song turned out a year, and a great success such as 'On the Banks of the Wabash' is not written once in ten years." [6] Times have changed since 1896.

Less familiar, even to Dreiserians, is the association of Theodore Dreiser with the firm of Howley, Haviland and Dresser as editor. Riding the crest of the wave, the flourishing partners conceived in 1895 the idea of a magazine, to be called *Every Month*, and, with its reading matter and four complete pieces of music, to be addressed chiefly to women. Dreiser was placed at the helm; he edited *Every Month* from October, 1895, to September, 1897,

[6] *Birth and Growth of a Popular Song.* By Theodore Dreiser. Metropolitan, November, 1898, pp. 497-502.

and kept his employers on the anxious seat with his outspoken manner and his uninhibited philosophy. The publishers lost $50,000 on the venture, which represents Dreiser's initiation into magazine editing. But what, in those days, was a mere $50,000 to Howley, Haviland and Dresser?

We shall meet them again, in sadder circumstances.

A Witmark Song?

The House of Witmark began with a toy printing-press. A prize won at public grammar school, the press determined the future of the brothers Isidore, Julius and Jay. They were an enterprising trio, imbued with the spirit of business and showmanship from their earliest days. When Isidore, as a child, had received a hobby horse as a gift, he had not been slow to ask his father for —an umbrella. "And why umbrella?" asked the puzzled parent. "So that I can start a merry-go-round," answered the precocious first-born.

The toy press turned in real dollars for the three musketeers. They printed New Year's cards for the neighborhood, up in their bedroom printery. Later, their father would establish them, still youngsters, in a printing-shop that was not slow to flourish. Meantime, however, Julius had developed a surprising voice, and before long he was being billed in the leading theaters of America as "the wonderful boy soprano," with that great minstrel organization, Thatcher, Primrose and West, introducing and making famous Jennie Lindsey's "Always Take Mother's Advice." He had first appeared with the San Francisco Minstrels in 1883, before he had reached his thirteenth year. Later, with the breaking of his voice,

Julius became the "celebrated boy baritone," appearing with Hoyt's *A Trip to Chinatown*, *The City Directory* and other musical successes and creating hits for the house of Witmark. Music publishers were not slow to realize the value of a child prodigy as a publicity medium; they overwhelmed young Julius with offers of big money to push their songs. Long on promises, they fell short on payments. Isidore, who had been writing music on the side, had begun to discover from his standpoint, too, that publishers weren't always on the square. There was but one thing to do: print their own music as they had printed their own cards.

The real début of the brothers as publishers came near to being a fiasco. It was during the time when rumors of a marriage in the White House had the readers of the nation astir. The Witmarks had an inspiration. Why not a President Cleveland Wedding March to celebrate the occasion? Tin Pan Alley lives, not on private emotions, but on tie-ups with current events, passing moods. Accordingly, brother Isidore left a large rotary press he was kicking, went upstairs, sat him down to the piano and arose, after his labors, with a piece ready for the engraver's.

The President, however, was not in a hurry. Indeed, to crown the Witmarks' uncertainty, the newspapers appeared with stern denials from the White House. That settled it; if any of the important publishing firms had intended to signalize the occasion, this was a definite answer to their plans. Well, here was a presidential wedding march on the boys' hands at a time when they couldn't afford a loss; perhaps they could hold it for the next national event, rename it, and recoup expenses. Even as they sought to solace themselves, official announcement of the wedding was made. The boys had the composition already off the press.

Literally, they had stolen a march upon all the other publishers.

Not one of the youngsters was yet of age. If the firm, to this day, is known as M. Witmark & Sons, it is because the father had to be taken in to sponsor his children and to provide for the budding concern a responsible head. (Witmark père, before the Civil War, had owned large business interests in Alabama and Georgia. He saw service as an officer, and after the peace came North, having lost much of his property.) M. Witmark & Sons it has remained, through the four uninterrupted decades of its success.

Before the turn of the century they would become known not only for such contemporary hits as "Her Eyes Don't Shine Like Diamonds" (1894), "I Love You in the Same Old Way" (1896), "Honey, You'se Ma Lady Love" (1897), "Just One Girl," "Just as the Sun Went Down," "When You Ain't Got No Money You Needn't Come Around" (1898), and "Stay in Your Own Back Yard" (1899), but as the publishers of songs from the operas and extravaganzas of Victor Herbert, Chauncy Olcott, George M. Cohan and Weber and Fields. They would, throughout their history, remain prominent as publishers and sponsors of productions as well as of songs,—"The Picture Turned Toward the Wall," "The Irish Jubilee," "Tammany," "Good Bye, Little Girl, Good Bye," "My Wild Irish Rose," "Sweet Adeline" . . . the musical comedies of Gustav Luders and Karl Hoschna . . . the "semiclassics" of Ernest R. Ball, Arthur Pann and Caro Roma.

No grass grew under their feet. The Witmarks were the dynamos of the growing Alley. Plugging, as we understand it to-day, was in its infancy. There were few singing companies, hence the necessity for modern plugging was at a minimum. The minstrel and burlesque shows were still the chief source of popularization—

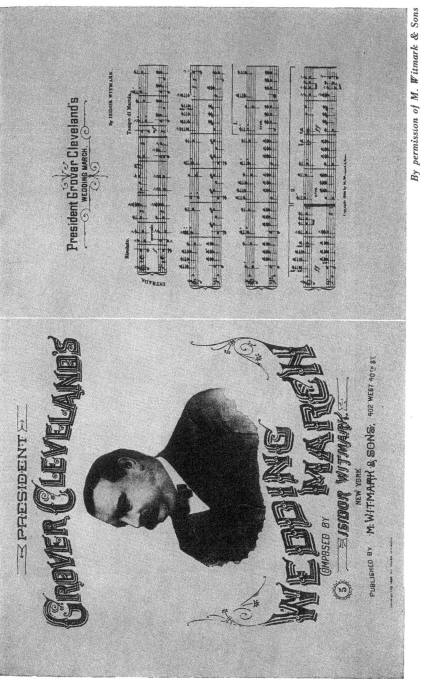

THE HOUSE OF WITMARK BEGINS ITS MARCH TO FAME AND FORTUNE

By permission of M. Witmark & Sons

these and such institutions as Tony Pastor's, and Koster and Bial's where youngsters with sympathetic voices would nightly rise from their seats in an upper box and regale the audiences with a repeated chorus. The outstanding personality who pilots a song into national popularity has always been important to the music business. In the days when Tin Pan Alley was still a single block on the Way that was not yet White, the fate of songs lay in the hands of such singers as J. K. Emmet, Gus Williams and their plays in Irish and German dialect, William Scanlon and his Irish dramas, J. Aldrich Libbey, Bonnie Thornton, May Irwin, Lizzie B. Raymond, and the vaudevillians.

The Witmarks saw that if they were to win wider audiences for their songs they would have to effect a minor revolution in the method of popularizing them. The experience of brother Julius had taught them what singers with personalities mean to song sales. If the singer didn't come to the publisher, the publisher would go to the singer. To-day, after forty years of evolution, something like an entente cordiale reigns among the Alleyites. The Radio companies and the Moving Picture interests have bought most of them up, so that the lion and the lamb have lain down together through the simple expedient of the lion swallowing the lamb. It was not so in the declining years of the nineteenth century. It was dog eat dog. Music publishers were hardly on speaking terms. They were out to steal singers, songmakers and songs from one another, and devil take the hindmost.

The Witmarks needed a catalogue and vocalists to popularize that catalogue. Did singers pay for their music? Then they would issue professional copies, *gratis*, teaching the singers into the bargain, and thus creating the modern professional department. Not this only, but they would furnish, likewise free, orchestrations to go with the vocal arrangements. They haunted the theaters, at rehearsals and at performances, seeking to cajole the artists into singing the biggest find of the year. Every song published has always been and ever will be the sensation of the century. Song publishers talked like theater posters and gay book-wrappers long before Gelett Burgess coined the word "blurb." It is in the theatrical tradition of which they are a picturesque part. To be sure, the language of the contemporary talkie trailer howls down the swellest efforts of the old-time ballyhooer of songs. When new adjectives are invented, the talkie trailers will blare them forth.

It was between the Witmarks and the firm of Stern and Marks that Mayor Walker of Gotham lived his short but successful career in the Alley of the Tin Pans. Walker, born in Greenwich Village of the Eighties, then known as Washington Square and Fourth Street Park, had music wished upon him by his mother. He played fife in St. Francis Xavier's Fife and Drum Corps. He haunted the band-concerts where pretty Kitty Rampone sang songs by her father, who conducted the band. He thumped away at piano scales, running the risk of being stigmatized as a "sissie," all for dear mother's sake. He struck up an acquaintance with Paul Dresser, then at the height of his "Wabash" fame. He became a favorite at house parties. (Something of this digital dexterity still remains, for Jimmy has been known to accompany Paul Whiteman's violin.)

So that Jimmy, under the jovial Dresser's inspiration, glided easily into the groove of Tin Pan Alley. With words, however; not music. When war with Spain had the nation roused, and "Good-Bye, Dolly Gray" was the leading hit, Walker entered the lists with "Good-Bye, Eyes of Blue." Witmark printed it;

Walker, at the time, was seventeen. Mother liked the song and sang it; nobody else did, and it looked like the end of Jimmy's lyric flight.

It was at this period that Ernest R. Ball began his phenomenal rise as a balladist. Witmark made him, and he, in turn, helped to make Witmark. How Jimmy ever plucked up the courage to approach the reigning popular composer of the day with a new set of verses is untold. "Will You Love Me in December as You Did in May,"—that was the song. With Ball's setting it shot up sky-high into the class of real money-makers. Walker collected $10,000 in royalties; in the latter half of 1929 he received a check for $30 on the song, thirty years after.

Edward B. Marks was around the corner with a steady contract. Walker signed, and the first fruit of the new arrangement was "I Like Your Way" (1905). There were other lyrics: "Kiss All the Girls for Me," "After They Gather the Hay," "So Long, Mr. Jasper Long," "With the Robins I'll Return," "Black Jim," "In the Valley Where My Sally Said Good-Bye," and "There's Music in the Rustle of a Skirt."

Yet Walker, like a surprising number of his erstwhile Alley associates, remains a man of one song. He might have added to his bank balance by writing, as one firm eagerly urged him, a theme song for his latest campaign. Mayor Walker, however, is through with the "J. J. Walker" who ranged Racket Row from the days of the Spanish-American War to the middle of the new century.[7]

[7] See *The New York American*, Monday, September 30, 1929, pp. 6 and 7; in a series, by O. O. McIntyre, devoted to the career of Mayor James J. Walker. See also a note, "Old Songs," in *The New Yorker* for September 13, 1930, pp. 20 and 21. The note errs in placing the beginning of Walker's career as a lyrist as late as 1905, when he joined Marks and Stern.

A Stern and Marks Young Song?

The house known to-day as the Edward P. Marks Music Company was, from 1894 to 1920, under the aegis of Joseph W. Stern. Stern (music) and Marks (words) had begun their joint career with "The Little Lost Child"; the passing policeman who found her, and, incidentally, his long lost wife, founded also a flourishing business. Stern and Marks took over from the Woodward catalogue such favorites as "White Wings" (1884), "Always Take Mother's Advice" (1884), Rosenfeld's "With All Her Faults I Love Her Still" (1888) and Dresser's "Convict and the Bird" (1888).

"The Little Lost Child" was not only the foundation of the Stern-Marks collaboration; it is justly celebrated as the song which, through the enterprise of its collaborators, inaugurated the illustrated song-slide. Innovations of song-exploitation and of business methods were, in those days, a necessity, if a firm was to keep its head above water. Mr. Marks still recalls with gusto the making of the photographs, at the Lee St. police station, Brooklyn, New York. A day was spent at the arduous task, and before the negatives were ready for development the station had been virtually dismantled, what with unhinged doors and curtains removed to allow for plenty of light. When, at last, the slides were in place for projection, and Allen May, of Primrose and West's aggregation of minstrels, was prepared to sing the song for the first time in public, a sad contretemps came near wrecking the ballad. Geo. H. Thomas, in charge of the stereopticon, was not too well acquainted with the vagaries of optics. A twenty-foot image was thrown upon the screen, and to make matters more pleasant, the image appeared inverted. Only tears in the author's eyes won for the author-publishers a second chance to plug the song into success.[8]

At its height, the song-slide was an important item of expense to the publisher. A set cost between five and ten dollars; there are records according to which, for the exploitation of a single song— in this case "Red Wing," published by F. A. Mills—eleven hundred sets of colored slide were used. Mills was as much the realist as were Harris and Marks. "Real Indians were engaged from a show playing in New York at the time, and the slide man had his own troubles persuading the Indians to pose before the camera, as many of them were under the impression that every time the camera clicked it cut away one day from their lives. On another occasion when Indians were brought into play, the pretty young girl engaged to pose had to promise a young buck several kisses, in addition to the five dollars a day he was to receive, before he could be induced to sit and watch the camera man chop away many days from his precious life." [9]

The cinema, in its early days, was used as a plug for songs; little did it imagine that it would be replaced by animated car-

[8] Charles K. Harris, in his autobiography, *After the Ball* (see Chapter VIII, on "The Rise of the Illustrated Song"), seems to contest the priority of "The Little Lost Child" as the first illustrated song. He relates how, having written "Is Life Worth Living," he got Joseph E. Howard to sing it against a background of painted curtains made expressly for the piece. Then, having attended a stereopticon lecture given by a minister in a church, Harris conceived the idea of adapting the apparatus to the illustration of songs. He then wrote "I Love Her Just the Same" and arranged for the Silvers, a vaudeville team, to introduce the ballad. "Naturally, the popular-song publishers, who were then springing up in New York like mushrooms, grasped the idea immediately and soon were having their ballads illustrated, too." For his song "One Night in June," the Thanhauser Stock Company, then playing in Milwaukee, did the slide-posing. Thanhauser later made a fortune in the movies. "Let me say here," adds Harris, "that this was more than merely a new method of staging songs; it was the first artistic illustrated song-slide thrown upon a canvas." All of this, however, occurred after "The Little Lost Child" was written.

[9] *Writing the Popular Song.* By E. M. Wickes. Springfield, Mass., 1916. See pp. 162-163.

toons. Thus does history reverse itself: the first song-slides were devoted to the ballads; such illustration of comic songs was the exception. To-day the moving caricature, as wildly fanciful as effective, is restoring many old songs to new favor, and adding, incidentally, to the creative contribution of the moving-picture technique.

Before the war with Spain had come to swing the country for a while into martial rhythms and sentimental good-bys, Stern and Marks were entrenched with a list that may serve as part of the graph that traces our slow progress toward ragtime. Tears were still in fashion: "His Last Thoughts Were of You" (1894); "No One Ever Loved You More Than I" (1895); "In the Baggage Coach Ahead" (1896), by the well-remembered Negro, Gussie L. Davis; "Mother Was a Lady" (1896). Mother is still a lady. Only last year the Victor company reissued the song, using as the new title the last line of its refrain, "If Jack Were Only Here." As a result, after thirty-four years, there was a sale of no fewer than 200,000 records, and the original publishers, who thought the song as dead as Tutankhamen, reissued the vindication of un-sullied womanhood under its new name. In '96 and '97 you were still bidden to "Whisper Your Mother's Name" and to "Take Back Your Gold." But a new type of raffish, rakish words and melody was invading our politer circles.

"My Best Girl's a Corker" (1895) was in waltz time, as was "Elsie From Chelsea" of the same year. Their spirit, however, was bubbling toward the newer rhythms.

"I Don't Care if You Never Comes Back" . . . "Take Your Clothes and Go" . . . "I Don't Like No Cheap Man" . . . These are all of 1897, and not at all in the vein of early minstrelsy. Not take back your gold, but bring it forward, becomes the new motif. The gold digger has begun to get in her spade work.

Leo Feist, in the early Nineties, was sales and field advertising manager for the R. & G. Corset Company. Also, he was writing songs. Everybody who remembers those songs is eloquent upon the prowess of Feist as a plugger of corsets. There is a theory in the business world that salesmanship is a science—perhaps with a dash of artistry—having little relationship to the article sold. He who can sell a corset can sell a song, or a shirt, or a foot-warmer. Feist, indeed, even managed to sell his first songs to Stern and Marks; "Those Lost Happy Days" signalized his beginning, and ere long he was spending his last happy days with the firm. Feist was not made to be an underling. Early he demanded partnership with Stern and Marks and was refused. At a later, more prosperous day, he would confess to Mr. Marks that his demands had been unreasonable. There was little harm in making the confession, for Feist had prospered in remarkable fashion. Publish Your Own Song is to-day the slogan blared forth by sharks who profit upon the inexperience and the vanity of the tyro. With a blithe unconcern for the three decades of intensive evolution that have characterized the music business, the profiteers point to the fortunes once made by self-starters in the Alley. Feist, rejected by the rising hierarchy of his day, in partnership with Frankenthaler began to print and push his own ditties; he got the orchestras to play them; he peddled them himself at the music-stores, and accumulated, in due season, some two hundred dollars. Howley, Haviland and Dresser had been incorporated for no more.

There was, in the kindly fellow, a vein of self-criticism. His sales charts told him that he had not been born to be a popular composer. Yet something in the life of the growing Alley held him in its thrall. If not a composer, then let him be a publisher for other composers. He opened a two-room office and was off. Von Tilzer—the ubiquitous Harry—helped launch the new firm with "Nobody Cares for Me," and "Oh, Oh, Miss Liberty." "Smokey Mokes," in 1895, cake-walked its publisher into the ragtime hit class.

He was one of the first to adopt a house slogan that served as the leitmotif of his business: You Can't Go Wrong With a Feist Song. His importance to Tin Pan Alley was not as a founder, but rather as an organizer.

Von Tilzer and Rosenfeld.

Among the notable free-lances of the Alley in its formative Nineties two figures stand out: Harry Von Tilzer and Monroe H. Rosenfeld. Rosenfeld, restless, versatile, fairly volatile, would never find a haven. Von Tilzer, in the early 1900's, we shall discover striking out for himself.

The circus, before the minstrel show, was America's one undisputed contribution to the forms of popular amusement. Minstrel songs, as we have seen, had been sung in circuses from horseback. Adventurous youths on the coast ran away to sea; adventurous youths inland ran away to the spangles and the sawdust. Showmanship must have been in little Von Tilzer's blood, for no sooner had he taught himself a tumbling act in his father's Hoosier barn than he left home for Barnum and Bailey's. Before he had got any farther than Ohio he was apprehended by his parents and his acrobatic career was thrown for a fall. A small repertory troupe appeared in his town shortly after, and Harry decided this time to become an actor. Perhaps he thought of this first venture in dramatics when, years later, he wrote "I'd Leave Ma Happy Home for You." In any case, for this troupe, Von Tilzer left his happy—perhaps not too happy—home. He was always leaving it. The next time it was to beat freight to Chicago; luckily for him the trainmen had hearts, and instead of red-lighting him and his improvised bed—a mere board tied beneath the car—they took the frozen lad into their caboose and landed him penniless in the big city.

He was compelled at once to turn his protean talents to the stern necessity of making a living. He did his tumbling act and other acrobatic stunts; he sang; he acted; he did tricks in the occult arts; he became a "spieler" for a medicine show. After this, the writing of songs—a notion that had always been at the back of his head—must have seemed, even in the face of long discouragement, something of a sinecure. It was in Chicago that the youngster penned his first song: "I Love You Both," a juvenile "ballad" that anticipated by several years the Harrisian child cycle.

> I love you both,
> Papa, with all my heart.
> I love you both,
> From mamma I never could part.
> Father, you've always been good to me,
> And a mamma that's sweeter there never could be.
> So, to answer that question it's quite hard, you see,
> I love you both.

The song was actually published, in 1892, by Willis Woodward, one of the most eminent of the pre-Tin-Pan-Alleyites. Von Tilzer had been aiming at Gotham, the Mecca of song-writers and actors.

And there he entered, at the head of a troop of horses—in a freight car—as their traveling custodian. New York, in 1891, was no place for a fellow with less than two dollars in his pocket. Six lean years lay ahead of him. He wrote, wrote, wrote, and then tramped the streets of the city with songs that could be purchased for a dollar, and nary a buyer to take them. Who'll buy my songs? Two for five? Fifteen dollars was a lofty figure; that was what, as late as 1898, "My Old New Hampshire Home" would sell for; nor did "Jack How I Envy You" command a higher price.

Von Tilzer had been introduced to Tony Pastor by Woodward. The bills of the week of June 1, 1896, discover Von Tilzer and Sidney in their act of The Humorous Germans. "My Old New Hampshire Home" was still two years away. Meantime, however, Von Tilzer was learning, from behind the footlights, what the public desired in the nature of songs. There were years during this lean period when Harry and his partners in rhyme wrote three songs a day—one thousand in a year. Ideas were never lacking.

It was during these first six struggling years in New York that Von Tilzer decided definitely upon his career.

Eventually, he so impressed Weber and Fields—themselves, at the time, only in their 'teens—that they formed a publishing partnership with him based on an even division of the profits. The association inspired him to write "I'd Leave Ma Happy Home for You," which would sell more than a million copies. With "On a Sunday Afternoon" he was to inaugurate the seasonal song. At its height it was selling, in a single department store of New York, at the rate of 10,000 copies per day. We shall meet Von Tilzer again. His career, like that of a few noted confrères, epitomizes the history of Tin Pan Alley.

Monroe H. Rosenfeld weaves in and out of the tale of the Alley in the guise of a mystery. He flourished throughout the Nineties as versifier, composer, press-agent, journalist, short-story writer and man-about-town. He hailed originally from Cincinnati, and it was Frank Harding who brought him to New York. Rosenfeld wrote a veritable catalogue of songs, now words only, now music, now both. He had at least three pseudonyms: F. Heiser, F. Belasco and Monroe Rosevelt. His voice was an open sesame to Newspaper Row and the journals were always ready to print whatever he brought in. He was, in brief, a "character," a happy-go-lucky sport who one day would flash a bank-roll of a thousand dollars, and the next would be borrowing car-fare of his friends. He earned big royalties for his day, but the race-track took what his words and music brought. Generous to a fault, he was everybody's philanthropist. There was something of the gypsy in him.

He added plentifully to the sobs of the Nineties. Thumb back in the files of the old *New York Clipper*, 1891 to the war of 1898, and you will discover reams of sentimental doggerel from his dripping pen. These verses, written especially for the old-time theatrical sheet, deal naturally with the playhouse; their spirit, however, is the spirit of the sad "ballads" that Rosenfeld wrote for the weeping sorority of our *fin de siècle*. Here is a sample from a four-stanza effusion in the *Clipper* of June 17, 1893; it might have been set to music for the delectation of the era:

> Oh, dear little maid so demure,
>   Has eyes that are filled with devotion;
> That other you scarce can endure,
>   So spiteful she is to your notion.

Alas! See them when they are wed,
  How strangely deceived was each lover;
There's only one word to be said—
  You can't tell a book by its cover!

Rosenfeld, one has a strong suspicion, is one of these books whose cover is deceptive. As far back as 1888 he had written "With All Her Faults I Love Her Still." He wrote, toward the end of the century, and well after ragtime had set in, the music to such lilliputian tragedies as "I Was Once Your Wife," "Don't Ask Me to Give Up My Mother," "Don't Say I Did It, Jack," "Those Wedding Bells Shall Not Ring Out," and at least two classics of this most un-classical genre: "Take Back Your Gold," and "She Was Happy Till She Met You."

Did he mean these things? Or did he write them with his tongue stuck derisively in his cheek? Rosenfeld wrote the music to Felix McGlennon's "And Her Golden Hair Was Hanging Down Her Back"; the tune suggests a sense of humor, and a Rosenfeld who, in his sighing symphonies, may have been writing—like the rustic Jane when she came back from the city—"with a naughty little twinkle" in his eye. On the other hand, there is the Rosenfeld of the *Clipper* doggerel, and of an article on "Popular Songs and Their Writers" in the *Metropolitan Magazine* for August, 1897, in which he quotes with approval such current "lyrics" as these:

Say, Mamie Reilly, I love you, yes I do;
You can't blame me, and though you try to shame me,
I'm your Jamie just the samie, Mamie Reilly.

That was from Maude Nugent's waltz hit. Our contemporary cultists of the inner rhyme are respectfully referred to the Mamiable vowels of this refrain. The waltz movement was still the fashionable one in Tin Pan Alley, and Rosenfeld was pointing to Sutton's "Rose, Sweet Rose" and to Pritzkow's "Take Back Your Gold." "Much of this song's fame is due," he was telling his readers, "to its exquisite rendering by the phenomenal contralto, Miss Emma Carus, who is also a musical composer of striking merit, she having just completed a grand descriptive song entitled 'The Crimson Chain.'" Rosenfeld did not add that he was the composer of the golden refusal; it might have spoiled the plug. He found it in his heart, too, to praise Ed Marks' verses to the music of his partner Sterns' "I Don't Blame You, Tom":

> I don't blame you, Tom, for marrying an heiress,
> But I loved you best, you'll find when you compare us;
> She may be rich and proud, but I was fond and true.
> You break your vow and leave me now, but I still love you.

They took marriage seriously in the Nineties. Every other song, it seems, was a sermon—in 3-4 time—upon the sanctity of the nuptial promise. Perhaps already "O Promise Me," interpolated into De Koven's *Robin Hood* to lend new life to the operetta, was beginning to rival Wagner and Mendelssohn at wedding ceremonies.

As late as 1917 Rosenfeld is discovered as the very vigorous editor of a musical magazine—*The Tuneful Yankee*—founded by the firm of Walter Jacobs, which is still active in Boston. He was ardently defending ragtime and—pure English in Tin Pan Alley!

The sentimental song of the declining Nineties betrayed no diminution of fervor. George Taggart (words) and Max S. Witt (music) who were soon to achieve fame with "The Moth and the Flame," were in the Rosenfeld–Harris–Marks & Stern–Dresser tradition with such pieces as "Grace O'Moore" (one of the thousand reincarnations of "Little Annie Rooney") and "Don't Let Her Lose Her Way." Virginity, too—at least, the virginity of girls —was also, forty years ago, a deep source of maternal—and music-lyric—solicitude.

Yet already the trumpet blasts of a new day had been heard throughout the land. Up from the South and out of the Middle West, from the dives of the despised negro, was coming once again the temper and the tempo of a new song, to restore life to the melodious languor of the Alley—to wreck the prunes-and-prism rigidity of the 3–4 school of morality—to undermine, as new rhythms always undermine, the order of things-as-they-were.

6. The Rise of Tin Pan Alley: Ragtime

RAGTIME in itself was nothing new under the moon. It was inherent in the oldest spirituals. It was latent in the songs of the minstrel era. Stephen Foster and James Bland had many a ragtime strain in their Negro and negroid melodies. The rhythmic ecstasy of the spiritual, sped up to the tempo of a new day, is rediscovered in what comes, in the latter half of the Nineties, to be known as Ragtime. Ragtime, then, far from being an invention of the Mauve Decade, is a rediscovery. It is, in its original haunts, as spontaneous a product as the most solemn black choric chant to the Lord. As spontaneous, but not so pious. . . . The spiritual yearns to God. Ragtime, not to put too fine a point upon it, yearns to the Devil. The spiritual is holy; ragtime, in its unleafy state, is, more than profane, obscene. We whites, in the pride of our civilization, placed a too transparent leaf over the nakedness of this black Eve; but we ourselves saw through our transparent sanctimoniousness. Ragtime is then, in part, the release of the Negro from his own addiction to holiness, and his rhythms brought to us something of that profane deliverance.

The spirituals translate the Bible; ragtime translates the other six days of the week. Small wonder that the moralists of both races should have hurled, from the beginning, their anathema against ragged meters that ragged all the tenets of the decent life. Ragtime is the materialism that balances the loud but tenuous religiosity of the spirituals. It is the raucous belly-laughter of the black after his awed service to the white man's and the Hebrew chillun's Jehovah. It is, in brief, a balancing of psychological accounts.

So, too, does it work for the white. It is rediscovered just in time to save us from the dismal melodramas of the hearts-and-flowers period. For us, too, it balances accounts. It brings up, from the dives of the South, from the levees and the swamps of darkest America, a robust humor that acts like a transfusion of blood. The Harris-Dresser forces by no means succumb at once; they linger on well into the 1900's, not only through sheer inertia, but because the "ballad" type of song answers to something eternal in that nest of illusions, the human breast. With songs it is as with theatrical forms—burlesque, musical comedy, operetta, vaudeville; the forms, though evolving from one another into their various perfections, yet live a life of their own that maintains the old simplicities.

No sooner has Ballad been buried than Ragtime arises to do a *danse macabre* at the obsequies. Yet Ragtime, too, shortly will listen to the threnody of the critics, while Ballad plays at resurrection. It is a see-saw rhythm; popular taste, like the taste of academicians, swings pendulum-like between fast and slow, merry and moody, high and low.

Tin Pan Alley takes over the heritage of minstrel days and speeds up the process. It does not mean what it says or sings. It is the paradise of Pseudo. Songs are not made, primarily, to sing; they are made to sell. Happy? Sad? Profit is the wind that fills this sail and points this weathervane. In the Alley, song becomes synthetic; one weeps, one laughs, at so many per cent. When You Ain't Got No Money, Well, You Needn't Come Around.

Etymology.

Ragtime . . . Where does the word come from? The etymologists, in the late Nineties, had a raggy time of it chasing these panting syllables through time and space. There were the *rags* of the Hindus.[1] There was the Latin *rado,* related to the Spanish *raer,* to scrape. There was the French naval term, *ragué,* meaning "scraped." Of course, there was the good old English word rag; if one could tear a passion to tatters, why not tear a melody to rags? The Negro term for clog-dancing is "ragging"; the dance is a "rag." Really, one needn't have left the country for an explanation of the word. Before the Negroes called these tunes and dances by the name of rag, I believe the word was "breakdown." It is helpful, in this connection, to recall the word "break" as used to designate the improvisations characteristic of the later jazz bands. To break down the rhythm, to rag it, would mean simply to pep it up with off-beat rhythms and effects of syncopation.

The deed came before the word. Handy, the recognized pioneer of the "blues," insists that ragtime, essentially, is nothing more than a pepped-up secular version of the Negro spirituals. He recalls how, in the old minstrel days, they rendered such haunting exhortations as "Git on Board, Little Chillun." To sing it in the traditional fashion of the earnest, if ecstatic, spiritual, was too tame. So, instead of repeating the call, "little chillun," his aggregation sang

---

[1] For this fanciful excursion see the *Musical Courier,* May 30, 1900: editorial entitled "A Ragtime Communication."

TIN PAN ALLEY

Git on boa'd, *little* chillun'!
Git on boa'd, *big* chillun'!
Git on boa'd, *all* de chillun'!
Dere's room fo' many a mo'!

To hear him sing it, to the accompaniment of hand-clapping and gestures toward the various components of the audience—a relic, perhaps, of the church atmosphere, where "brothers" and "sisters" sit in different sections of the building—is actually to hear the spiritual disintegrating, "breaking" up, into its ragtime successor.

Ragtime thus begins (like jazz), and perhaps ends, as a spirit derived from a spiritual. To-day, hearing Handy jazz up the invitation to a ride on the heavenly railroad, one would exclaim, "Why, he's simply jazzing it." In Handy's minstrel days they called it "jubing," from the word "jubilee." Ragtime, then, is already found lurking beneath the ecstasy and the rhythms of the more jubilant songs to the Lord, just as, in the slower-paced spirituals, one hears the mood, though not the peculiar pattern, of the "blues."

Yet, from the first, ragtime was bound to meet with passionate opposition. And, be it added, with passionate defense. There is something in moral man that fears mirth—that mistrusts those moods in which we abandon ourselves not to sorrow but to gladness. Ragtime was happy; *ergo,* it must be in some subtle way reprehensible. It came up from below, the product of an inferior race. It was the slum music of the slum proletariat. It crossed the color line of tone. It would lead—it has, indeed, led—to psychic miscegenation, to a sort of intellectual and emotional intermarriage. It had dared to leave the Jim Crow car of the arts and to take a seat in the white man's Pullman, not as servitor but as fellow passenger.

Ragtime . . . What, musically, is it?

It is usually, and carelessly, dismissed as syncopation. The definition is too easy. It is as difficult, in fact, to define ragtime as to play it. Into the definition must go something of the *rubato*, the nonchalance, the uncertainty of accent that characterize the ragtime player; something of the glorious indifference to precise pitch that stamps the true—and now almost extinct—singer of ragtime tunes. Syncopation alone—the regular dislocation of regular rhythmic accent—is as orthodox as the common triad. It is no more ragtime, *per se*, than Beethoven's choric capers in the Ninth Symphony, for all their jumping jollity, are jazz.

Louis A. Hirsch, one of the pioneers of modern popular music in America, once pointed out to Carl Van Vechten that ragtime syncopation had a quality all its own. "The melody and harmony are syncopated separately." Seventeen years ago Van Vechten himself, attempting to discover the secret of negro syncopation, was compelled to accept Hirsch's explanation as the most practical, even if not altogether satisfactory, and went on to show that many trained singers found it impossible to read ragtime properly, while European orchestras faced a similar problem. Later still, Van Vechten was to declare that no white woman should ever attempt to sing a "blues." The flesh would be willing, but the *spirit* would be weak. . . .

Academic syncopation may be set down on paper. The notes of ragtime, as of jazz, may be set down likewise, but unless there is added that something which defies notation, one hears sounds, not ragtime. Ragtime is in an aural, not a notational, tradition. It

[143]

has come down from ear to ear, not from sheet to sheet. There is in it a gypsy quality that the Hungarian or the Spaniard should understand.

When ragtime burst upon a jaded public there was, indeed, an attempt to deprive the Negro of his contribution. It was Scotch, said some; listen to the Scotch "snap." (Listen; and you can make out a case for the Black Bottom's ancestry.) It was Spanish, Mexican, Cuban, said others. (Listen to the *habanera* or the *tango* and you will know what they meant. Take the characteristic accompaniment of the tango and emphasize the two middle notes; you have the Charleston's characteristic rhythm.) Yet who would mistake the *habanera* of "Carmen" or Saint-Saëns' "Havanaise" for ragtime? No. Ragtime is something that music did to the Negro and that the Negro did to music. It began, as more than one Negro has assured me, in the restless feet of the black; it rippled through his limbs, and communicated itself to every instrument upon which he could lay his hands. It broke through his speech, especially in the shifted accents of his vocabulary. It still remains a racial accent which the white, for all the uncanny skill with which he has translated it from its original black, has not fully mastered. And yet, by paradox, it is the white—the Northern white in association with the Negro—who has developed ragtime and jazz to their fuller (not yet their fullest) possibilities.

The rag dance, as Rupert Hughes pointed out in an early eulogy of ragtime,[2] is "a sort of frenzy interrupted with frequent yelps of delight from the dancer and spectators, and accompanied by the latter with banjo-strumming and clapping of hands and stamp-

[2] *Musical Record*, Boston, April 1, 1899, pp. 157-159. When, in the following year, Hughes published his *American Composers* all this fine enthusiasm for the new musical phenomenon was, so far as the book was concerned, forgotten.

ing of feet. The banjo-figuration is very noticeable in the rag-music and the division of one of the beats into two short notes is perhaps traceable to the hand-clapping; every American is familiar with the way the darkey pats his hands with two quick slaps alternating with the time-beating of the foot. Something of this effect is seen in the Bolero and in the accompaniment to the Polonaise. The so-called 'snap' may be traced to the quick slap of the heel and toe of the foot in sharp succession. . . .

"To formulate ragtime is to commit synecdoche, to pretend that one tone is the whole gamut, and to pretend that chaos is orderly. The chief law is to be lawless. The ordinary harmonic progressions are not to be respected; the dissonances are hardly to be represented by any conventional notation, because the chords of the accompaniment are not logically related to the bass nor to each other, nor to the air. It is a tripartite agreement to disagree. In this beautiful independence of motion the future contrapuntalist will fairly revel; the holy fugue itself offers no more play to ingenuity."

There was reason in Mr. Hughes' irreverence. His prophecy about the contrapuntalist of the future came true in the Tin Pan Alley of the jazz arrangers—that noble, learned crew who are responsible, by half at least, for the vogue of jazz, and who, so far as the general public is concerned, like mute, inglorious Miltons, have wasted their fragrance anonymously, upon desert airs.

"The bass," continues this pioneer defender of ragtime, "is metronomically exact, as a rule, and as thumpily discordant as you might imagine it to be if a heavy-handed Negro should give all his eyes to his right hand, and let his left thump where it would." This may have been true of the first ragtime players. Listen to

[145]

Jimmy Johnson to-day—and watch his fingers—as he plays his rhapsody on themes from the music of the Georgia Negroes entitled "Yamekraw." . . . Abandon and rubato there are, in abundance; but every finger at every note knows just where it is going. The blending of the improvisatory spirit with the precision of the virtuoso makes for a delicious uncertainty that at no moment slips out of control.

The instrumental background of ragtime, as of the plantation songs and dances whence it derives, is the banjo. The spirituals are a group phenomena of worship; they are purely vocal, unless we consider the limbs an instrument. They sing, *en masse*, to God. The secular songs and tunes are for the entertainment of one's masters, the master's guests, or for one's self. "On the old five-string banjo," William C. Handy has told me, "you could get every syncopative effect that you find in the jazz bands of to-day." It was, in the hands of a competent player, a jazz band in itself.

Ragtime reached the whites through a process of slow insinuation. It worked its way up, as it were, from the accompaniment to the melody. I do not believe that the name itself appears on the covers of our sheet music before 1896. There was Bert Williams' expression of thermometrical dubiety entitled "Oh, I Don't Know, You're Not So Warm," carrying, in addition to the regular chorus, a "refrain with ragtime accompaniment—arranged by D. A. Lewis." There was Ernest Hogan's immortal "All Coons Look Alike to Me," with an additional chorus arranged by Max Hoffman: "a choice chorus with negro 'rag' accompaniment." W. T. Jefferson's "My Coal Black Lady" is subtitled Symphony de Ethiopia—a relic of the minstrel days—and the serviceable Max Hoffman again provides a "rag accompaniment." Hoffman, the husband of the danseuse, Gertrude Hoffman, was the first of the orchestral arrangers of ragtime. The prolific J. Bodewalt Lampe would follow fast upon his footsteps.

Ben Harney.

Of especial historical importance are Ben Harney's "Mister Johnson Turn Me Loose" and "You've Been a Good Old Wagon but You've Done Broke Down." Harney is generally credited with having been the first white to transcribe ragtime for the piano. He had served as accompanist to a Negro, and had toured the West and the Middle West long before he came East to start the rage in Gotham. His work was to be carried on by the unjustly forgotten precursor, Scott Joplin, composer of the *Maple Leaf Rag* and a dozen other pianistic intricacies, even as Joplin himself, who was twenty years ahead of his times, would find completion in the feline animadversions of Zez Confrey.

As early as 1897 Harney issued through the Witmarks his *Rag-Time Instructor,* "the only work published giving full instructions how to play rag-time music on the piano." The instructions were anything but full; they are interesting, however, both the text and the music, not only as precursors of Zez Confrey's truly admirable series upon the piano technique of jazz, but as showing the uncertain approach to ragtime at the period in which it was beginning to echo through Tin Pan Alley. There were few competent theorists in the Alley of the Nineties. Arrangements, even for piano scores, were not done with half the skill that is put into sheet music to-day. Even had they been done with such skill, the effort, largely, would have been wasted. Upright pianos were still luxuries in the land.

[147]

The installment business had not yet developed its high-pressure salesmanship. If you would judge the pianist technique of the Nineties, con the accompaniments to the heart-breakers.

Harney's explanation of ragtime was simple to the point of naïveté, yet few could have had better opportunity to absorb it in its native habitat. His instructions and his musical examples are important as revealing ragtime in the nature of a formula that could be applied to any orthodox tune.

"Ragtime (or Negro Dance time)," wrote Harney at the moment when the new rhythm was beginning to captivate the feet and the hearts of Broadway, "originally takes its initiative steps from Spanish music, or rather from Mexico, where it is known under the head and names of Habanera, Danza, Seguidilla, etc., being nothing but consecutive music, either in the treble or the bass, followed by regular time in one hand. In common time the quarter note of the bass precedes the melody, and the same in 2–4 time, where the eighth note is the marked tempo accentuated to the eighth in common time, and the sixteenth in 2–4 time." I copy this verbatim from Harney's *Instructor*. I confess that the words are written in a ragtime that I cannot quite make out. The meaning, however, is made clear by the examples. All that Harney asks of the executant is to give the bass a handicap of an eighth note in common time, and of a sixteenth note in 2–4 time. It was very simple, and it was, moreover, vastly encouraging to read that "by following this rule, the pupil will, after a few trials, be able to play the most difficult rag music written in any time or key." Harney then proceeded, mechanically, to rag "Old Hundred," "Annie Laurie," "The Man That Broke the Bank at Monte Carlo." Better was an original rag—"Ma Black Mandy"—that he threw in for good measure. His explanations, however, were as baffling as ever: "In this number the player will observe that both hands are playing consecutive time, and in places directly at variance with each other; by counting time with each hand separately, then playing slowly, increasing ad lib., the effect will be attained, and the most intricate rag can be played."

Meet Black Mandy:

Harney's example was far superior to his precept. Twenty years later, Monroe Rosenfeld was extolling and expounding ragtime for the readers of his *Tuneful Yankee*, and getting no further technically. The early public was not learning ragtime from printed instructors but from singers and songs and public performers. The "Georgia Camptown Meeting" by Kerry Mills, had already established itself as the representative cake-walk of the day; when Debussy was to write his "Gollywogs' Cake-Walk"—

which contains more ragtime than the Mills song-dance—he would clearly have the rhythms of the "Georgia Camptown Meeting" in his ear. . . . The establishment of ragtime as a national hysteria was still a few years in the future.

Out of her travels on the Western Coast and in Chicago, May Irwin was coming East with a new tune that she had picked up in a Pullman car from the guitar of Charles E. Trevethan, a sport scribe. Trevethan, in turn, had brought it up from the South. The irrepressible May was so struck with the tune that she ordered a supply of words for it, and into *The Widow Jones* went the song. A try-out at Brockton was followed by performances in Boston and New York. The "New Bully" was a knockout over night. Coon-shouting, as translated into Caucasian, was born and we were not to hear the end of it until a more slender age would introduce the jazz-baby. Your coon-shouter was a lusty, rounded lady. She was all curves. Her voice was a wild, raucous yell, and perfect intonation was her least concern.

As a matter of fact, the more subtle technique of singing ragtime and jazz is founded upon a rubato of pitch as well as upon a rubato of accent. Hughes recalls Ernest Hogan's singing of "All Coons Look Alike to Me" "with an impudent determination to keep out of key and out of time that was simply fascinating." The instrumental jazzification of Negro tunes, indeed, is a more or less conscious imitation of the Negro's vocal practices. And here we may note a queer interchange of functions. The voice becomes an instrument; the instrument becomes a voice. Jazz completed a process that ragtime began.

The voice came before the instrument. If, to-day, we speak of harmonic voices, it is because we sang before we played. The technique of instrumental writing, when it first appeared in Europe, was borrowed from singing. Contrapuntal writing for orchestra mirrors the development of vocal patterns. Instrumental music, in its earliest stages, was but a support for the human voice. The voice, however, has gradually taken over the prerogatives of the instrument. Listen to any first-class quartet over the radio and hear how, in their attempts to capture new effects, they mimic instrumental music, whether of the classic or jazzic variety.

The jazz-baby is line rather than curve. She, like the tunes that she chortles, is boyishform. She has caught, has been transformed by, the precision of the newer popular music.

The earlier ragtime, for all its debt to the white writers and the white performers, was definitely and refreshingly black. The rule of the white upon the pseudo-Negro minstrel stage was virtually over. The Negro, upon the vaudeville and musical stage, was achieving a certain revindication. The coon song and the rag were born anew in the image of a more sophisticated, yet still ingenuous, day.

The vogue of Weber and Fields in the New York of the late Nineties and the early Nineteen-Hundreds gave Gotham a taste of what the Greek burlesque may have been. Brander Matthews, who was not too solemn to have an eye and an ear for our vulgar entertainments, and who had audaciously mentioned Ned Harrigan in the same breath with Molière, now gazed upon the mock-corpulent Joe and the elongated Lew and went home to write: "An American professor of dramatic literature, whenever he came to discuss the lyrical-burlesques of Aristophanes, was in the habit of sending his whole class to Weber and Fields that his students might see for themselves the nearest modern analogy to the robust fancies of the great Greek humorist." It is quite Weberfieldian that this precious indorsement should have been overlooked by their lively biographer.[3]

So much for the antics of the slapstick duo. To us, at the moment, they are important rather for presenting to popular music the busy John Stromberg, who directed their burlesques upon the current drama and wrote the musical scores. Usually, the words were by Edgar Smith, a fellow with a flair for Gilbertian effects. Would that Stromberg had known his Sullivan to equally good effect. As it is, little is left to-day of the Stromberg songs except "Kiss Me Honey Do"; better known as "Dinah" (de moon am shinin'), made popular by the irrepressible Peter Dailey; "When Chloe Sings Her Song," which was the first coon song to be sung by Lillian Russell; "I'm a Respectable Working Girl," which none can blame Fay Templeton for having rebelled against; "Ma Blushin' Rosie"; "Say You Love Me, Sue," "Come Back, My Honey Boy, to Me," "My Best Girl's a Corker" and—his simple best—"Come Down, Ma Evenin' Star."

The Rogers Brothers—Max and Gus—had hatched their eggs in the nest of Weber and Fields, having begun as shameless imitators of their East Side companions. They would find their composer in Maurice Levi. Levi wrote for the Rogers many singable tunes, but neither he nor Stromberg could match the authentic spirit with which the colored composers had already begun to captivate Broadway.

Coincidental with the vogue of Weber and Fields in New York had been the rise of the Negro musical comedy.

[3] *Weber and Fields: Their Tribulations, Triumphs and Their Associates.* By Felix Isman. New York, 1924.

In 1890, Sam T. Jack, a leading manager of burlesque, originated the *Creole Show* upon the principle, as James Weldon Johnson has happily phrased it, of "glorifying the colored girl." It was, although it adhered to the pattern of the traditional minstrel show, a radical departure from that then decaying form. The show opened at the Howard, in Boston—cradle of so many theatrical enterprises—and within a year was in Chicago. Indeed during the entire season of the Fair the *Creole Show* played Porkopolis at Sam T. Jack's Opera House and prepared for a sensation in Gotham. The show ran for five or six seasons, enlisting such salient talents as Sam Lucas and Irving Jones. Here, in embryo, were the musical comedies of Cole and Johnson, Williams and Walker, and Ernest Hogan. There followed, upon this pioneering effort, similar aggregations: *South Before the War, The Octoroons,* and *Oriental America,* the two latter produced by John W. Isham, who had been the advance agent of the *Creole Show.* These productions are important for having assembled the finest negro talent available and especially for having encouraged a number of significant negro composers. When Sissieretta Jones, the "Black Patti," returned from her European tour of 1893, she was featured in an all-Negro show composed for her by Bob Cole, who had been for a time with the *Creole Show* and had later headed the negro stock company that occupied Worth's museum. Cole, fortunately, soon broke relations with the managers of "Black Patti's Troubadours." Fortunately, because in the season of 1898-9 "he came out with *A Trip to Coontown*"—obviously written under the influence of Charlie Hoyt—"the first Negro show to make a complete break from the minstrel pattern, the first that was not a mere potpourri, the first to be written with continuity and to have a cast of characters working out the story of a plot from beginning to end; and, therefore, the first Negro musical comedy." The show enrolled Sam Lucas and Billy Johnson; Johnson, entering into partnership with Cole, became the first Johnson of the famous Cole-Johnson alliances. The rejuvenation of our popular music by the Negro now assumed the proportions of a school. William Marion Cook— a thorough musician who had studied the violin under Joachim and musical theory at the Hochschule in Berlin—in 1898 wrote the score of *Clorindy—The Origin of the Cake-Walk*, to words by Paul Laurence Dunbar. Produced by the great Lederer, it ran for the whole summer. James Weldon Johnson, who speaks with authority upon negro music, discovers in *Clorindy* the "first demonstration of the possibilities of syncopated negro music. Cook was the first competent composer to take what was then known as ragtime and work it out in a musicianly way. His choruses and finales in *Clorindy*, complete novelties as they were, sung by a lusty chorus, were simply breath-taking. Broadway had something entirely new."

Cook was to be heard from in the musical gambols of Williams and Walker, those dark Lochinvars from out of the West.

The black and tan team came to New York in 1896; the play in which they first appeared proved a failure, but so great was their personal success that Koster and Bial's billed them for forty riotous weeks. They made the cake-walk the society dance of the day, as later, in England, they made it the rage with their *In Dahomey*. Their true vogue, however, belongs to the 1900's. Their first real hit was *The Sons of Ham*. During the eleventh year of their metropolitan career—in 1907—they were to produce "Bandana Land," after which the declining health of Walker ended "the strongest Negro theatrical combination that has yet been assembled." [4]

New Words for New Music.

The words of the new black music were as different from the words of the waltz-tragedies as was the music of those waltzes from the jagged melodies of the raging "rags." They rioted in materialism, in cynicism, in the platitudes of mundanity. Babies, in the Harrisian sense, disappeared; they gave way to "babes"— a different species of infant entirely. One ceased from breaking the news to mother, or even to "mammy." Mammas were no more mothers than babes were babies. The temperature of our popular song shot up to the top of the thermometer. The waltz-type, the sentimental ballad—these, for all the language of intense devotion that they suggested, registered at somewhere between zero and temperate; the coon song, in its variegated manifestations, went without delay to fever heat. Ragtime could laugh not only at the world, but at itself. The colored composers of the era wrote with an engaging dash of self-criticism that was not matched by their white contemporaries.

Listen to Irving Jones:

> I'm living easy,
> Eatin' pork chops greasy,
> Always got money,
> To give my honey.
> I'm always pickin'

[4] The data and quotations are from *Black Manhattan*, by James Weldon Johnson. New York, 1930. See the various chapters on negro music and drama in New York.

TIN PAN ALLEY

On a spring chicken:
Yes, I'm livin' easy
And cert'nly livin' high.

And again, to the same dusky troubadour of the tenements:

Enjoy yourselves,
Keep all your razors in yer inside pocket.
Enjoy yourselves,
But don't cause no disgrace.
Enjoy yourselves,
Gals, keep yer hands upon yer chains and lockets,
Jes' 'member you is ladies and genmen,
An' represent de colored race.

This is not only graphic and comical; it is social criticism, and
not of a low order. If you think that the gold-digger is a recent
blonde phenomenon, recall Ernest Hogan's

All coons look alike to me,
I've got another beau, you see,
And he's just as good to me
As yon nig ever tried to be.
He spends his money free;
I know we can't agree;
So I don't like you nohow.
All coons look alike to me.

What the whites were thinking in the gilded Nineties, the blacks
were singing. The ragtime songs, among other things, were more
honest than the dreary melodic tales that they helped to drive out
of fashion. They provide, too—it is a function of song—a vocabulary of unadorned passion,—a crude *ars amandi*.

Even Paul Laurence Dunbar paid his tribute to the national bird:

> Who dat say chicken in this crowd?
> Speak de word agin, and speak it loud.
> Blame de lan'; let white folks rule it,
> I'se looking fer a pullet;
> Who dat say chicken in this crowd?

In "Ev'ry Race Has a Flag but the Coon" there is a remarkable synthesis of the coon song's salient interests:

> Now I'll suggest a flag that ought to win a prize:
> Just take a flannel shirt and paint it red,
> Then draw a chicken on it with two poker dice for eyes,
> An' have it wavin' razors 'round its head.
> To make it quaint
> You've got to paint
> A possum with a pork-chop in his teeth;
> To give it tone
> A big ham-bone
> You scratch upon a banjo underneath.
> And be sure not to skip
> Just a policy slip
> Have it marked four-eleven-forty-four.
> Then them Irish and Dutch
> They can't guy us much;
> We should have had this emblem long before.

It's all there but the gin.

The colored lyrists and composers—Hogan, Cole and the Johnsons, Will Marion Cook's "Darktown Is Out To-night," Chris Smith ("Good Morning, Carrie"), Matthew Bivens, Irving Jones ("Get Your Money's Worth," "Take Your Clothes and Go"), Al

Johns' "Go 'Way Back and Sit Down" and "I Thought I Heard Somebody Calling Me"; Will Accoe's "My Samoan Beauty"; Brymn and McPherson's "Josephine, My Jo"; Edmonds' "I'm Goin' to Live Anyhow Until I Die"; Hillman and Perrin ("Kill It, Babe," "Little Pumpkin Colored Coon"), Fred Stone of Detroit ("Ma Ragtime Baby"), Tom and Charles Turpin of St. Louis— these brought to our popular song a new vitality. After the middle Nineties, the white man's street and dance music would never be again what it had been.

Cole and Johnson belong, like Williams and Walker, in the 1900's, but their contribution to the ragtime craze is best considered here with that of their fellows. It was not only their songs that infected us—Cole and Johnson's "Under the Bamboo Tree," "Nobody's Looking but the Owl and the Moon," "I Must Have Been a-Dreaming," "Oh, Didn't He Ramble"; Bert Williams and Rogers' "Nobody," "I May Be Crazy but I Ain't No Fool"—it was their singing, which inspired to various felicities of imitation a whole troupe of white vocalists.

The higher temperature of the coon song glistened in the titles, especially from 1896 to 1901. "Dar's No Coon Warm Enough for Me" . . . Bert Williams' "Oh, I Don't Know, You're Not So Warm" . . . George M. Cohan had struck his stride before 1897 —he wasn't yet twenty when he produced "The Warmest Baby in the Bunch." He could blow in the other direction, too, with "You're Growing Cold, Cold, Cold," advertised as "the story of a coon with an iceberg heart." There were Cole and Walker's "A Hot Coon From Memphis," Gene Senarens' "A Red Hot Coon," Reed and Ward's "She's My Warm Baby," Will Cook's "Hottest Coon in Dixie," Kerr and Nichols' "The Warmest Colored Gal in Town,"

Williams and Walker's "I'm a Cooler for the Warmest Coon in Town." And who that has sung Metz's "Hot Time in the Old Town To-night" remembers, or ever knew, "Another Baby," which he did with John Boyce in 1899—"as warm as the original warm baby by the same composer"?

Ragtime warmed us up. Jazz would merely add fuel to the flames. Ragtime also sent new currents of energy into our feet. What it did for our song it did for our dance; whatever raises the temperature quickens the pulse. Songs have always been written around and in celebration of the dance. Strangely enough, the waltz-type of song was frequently used to condemn addiction to the whirling pastime. Our fathers and mothers danced to songs that frowned upon dancing. How often, did we but know it, are words and music linked in unfriendly tether.

The speeding-up process began with the introduction of ragtime. Perhaps the classic ancestor of the species is "La Pas Ma La" of 1895, the name of which may be traced to the French *pas-mêlé*, or mixed step.

> Fus yo' say, my niggah git yo' gun
> Shoot-a dem ducks an' away you run.
> Now my little coon come-a down the shute
> With the Saint-a Louis pass and Chicago Salute.
> Hand upon yo' head, let your mind roll far.
> Back, back, back and look at the stars.
> Stand up rightly, dance it brightly,
> That's the Pas Ma La.

And this, from some extra verses:

> Fus you say, my niggah, Bumbisha
> Than turn 'round and go the other way

To the World's Fair and do the Turkey Trot
Do not dat coon tink he look very, very hot . . .

The Turkey Trot here antedates the true vogue of the dance by some sixteen years.

The next few years were rich in dance-songs, which have marathoned into our own day in an uninterrupted succession of increasingly complicated patterns. In 1896 appeared "De Coonville Grand Cake Walk," "Miss Brown's Cake Walk," and Gussie L. Davis's "When I Do the Hoochy Koochy in de Sky." This Midway Plaisance inspiration was, in its way, fairly paranoid:

> They'll turn the X-rays on me when the music plays
> So dat ev'ry one can see into the dance.
> I'm goin' to do the coochy seven thousand diff'rent ways
> And I'll knock the Midway people in a trance. . . .

Followed in rapid succession—all of 1897 and 1898—"The Possum-a-la" and "Bom-Ba-Shay"; "My Ann Eliza, the Ragtime Gal," "Mister Johnson, Don't Get Gay," "My Honolulu Lady," Rastus Thompson's "Rag-Time Cake Walk," and the Sterling-Von Tilzer "That's How the Ragtime Dance Is Done," which goes back to the original "Pas Ma La":

> First you do the rag, then you Bombershay
> Do the side-step, dip, then you go the other way,
> Shoot along the line with a pas-a-ma-la,
> Back, back, back don't you go too far . . .

The hoochy whoopee at the World's Fair was bound to produce an epidemic of dances; relatively few found their way into print at once. Two years after the Fair, Henry Berti (Alberto Himan) and Percy Armand published, as piano pieces, respectively, "Kutchy Kutchy or Midway Dance," and "Hulla Hulla." Two years after that there was a song named "Coochy, Coochy, Coochy, Coo." In this selfsame year a jungle jongleur complains that

> There ain't nowhere the coons can do
> The hoochy coochy dance

yet in 1896 Will C. Carleton's "I Love My Honey, Yes I Do" promises to buy the girl of his tandem—built for two

> a pair ob dem bloomer pants
> Like dem gals in de Koochi Koochi dance.

This punctures an illusion. Could the original umbilical centripetalists have worn pants, or were the pants, like so much else in our light ditties, inconsiderately put on—rather in—because they rhymed?

In "Get Your Money's Worth" the darkies had been bidden to prance and do the Hoochee-Koochee Dance, but the song itself is a glorification of the then popular cake-walk. It was not until the 1900's were well advanced that the abdominal gyrations achieved their proper status in our catalogue. The Marriuccia series, begun in 1906 with Al Piantadosi's "My Marriuccia," restored the dance in popular verse. For this, there was perhaps no more subtle reason than the fact that hoochee-kooch could be made to rhyme with Marriootch.

Ragging and Jazzing the Lingo.

Very early there developed, in the singing of ragtime, the use of an interpolated vowel: "I'm a hust-a-ling-acoon-a, and-a that's-a

[161]

just-a what-a I-a am"; or, in the classical example of "Under the Bamboo Tree":

If you lak-a me, lak I lak-a you
And we lak-a both the same,
I lak-a say, this very day,
I lak-a change your name.
'Cause I love-a you
And love-a you true,
And if you-a love-a me,
One live as two, two live as one
Under the bamboo tree.

There are several possible explanations of the practice. It may be an aid to breathing in song. The minor explosions of Italian tenors into just such half-breathed terminal vowels is not due alone to the nature of the Italian language; it serves as a respiratory exhaust. The phenomenon is not unknown to English balladists, who doubtless consider it an added touch of artistry and a sign of passion that overflows its banks. Again, it may fill out a rhythm that otherwise would be purchased at the expense of artificial pronunciation. Consider the effect of the first line quoted above, if, instead of the verse as it stands, one were to sing

If you like me like I like you

and give the two notes of "lak-a," in each case, to the vowel i of the single word "like." It would not be at all likable.

Again, the Negro rags, not only his tunes and his verses, but his speech. His fondness for long words that he but half or quarter understands may be, at bottom, not only a desire to impress his hearer but a response to their rhythms. He shifts his accents. He breaks up his words and inserts syllables; *hot dog* becomes *hot diggety dog*, in which *dog* is ragged into *diggety*. I recall singing, as a child, the familiar chorus of "Hello, Ma Baby," in something like the following fashion:

> He-ge-dello, ma baby,
> He-ge-dello, ma honey,
> He-ge-dello, ma ragtime girl.
> Se-ge-dend me a ke-ge-diss by wire,
> Ho-ge-doney, ma heart's on fire!

We carried the process into ordinary conversation, adding it to the various "secret" languages of our catalogue. The vowel of the word was split into two of itself, and between these vowels created by fission we inserted the combination "ged" or "gad." *What's the matter* thus became *Wha-ga-dat's the ma-ga-datter.* I do not believe that it was altogether a coincidence that this was at its height during the hey-day of ragtime. In our less patient day we shorten, not lengthen, our speech. "Don't be sill—" "Don't be ridic—"

Ragtime, as was natural with the less original spirits, soon became a plaything. It was, almost in its infancy, impatiently applied to orthodox music, even as we had applied it to orthodox speech. The "Star-Spangled Banner," Mendelssohn's "Wedding March," the "Miserere" from *Il Trovatore,* and numerous other "popular ' classics" were subjected to the process in the rather automatic manner of Harney's *Instructor.* The humorless business was a forecast of what would happen to jazz when it ran out of novel ideas. The parallels between the evolution of ragtime and the evolution of jazz are almost mathematically exact.

"Rags" became as common as, in some fifteen years, the "blues" were to become. The titles meant little: "Maple Leaf Rag," "Temptation Rag," "Black Diamond," "Frisco," "Haunting," "Moonlight," "Mocking Bird," "Porcupine," "Red Pepper" . . . You could remove the names, mix them up in a hat, pull them out again and retitle the rags at random without in the least disturbing the music.

The rags were not written with any salient skill. They bore a marked family resemblance. This may have been owing, in part, to the relatively undeveloped piano technique of the day. Perhaps, also, to solicitude—commercial solicitude—for the home pianist. The few ragtime pianists who acquired a reputation on the stage and the band pianists of the new musical dispensation must have played ragtime somewhat differently from what the printed notes suggested. Here, too, must have begun the pianistic virtuosity that was to flower in the pre-jazzian era.

Ragtime, in its early phases, produced fine melodies and a few characteristic rhythms that easily grew monotonous. It fastened more firmly than ever upon our popular music the pentatonic (five-note) scale, which is still a powerful influence in jazz. It gave us, however, no characteristic harmonies.

The ragtime era had its orchestral arrangers, but interest was so intensely concentrated upon purely rhythmical effects, and so orthodox was the constitution of the ragtime band, that little progress was made in tone-color, contrapuntal humor and the other devices characteristic of jazz.

The ragtime band, indeed, especially as it was known to the whites of the middle Nineties, was the same band that played in the orthodox ball rooms of the day. No banjo plunked its staccato emphases; no saxophone dripped its oily moaning; the violin was still the chief singer; the clarinet was an unobtrusive alto, usually, and altogether too well-bred to emit tedlewisian squeals; the trombone, to be sure, permitted itself an occasional slide of commentary; the battery was just that—drums, triangle, cymbals and not a forest of noises issuing from gourds, wood-blocks, ash-sifters, steam-pipes and what had they.

The ragtime band, in its way, was refined. It abandoned the uncouth array of the early minstrel music-makers. It was, by a curious paradox, white. Not until 1905 would a genuine jazz band appear for the first time upon a New York stage; this was the Memphis Students—"a very good name, overlooking the fact that the performers were not students and were not from Memphis . . ." [5] The twenty pseudo-intellectual-Memphisians, who were drawn from the roster of players at private parties, had been trained by Will Marion Cook; their success at Proctor's Twenty-third Street Theatre was so great that it eventuated in a European tour. Jazz organizations had already appeared at dances and the lower grade of outdoor entertainments. Not until the eve of the Great War would they establish themselves.

Metz and "A Hot Time."

The war between Spain and America produced very little music worthy of remembrance. The war itself, and some of its attendant scandals, hardly merit too much space in our history books, though the fetor of canned beef is still in our nostrils after more than thirty years. The songs that we now associate with the short conflict were not all written for the war; they had been done before

[5] James Weldon Johnson. *Op. cit.* p. 120.

the blowing up of the Maine. Indeed, "A Hot Time in the Old Town," credited to Theodore Metz as composer, though published only a year before the hostilities, had been written and played no fewer than twelve years before Theodore Roosevelt catapulted it into fame by adopting it as the official song of his Rough Riders. The piece became the theme song of our soldiery in Cuba; during the Great War an attempt was made—with what success I do not know—to revive it as the marching song of the A.E.F. Other wars, other songs.

As the war of 1898 caught up with "A Hot Time," so it caught up with Harris's "Break the News to Mother," which had been published some years before. So that, in the climactic year of 1898 we have, as outstanding war songs, an example of the evanescent ballad type and a forerunner of the ragtime rage. Originally, "A Hot Time" was wordless.

"Mr. Metz, however, was important in his day. He composed 'A Hot Time in the Old Town To-night.' He wrote that back in '86 when he was band-leader with the McIntyre & Heath Minstrels, and this is the story of it: The troupe's train was held up somewhere in Louisiana because a house near the railroad station was afire. The townsfolk were frenziedly rushing water to put it out. The name of the village, posted on the railroad station, was Old Town. McIntyre spotted the sign and remarked: 'They're certainly having a hot time in the Old Town to-night.' 'Yes,' replied Heath, 'and that's a good song title'—he was quick at such things. He told Metz about the idea and Metz set to work and wrote the music. He had it done in time for the band to play it for the street parade in New Orleans.

"The song didn't make any special hit then or in the next few years although Metz plugged it with various minstrel shows he was connected with. In '96, however, a man named Joe Hayden wrote some words for it and it was published. Came the Spanish-American War, the soldiers took it up, and in no time the whole nation was singing it.

"Metz came to New York originally in the seventies and got a job sweeping out and doing chores in a drugstore. His ambition was to become a fine violinist. He had with him when he came a Guarnerius from which he refused to part. He took lessons from Joachim and at the same time played in a saloon for three dollars an evening. After that he barnstormed around with bands and minstrel shows, mostly in cow towns and mining camps out West. He went into mining in Colorado and made fifteen thousand dollars but was shortly back in music circles as the leader of a women's orchestra. He couldn't get a woman clarinetist so he persuaded a friend of his, Joe Weber, to dress up like a woman and fill in. Weber got by all right. He is now the president of the American Federation of Musicians and dignified. It was after all this that Metz became a bandmaster, one of the most famous of his day. Still later he became a music-publisher in New York. It was then that he dug out 'Hot Time' and sought words for it." [6]

Metz appears, too, among the precursors of the jazzband leaders, and fancies himself as one of the granddaddies of jazz. Fifty years ago, he will tell you, in a Denver concert hall, he jazzed up the "Jolly Coppersmith Medley," and played it on whistles, with two pieces of iron to serve as the anvil effect. In 1884 or 1885 he had

[6] *The New Yorker*, August 2, 1930, p. 11. The unsigned note is by that paranomastic connoisseur, Sigmund Spaeth.

a cornet, clarinet and trombone play "The Last Rose of Summer" in three different keys.

Though Metz wrote numerous songs and instrumental pieces— "Diana Valse," "A Warm Baby" (ragtime two-step, and one of the first on the market), "One Sweet Smile," "Once Again," "Merry Minstrels," "Olympia March," "Never Do Nothin' for Nobody," and others—he remains, like so many in Tin Pan Alley, a man of one song. And of one operetta, *Poketa*, on an Indian theme. The librettist? Monroe H. Rosenfeld. Metz, too, bears testimony to the facility of the ubiquitous Monroe. "You could sketch out a topic for Rosenfeld to work on, and he'd have the job done before you were through talking. As 'for *Poketa*, that's just how we did it. I outlined the plot, situations, and the rest, and that very night the libretto was finished in Rosenfeld's room."

Metz, the oldest active conductor in the game (for Sousa is only 76, as the composer of "A Hot Time" will remind you), distinguishes between the classical and the mass-ical; he believes, however, that popular taste shows an increasing appreciation of the masters.[7]

The history of music publishing immediately after the Spanish-American war may be summed up in the phrase "more of the same." Jewish names were becoming more prominent, and with them, Jewish commercial methods. To assume that there had been no hustlers on Music Row before the Jews arrived would be stupid; perhaps it is a coincidence that with their coming the industry began to hum. It is reasonable, however, to attribute much of Tin Pan Alley's early progress to the more intense competition introduced by the Jewish firms.

[7] The foregoing paragraphs are based upon information kindly furnished by Mr. Metz himself.

Thus more than one new organization was founded in frank rivalry of the amazing Witmarks, of Stern and Marks, of Charles K. Harris. Music publishing in Tin Pan Alley grows as often as not by a process of fission. Firms could be formed—and they were—on the basis of a single hit. As pluggers were stolen, so were lyrists and composers. When Feist went into business for himself he had no scruples about annexing word and music men from his friends Stern and Marks. Morale was easily destroyed. Royalties are one thing; in the primitive days of book and music publication they were neither too certain nor too accurate. Publishers' profits are yet another. The story of the well-known publisher who once employed as bookkeeper a chap named Anderson still goes the rounds. Every time he submitted to one of his chief lyrists and humorists the latest royalty statement, the gag-man would counter with, "Another one of Anderson's fairy tales."

To write a hit and "make" your firm was flattering; but why should the firm take the cream of the earnings? Ergo, into publishing for yourself, and make both royalties and profits. It was simpler then than it is now. It took the lyrist and composer a long time to discover that there is many a slip twixt the studio and the sales counter—that it required more than a good song to achieve a good sale. By the time a song has sold its millionth copy, so many agencies have intervened between creators and purchaser that the actual writers are all but forgotten. You remember the artist or the band that played it; could you, for the life of you, except in a few outstanding instances, name the gentleman who merely wrote the darned thing?

With the optimism of an industry on the make, Shapiro and

Bernstein threw their hats into the ring. Their policy, from the beginning, was to go after the singing stars by the wholesale. Every publisher was being compelled, if he would make his pieces known, to effect a tie-up with a prominent vocalist who, in more senses than one, would "sell" the song to the public. The Alley was moving up Broadway. Always it has followed the theater. Accordingly, Shapiro and Bernstein decided to establish themselves at Broadway and 6th Avenue, near Twenty-eighth Street. With Morris's booking agency on one side, and the *New York Clipper* on the other, the new firm would be in the heart of the theatrical market, camping, as it were, on the very doorsteps of the profession.

Burlesque and variety—the various beer gardens at the open-air resorts—were the goal of the contemporary plugger. The press, too, then as now, was eager for news of song and dance. "Harry Von Tilzer," remembers Mr. Bernstein to-day—we meet Harry everywhere—"was the greatest plugger in America." He had already written "My Old New Hampshire Home," and sold it for $15 to W. C. Dunn. Shapiro and Bernstein took it over—publishers in those days seemed to live by taking in each other's tunes—and built it into a hit. Lottie Gilson was singing the new firm's songs, taking them all over the country and teaching them to fascinated audiences. Artists were modest in their expectations; when, at the end of a season, Shapiro and Bernstein presented her with a diamond ring that was worth all of $500, it looked like a big stone.

Bernstein, as his special contribution to the technique of the era, helped to evolve the song-with-action. As a frequenter of the burlesque houses, and as a publisher, he was interested in encores.

HARRY VON TILZER

The Man Who Launched a Thousand Hits

Encores engraved the song upon the memory of the audience and sent them to the counters for copies. "My Old New Hampshire Home" had originally been done in burlesque, and Bernstein, by suggesting action to accompany the singing—chorus work in particular—had been able to produce as many as seven or eight repetitions.

It would not be long before Shapiro and Bernstein would add Von Tilzer to the firm. Good men, before they become rivals, had better be made into partners. It would not be long before Von Tilzer would subtract himself from the firm. Good men, before they sink their identity, had better strike out for themselves.

Von Tilzer is one of the most interesting products of the Alley that he helped to make. He is, and has always been, dynamic, irrepressible. He was the Beau Brummel of the Alley, and thought nothing of ordering a dozen suits at a time. For long he affected a high stiff collar that was as much a trade-mark as Belasco's collar in reverse. Von Tilzer is one of the few word-and-tune men to have exhibited, since his beginnings in the late Eighties, a principle of self-adaptation and growth. Harris, for example, never escaped from the groove that he had dug for himself with "After the Ball." Contentedly he ran along its narrow track, ringing the changes. With Dresser and Rosenfeld and most of the others it was much the same. Von Tilzer proved himself equally adept at fashioning waltz songs, ragtime, comic ditties. It is not only that he has issued thousands of popular tunes, the aggregate sale of which runs into the numerous millions. He has been shrewd at satisfying the public taste, at forecasting it, at shaping it. If the Nineties may be christened the Harrisian age, so may the 1900's be christened the age of Harry Von Tilzer. It is in this decade

[171]

that he rides the crest of the wave, with songs for every heart. Down to the threshold of the jazz régime he maintains a popularity that is scarcely rivaled.

He rejuvenated the practice of nonsense syllables, as in "I'd Leave Ma Happy Home for You-oo-oo-oo-oo." (Someone should write a history of these, from the primitive tra-la-la to the erstwhile inescapable "vo-de-o-do" and "boop-a-doop." Frequently, they are equivalent to the jazz break, serving to fill in a gap of the words or the melody.) He glorified the bourgeois Sabbath with "On a Sunday Afternoon." Our contemporary metricians should glance over Andrew B. Sterling's words for samples of internal rhyming:

> They work hard on Monday
> But one day that's fun day
> Is Sunday afternoon.

Von Tilzer, with his "Cubanola Glide," began a new era of dance-songs. With "I Ain't A-Goin' to Weep No More" he successfully ragged even the raggy meter of the coon song. He has always insisted upon concise, hard-hitting, effective phraseology in his songs; he has written the words for at least seven-tenths of his choruses.

Irving Berlin was not a phenomenon that burst suddenly upon New York. The way had been paved for him, and in the office of Harry Von Tilzer. It was for Von Tilzer that little Izzy plugged in the balcony of Tony Pastor's music hall. It was Harry who published one of Berlin's first songs, to music by Al Piantadosi, entitled "Just Like the Rose." He was the first to publish a song by George Gershwin, to words by Murray Roth, now high in the councils of Moviedom. The song was entitled "When You Want 'Em You Can't Get 'Em, When You Get 'Em You Don't Want 'Em." If Von Tilzer hadn't written "Alexander, Don't You Love Your Baby No More" in 1904 the name of "Alexander's Ragtime Band" would have been another in 1911. When Berlin, in 1924, wrote "All Alone," he was remembering a title of Von Tilzer's dating back to 1911.

Tin Pan Alley Is Named.

To crown the tale of Von Tilzer, it is probably in his office, early in the 1900's, that Tin Pan Alley received its name. Here is the story as I received it from Harry himself:

It was Von Tilzer's custom, when playing the piano in his office, to achieve a queer effect by weaving strips of newspaper through the strings of his upright piano. It is not a musical effect; it is wispy, sometimes mandolin-like, and blurs the music just enough to accentuate the rhythms. Monroe H. Rosenfeld was a frequent visitor, not only as a composer and jingle-man, but as a newspaper writer in quest of material. He had just finished an article upon the music business—perhaps for the *Herald,* on which he worked for a number of years—and was casting about for a title. Harry happened to sit down and strum a tune, when Rosenfeld, catching the thin, "panny" effect, bounced up with the exclamation "I have it!" It was another "Eureka!"

"There's my name!" exclaimed Rosenfeld. "Your Kindler and Collins sounds exactly like a Tin Pan. I'll call the article Tin Pan Alley!"

There are those who doubt Rosenfeld's invention. The pianos

of the professional parlors in those days, they will assure you, sounded so unmistakably like tin pans that the metaphor must have occurred to hundreds of listeners simultaneously. Yet, to those whose curiosity has extended to Rosenfeld's articles and verses, and to inferences as to his peculiar personality, it is easily credible that he was just the kind of man to name Tin Pan Alley.

The Alley, at the opening of the new century, swarmed with names new and old. It was a kaleidoscope of ever-changing hue, against the background of a few solid firms who have weathered every storm in the trade.

Broder and Schlam, from San Francisco . . . Kerry Mills, whose real initials were F. A., was established opposite *The Clipper*. Mills, in the history of ragtime, is an overlooked figure. He wrote not only the "Georgia Camp Meeting," which became the cake-walk par excellence, but "Rastus on Parade" and "Whistling Rufus," two of the earliest ragtime piano hits. Mills, in 1912, wrote the theme song of the St. Louis Exposition, "Meet Me in St. Louie, Louie,"—a lively waltz that was reminiscential of the old days. . . . Feist was already convincing people that they couldn't go wrong with a Feist song . . . Petrie, who is remembered for one tune: "I Don't Want to Play in Your Yard" . . . Remick, who had come in from Detroit and whose name would appear upon an amazing succession of hits. Remick had entered the business through the Whitney-Warner Publishing Company of Detroit. They had issued the "Dance of the Brownies"; had "repeated" with Lampe's popular cake-walk, "Creole Belles." As a result, Lampe came on from Buffalo to join the firm as an arranger; he followed them to New York. The firm was still Whitney-Warner when it

accepted Chas. Daniels' "Hiawatha," which started the pseudo-
Indian rage. It was no longer possible to keep out of New York,
and Gothamward it came, as Remick's. When we were lucky
enough to sit near the band of the burlesque or vaudeville house
we could make out the name proudly strung across the covers of
the musicians' selections. Remick to-day is president of the Detroit
Creamery Company. His remembrances of the music business are
not happy. Yet the old name, carried by his successors, is still
synonymous with hits. . . . Charles B. Ward, as Harris remembers, was exceedingly popular. He had written "And the Band
Played On"—Casey may be heard still waltzing with his straw-
berry blonde through an old-timers' program on the radio—and
believed in flamboyant advertising. . . .

Howley, Haviland and Dresser were at their zenith. . . . In a
few years the phenomenally successful trio would be parted. As
their inception illustrated the hatching of the new in the nest of
the old, so their dissolution is typical of what, from the first, has
gone on in the Alley. That dissolution was sourced in its very success. The beginning of the end arrived after the firm had trans-
ferred its quarters to the Holland Building. Paul, it appears, had
a dear friend in Buffalo who convinced him that he was too gifted
whether as business man or as writer to split profits with Howley
and Haviland. Dresser at once began to make things unpleasant
for Haviland, who announced his willingness to sell out his interest
to his partners. We are looking ahead now, for the parting occurred in 1904; Haviland was bought out for $8000; his share,
he contends, was worth at least ten times that figure. Together with
the composer Theodore Morse he reëstablished himself as the
F. B. Haviland Publishing Company, at Thirty-seventh and Broad-

way, and ran into another series of hits: "Blue Bell," "Down in Jungletown," "Arra Wanna," "The Good Old U. S. A.," "Keep on the Sunny Side," "Keep a Little Cozy Corner in Your Heart for Me," "Way Down in My Heart I Got a Feelin' for You."

Music firms are not famous for their stability. After five years of this, Morse decided to go into business for himself, together with their then manager, Al Cook. The combination lasted just thirty days, and Haviland purchased Morse's interest.

To return, however, to Paul Dresser. He and Howley, about a year after Haviland's withdrawal, went into bankruptcy. It is no secret that, as much as from anything else, Paul died of a broken heart. Pat Howley tried a comeback; he purchased the Howley, Haviland and Dresser catalogue at a receiver's sale, for a nominal sum. The spell had been broken, however, and later the catalogue was dispersed among various publishers.

Harris, in his valuable autobiography, *After the Ball: Forty Years of Melody*, has told of Dresser's last day. "Paul," he said to the once so jovial troubadour, now bankrupt in purse and spirit, "I'll tell you what I'll do. I'm going to give you an office here with me. Put your name on the door, publish all your songs, exploit them, and we'll split fifty-fifty." They shook hands on it . . . and the next day Dresser was dead. He had lived and died like a popular ballad. Strange . . . the likeness in the difference between the brothers, Paul and Theodore. There is little humor in either. Paul's ballads are drenched in tears and bathos. The man who wrote "On the Banks of the Wabash" wrote also "Our Country May She Always Be Right, but Our Country Right or Wrong" . . . And "Your God Comes First, Your Country Next, Then

Mother Dear"—a peculiar inversion of Tin Pan Alley standards. Dresser, together with Harris, inaugurated and sustained the new school of weeping balladry in popular song. It was the antithesis of that realism which Dreiser had already inaugurated in American fiction.

7. Sousa, De Koven, and—Principally —Victor Herbert

PARALLEL to the two chief currents of our popular song in the Nineties flowed yet another stream: that of the polite musical comedy. Three names stood out: John Philip Sousa, Reginald de Koven and Victor Herbert. Sousa, the oldest, survives his compeers, and this may be a symbol. For, underneath the changing fashions of our popular music, the martial rhythms of the typical Sousa piece beat as strong as ever. The march, like the waltz, is a fundamental pattern. It was the historical function of Sousa, indeed, to quicken the tempo of our national life by introducing, as rival to the Strauss waltz, a two-step with all the time-beats of the national psychology. It is a pretty question for our musical historians—if they deign to consider so plebeian an inquiry—to discover just how the Strauss waltz degenerated into the almost undistinguished 3–4 measures of the waltz as Tin Pan Alley wrote it in the Nineties. Of the Straussian product, someone had said, not too untruly, that "it is calculated to strangle expiring virtue in its tendrils." Our Alley waltzes—read the words if you don't believe it—were calculated to strangle toughly resistant vice.

Sousa (1856-), though American-born and American-educated, was trained in the tradition of Offenbach and Sullivan. Before he was appointed, in 1880, leader of the United States

Marine Corps band, he had traveled with theatrical troupes as violinist and as director. When, in 1892, he resigned to head his own organization, he had served under five presidents—Hayes, Garfield, Arthur, Cleveland and Harrison. He qualifies, then, as a member of our club of Yankee Doodle Boys.

Later generations are wont to forget, if they ever knew, that many of the glorious Sousa marches come from comic operas to which the composer often wrote his own words. Nor, from the evidence at hand, were they at all inferior to what passes muster to-day. But then, Sousa is also a novelist, and wields words almost as easily as he wields the baton.

El Capitan, The Bride Elect, The Charlatan, not to overlook his first attempt, *Desirée*—these were old when Tin Pan Alley was young. The first of his marches to attract attention was "The Gladiator," written during his early days as bandmaster. Up to 1892 he was as badly underpaid as he was prolific. This march, as well as "The Washington Post," "The High School Cadets" (which, in Europe, would be asked for as an encore under the title Ice-Cold Cadets), "Semper Fidelis" and other marches of this era, were sold at a price from five to fifty dollars, outright.

Sousa, though never a playboy of the Alley, had the attention and the admiration of the swarming hacks. He had, too, their sensitivity to the advertising value of a catchy title. His "Man Behind the Gun" was suggested by the Spanish-American war; his world-famous "Stars and Stripes Forever" was a salute to Dewey's victory at Manila. He had a girl named after him: For She Is a Regular Sousa Girl. So he is enshrined in Tin Pan Alley after all, not to speak of the generous quotations which the scribes of Melody Lane have made from his endless list of compositions.

[179]

TIN PAN ALLEY

A Monocled Operetta.

De Koven (1859-1920), stands, in this respect, midway between Sousa and Herbert. His best was his first. His friend, Rennold Wolf, once wrote an article about him entitled *A Composer with a Monocle,* and the description is admirably illustrated by the music of *Robin Hood.* For this is a comic opera with a monocle. One eye sees English; the other, American. "O Promise Me" has sold into the millions of copies; it is still all but obligatory at properly self-conscious weddings. Yet, this happy accident aside, De Koven was never a truly popular composer in the sense that Sousa was popular, or Herbert. He never captured the imagination of the people. (This, be it understood, is not a criticism of his music; it is simply a statement of historic fact.) Yet he was keenly alive to the possibilities of ragtime, even though, as his later work revealed, he could not manage it with deftness or without the self-consciousness of one who had been reared in a higher tradition.

As early as 1897 he was discussing the possibility of a national school of music based upon the darky song and the plantation dance. He was not ready to side with Dr. Dvořák, the Czech proponent of a Negro-American school, but he saw the need of the vitality which such a school could bring. "We cannot," he was saying thus early, "look to the educated, highly-trained and able musicians who are turning out worthy and authentic work in America as the founders of such a national school. They are too wedded to formalism, too anxious to reproduce correctly the forms that they have been taught to admire, to be readily susceptible to purely national influences, did any such exist. No—rather must we,

I think, turn to those comparatively less learned, and therefore, perhaps, more natural composers who are now producing the popular songs heard in every music-hall, on every street corner, from ambulant pianos and itinerant organs, which are sold by the hundreds of thousands of copies among the masses of the people, as the early, and however crude, progenitors of the future American music."

The composer with the monocle was not a musical snob. He did not too greatly suffer from the Solemn Fallacy. There were, in his day, as in ours, publishers who scorned to print the current trash. For most of it was just that: trash. But—and it is here that the "classical" publishers made and make their amusing error—so was and is the great majority of musical publications trash, whether it bear the gaudy covers of Tin Pan Alley or the sober black-and-white of that abomination, the "semi-classic." Dignity is precious; its pompous mask is a worthy target for Chaplin's custard pie.

Victor Herbert, of all the early comic-operatists, became the darling of the American public. He was, temperamentally, of the Alley; in gifts, in ability, he rose far above it. When he entered it, academically he stepped down, but not with condescension. His career enfolds that of numerous younger contemporaries: Cohan, Rudolf Friml, Jerome Kern, Romberg, Gershwin. All, in varying measure, went to school to his glittering scores. Because he was so gifted, we judge him instinctively by a higher standard than that against which we range the humbler troubadours of his day.

TIN PAN ALLEY

Our Melody Man.

Said Andrew Carnegie once, in a moment of expansiveness, "My idea of Heaven is to be able to sit and listen to all the music by Victor Herbert that I want to." Certainly, if one is to judge by the trend of democratic amusements in this country, the people of the nation have ratified the sentiment of the great donor of libraries. Everywhere one comes upon the chief tribute that may be paid to a composer: the playing of his music and the singing of his songs. Herbert, within a few years after his death—he died on May 26, 1924—leaped into the position of "America's favorite composer."

There was, for a time, a downright Herbert rage, and it has not yet quite subsided. He achieved the dignity of a Herbert Album, issued by one of the leading phonograph companies, and was thus whirled into the company of the immortals. There was a time when it was difficult to tune out of a Herbert number on the air; every wave-length broadcast a favorite refrain, and one only wondered that, with the wealth of material to choose from, the program-makers harped on a wearying routine. Herbert himself, in his lifetime, got tired of the endless repetition of a few popular selections, not to speak of the fact that the radio had begun to cut in definitely upon the sale of his sheet music. They were playing him, almost literally, to death.

He did not live to enjoy his victory over the radio magnates, against whom he led the fight of the American Society of Composers, Authors and Publishers. He had been nobly instrumental —and vocal—in ensuring to the gentlemen who write our popular music the rights to their property in the air, as well as on land and sea. It was ironically appropriate that, as epilogue to that victory, he should become one of the most popular composers in the nightly broadcasts. He died just before the era of big money in the movies, the talkies and the radio. Although he was imposingly prolific, and was on the job to the very instant of his sudden death, he is said not to have made more than $20,000 a year in his hey-day. His estate, valued at $58,156, was not sufficient to pay all his bequests. By the time his wife had died (on February 27, 1927) his royalties had sunk to $10,000 a year. Harry B. Smith, his most constant collaborator, told us in *The American Mercury* (August, 1924) that he "died from overwork in the sixties." There are boys in Tin Pan Alley who would regard his income as a pittance. New days, new ways.

Herbert, convivial soul, was not out primarily for the money. With him, music and friendship came first. His motto might have been, "Easy come, easier go." It came, and it went. What he might have accomplished had he discovered a public that was interested in more serious music, it is difficult to say. He himself was of the opinion, to judge from a few scattered remarks, that to succeed in the United States it would be hazardous to stick to serious composition. Yet it is easy to believe, as in the analogous case of Sullivan, that in writing his musical comedies he was obeying a deeper fiat of his nature.

Now, on the stage, he is being "revived." It was interesting to watch how audiences trained to the speed and precision of the jazz *revue* reacted to the ditties and humors of an age when neither drink nor music was synthetic. Herbert, then, shows all the signs of becoming a national classic. The new Britannica allots him fifteen lines, mentions three of his light operas (about 6% of his output), lists one of his two grand-operatic ventures (*Natoma*) and has a line or two about his music for the movies. (He was the first important American composer to write an original score for a cinema production—*The Fall of a Nation.*) The commentary is not much, and it is almost noncommittal; however, Herbert's famous grandfather, Samuel Lover, is awarded but two lines more, so that perhaps the grandson came off fairly well. A book on our native opera and its composers gives grandson Victor a seven-page chapter; it appears, however, that four of these pages are taken up with the stories of *Natoma* and *Madeleine,* and that the light operas, which won for him his more enduring fame, are deemed worthy of some five lines. "He reached the musically untrained and taught them to appreciate the difference between music of the day and music of all time." So he did, but not with *Madeleine* and *Natoma.*

"America's favorite composer," like England's, was by heredity an Irishman. But he was really an international product, Irish by birth, German by education, and American by adoption. The Irish in him clung to his voice; he spoke with the decided suggestion of a brogue. A visitor to his home in New York found decorations in green on all sides, and a fitting climax was reached when the composer himself was discovered at his labors in a tweed suit of erin-go-braghish verdancy.

He was born in Dublin on February 1, 1859. His father, Edward Herbert, was by profession an artist; his mother, Fanny Lover Herbert, was the daughter of Samuel Lover, best known for *Handy Andy*. Samuel Lover, as a direct and an indirect influence, was of great importance in the early life of Victor. Edward Herbert died in Paris when his son was but three years old; the family then went to live with Lover at his estate, "Seven Oaks." Here it was that Victor spent an impressionable childhood, under the eye of a doting mother and an understanding grandfather.

He owed everything to his mother, he said years afterward to Miss Enid Stoddard, who at the time was painting his portrait. It was a proper sentiment from an American composer, and from a fond son; but it overlooked much that Grandpa Lover had given to him. Lover was not only a novelist; he had also made his beginnings as an artist, and had been elected, in his thirty-first year, a member of the Royal Hibernian Academy. He is said to have been an excellent musician, and fused his interests in a portrait of Paganini. He wrote songs. At the time when the Herberts came to "Seven Oaks," Lover was along in years—some sixty-five, in fact; he died in 1868, so that the most Victor could have spent under his tutelage was six years. Yet the home breathed an atmosphere of culture and especially of music. "Seven Oaks" was a rendez-vous of arts and artists.

It was Lover who, with the instincts of a musician, saw the talents of his grandson and insisted, from the first, that he be given the advantages of an education in Germany. This was the easier to accomplish since his mother, after his father's death, married a German physician, and soon established the family in Stuttgart. Yet the first plans for Herbert were that he should be, not a musician, but a doctor; he would enter his step-father's office. The child showed such unmistakable leanings toward music, however, and particularly such rare proficiency upon the violoncello, that his mother encouraged him in his ambitions.

His first teacher was Professor Cossmann, later to join the Hoch Conservatory at Frankfurt. Cossmann urged him to a musical career, and to the wide-ranging studies that are an indispensable preliminary to it. No more is heard of the plans to make a physician of him. At about the time when he would have been hanging out his shingle, he is discovered instead as first 'cellist of the Court Orchestra at Stuttgart. Dr. Emanuel Baruch, who knew him in those early, impecunious days, recalled upon his death that his talent for making friends was always as great as his talent for making music; he made both all the time. Leipzig, Munich, Berlin and other cities of Europe heard him on tour, and he returned to teach at the Stuttgart Conservatory, at the same time continuing his studies in theory and composition. He was polished off by Raff and Reinicke—two names that are not yet forgotten.

It was a love affair that brought him to the United States. Had it not been for Therese Foerster, who was about to set sail for New York to make her début at the Metropolitan Opera House under the baton of Dr. Damrosch, we should never have known *The Fortune Teller*, *Mlle. Modiste*, *The Red Mill* and their numerous companions. The opportunity held out to Fräulein Foerster was too good to let slip by—and Herbert, though still only an indigent musician, could not bear the thought of his sweetheart crossing the ocean without him. So, taking their courage in both hands, they crossed together, as man and wife. No sooner had Damrosch listened to Herbert's 'cello than he engaged him for the Metropolitan orchestra. The union began auspiciously, with Mme. Herbert on the stage and Mr. Herbert in the pit. In this household there had to be harmony.

As a musician, Herbert, in the United States, was a success from the start. He played under Seidl and under Thomas. In time he would lead, with equal grace, the famous Twenty-second Regiment Band (called Gilmore's) and the Pittsburgh Symphony Orchestra, not to speak of his own band, organized in 1904. He would lead, too, at the Worcester Festival, and write for it his oratorio, *The Captive*. His beginnings as a composer, however, were humorously dubious. His earliest efforts in composition he took to old man Schirmer, in New York. Schirmer shook his head and advised him to stick to his orchestra job and leave composition to composers. Herbert's revenge, however, was sweet and complete. Soon his music was appearing under the Schirmer imprint, including even the very pieces that had been rejected.

Herbert's Versatility.

He had arrived in 1886. Within six years his *Prince Ananias* inaugurated his career as a composer of light opera. From that date onward he was to be alert simultaneously on several fronts, but the violoncello was slowly relegated to the memories of his beginnings. In 1894 he succeeded Gilmore as bandmaster of the Twenty-second Regiment Band; in 1898 he was chosen as conductor of the Pittsburgh Symphony, and wrote *The Fortune Teller* for Alice Nielson. This was but one of four operettas completed during that busy year. Before the end of the same year, so important for Herbert—and for Spain and the United States—there arrived from Germany, on October 20, his mother and his half-brother, by now a well-known German actor. During 1899-1900 he completed his first symphony; there followed a suite for strings, a concerto for his favorite instrument, a symphonic poem. The conductorship of the Pittsburgh Orchestra stirred in him, it would seem, the ambition to write serious music—an ambition that can

[187]

never be put to sleep in the heart of him who was born to write strains of gayety. To this period belong his *Suite Romantique*, his tone poem *Hero and Leander*, and the suites, *Woodland Fancies* and *Columbus*.

Herbert here ran true to form; it was the story of Sullivan all over again, with one eye on the concert hall and the other in the pit of the Savoy; it pointed to the story of Gershwin to-day, with one foot on the stage of musical comedy and the other planted on the platform of the symphony hall. De Koven, too, the only true rival of Herbert in the pre-jazzian era of operetta, sought for such of his pieces as *Robin Hood* a category that should distinguish them from the more vulgar musical comedy. What, deep down in the hearts of those who bring us laughter with their music, is there that makes them at moments ashamed of that levity? Why should man, almost universally, feel a glow of guilt when he is having a good time? Herbert could not have been very happy in Pittsburgh. He confided to a friend that the real reason he dispensed with the services of the band's guarantors was that they wanted him to play "Annie Rooney" instead of Beethoven and Wagner.

He made his sacrifices to the Great God Sobriety. He wrote his symphony, and, with the aid of the public, forgot it. He wrote his operas in the grand style, and cherished for *Natoma*, with its Indian plot and its capable musical eclecticism, that affection which parents so frequently reserve for the more unfortunate of their offspring. Why, when he must write our great American operas, this passion for the Red Man? Or for a self-conscious archaism that takes us off the continent altogether? Sullivan, offering up his sacrifice, at least wrote an *Ivanhoe*. Damrosch at least chose *A Scarlet Letter*.

[188]

Herbert was definitely of the pre-jazzian era. He belonged, after all, to the period of the waltz rather than to that of the fox-trot. I should not be surprised to learn that, despite his willingness to contribute to the historical jazz programme of Paul Whiteman, he did not, in his Irish heart of hearts, care too much for jazz. It came too late in his life. It was the music of a generation that stepped too fast for his corpulence.

He was a burly fellow, who could never shed a certain boyishness of manner. Miss Stoddard, painting him, studied his head and thought at once of Franz Hals' cavaliers. He was round and florid. His hair was black and wavy; its curliness was accentuated by his favorite photographs. His eyes were blue—"a deep Irish blue," as someone has described them. He was by nature generous, jovial, convivial—the Falstaff of our popular American music—spendthrift of his earnings as of his gifts.

He composed with ease. An operetta like *The Wizard of the Nile* would cost him but a month, part of which would necessarily be spent upon other duties. *The Idol's Eye* took little longer. The melodies came almost unbidden. They were, as he told an interviewer, a divine gift arriving as he walked in the woods, rode on a train, or woke suddenly in the night.

"Some composers think in terms of the piano, but I pay little attention to it, and consider all the resources of orchestra and voices given me to work with. People often ask me if I work out my own orchestrations. If I did not, it would be as if a painter conceived the idea for a picture and then had someone else paint it." The real labor lay in the arrangements. Herbert, unlike so many of our popular composers, was his own master in the matter of orchestration. And, as musicians need not be told, a song that will take but a few minutes in the production may require many hours before it is scored with conscience and skill.

"He would come in," recalled Florenz Ziegfeld, shortly after Herbert's death, "and work out a new scene in my office, and the next morning appear with the full orchestration. Some composers will play a song or a chorus on the piano and it will sound pretty well. But when they write it down for the orchestra it sounds pretty bad. Victor was just the other way—not so good at the piano but very good in the orchestra. He used to say to me, 'I'm a rotten piano player,' when he was running over a tune, 'but it'll be all right when I fix the orchestra part.' And it always was."

Herbert's thorough technique stood him, as we shall see, in good stead. He was eager to impress upon the younger composers of his day the need of a solid grounding. Irving Berlin has testified that he tried to interest him in musical theory. "I remember his saying, 'It is a mistaken idea that a little science will hurt your natural flow of melody. On the contrary, a musical education will give you a background that will improve your work.' " Gershwin has told me, too, that Herbert, with his characteristic generosity, offered to teach him orchestration, gratis. At the time, Gershwin declined; since then he has been remedying his deficiencies.

It was natural for Herbert to achieve his orchestral fluency. He sat in the best orchestras of his day; he knew the band as a player and as a conductor; his wife sang in the grand operas. The geniality of the man is mirrored in his tunes and in the humor that he could write into his instrumental parts. De Koven lacked his flash, his bubbling spirits, his versatility. I am not sure that *Robin Hood* is not superior to any single score that Herbert ever wrote; yet De Koven was never ratified by the public as Herbert was; his attempts at popular ditties were commonplace, without the redeeming brilliancy—if too frequently also the tinsel glitter—of Herbert's orchestration. One has but to compare the frequency of De Koven numbers on the radio with that of selections from Herbert to appreciate their relative standing with *hoi polloi*.

Within a span of thirty-eight years, Herbert was to write some fifty light operas. This fertility, this prolixity—were they tokens of creative exuberance or of mere financial need? The answer, as in the case of so many similar queries, lies not in the middle but at both ends. His first operetta, *Prince Ananias,* was written when he was thirty-five. That was a late start, but he very soon caught up.

A Music Mill.

My experience with his lighter music has been, invariably, that it sounds better away from the opera house than in it. This may be an indirect commentary upon the general inferiority of the librettos. When in doubt, always blame the text. Or, as Herbert's librettist, Smith, once said in a curtain speech after the second act of *The Serenade:* "When an opera is successful, the audience always say, 'What pretty music!' And if it is a failure they say, 'What a bad libretto!' " The fact is that every text was grist that came to Herbert's music-mill. He was too hurried, too harried, to exercise discrimination. So that now we recall, not so much the various operettas as the outstanding music in them. The earlier pieces are quite as likely to contain the finest writing as the later. There is no curve of progress; there is a wavering level of accumulation. The wonder is that under such circumstances Herbert should have done as well as he did.

TIN PAN ALLEY

The names of the operettas come tripping to memory with the very lilt of Herbert's music. (And consider how, with the jazz vogue for double-time music, the lilt of triple-time has all but died out.) *Prince Ananias* had a libretto by Francis Neilson, long before the days of politics on the old lamented *Freeman.* Some critics found the score too ambitious, subtle, highfalutin. But soon the grace and humor of the composer and the richness of his orchestration were noticed. Then followed *The Wizard of the Nile,* and more praise for a tuneful score. *The Serenade,* and a charm that still endures. *The Idol's Eye . . . The Fortune Teller* and La Nielson. Huneker was jubilant, praising the versatility of the composer, his choral work, his polyphonic writing and his orchestration. *The Singing Girl,* with Nielson and Eugene Cowles, following hard upon the dubious *Cyrano de Bergerac* and an equally dubious Francis Wilson. *The Ameer,* with Frank Daniels—and already cries that Herbert was played out.

Now the names crowd into a crescendo of memories in which not the chronology but the totality is important. For Herbert will live, not for any single operetta so much as for the selections, the melodious anthology, that will be made from his repertory. An excellent operetta could be put together from his works in the same manner that *Blossom Time* was tessellated from the writings of Schubert. It would be well worth trying. It is too bad that the evaporation of the texts he set so blithely should carry off with it so much pleasurable music. *Babes in Toyland, It Happened in Nordland, Naughty Marietta* (with a Lilliputian Emma Trentini and an Orville Harrold of Brobdingnagian proportions), *Mlle. Modiste* (and the temperamental Fritzi Scheff, with her perennial invitation to the kiss), *Eileen,* which sounded more Irish to me, and essentially more tuneful than the unfinished *Emerald Isle* of the sick and wearied Sir Arthur Sullivan. . . . It's a rollicking roster—honest tunes, robust or charming, as the case called for, and usually finer to the ear when divorced from their words. Herbert belongs to the "ifs" of the operetta. If only he had had a Gilbert; if only he hadn't been rushed to death . . . If—the cruelest epitaph of all. And keeping him company in the shadows are the younger Sousa, Gustav Kerker, Luders, Reginald de Koven. . . . Much vigorous music of our own day—unless it is caught up by the tabloid versions of the talkie-operetta—is destined to go the same way.

Herbert, then, did not lack appreciation during his extremely active career. Perhaps our musical criticism had not, during the height of his productivity, acquired its present ability to deal understandingly with the lighter musical and literary forms. He was not so easily intellectualized, by the sophisticates, as of late our comic-strip men and our jazzophiles have been intellectualized. Indeed, as one thumbs through his scores one finds little of our contemporary sophistication. His melodies are forthright; his humor is robust and, in its simple manner, honest; by half, certainly, he is the conscientious craftsman doing his busy best by his job.

His death, of course, called forth from even the most critical of his friends, eulogy instead of criticism. "He was the last of the troubadours," wrote Deems Taylor. "His musical ancestor was Mozart and the family of which he was so brilliant a younger son numbered Offenbach, Délibes, Bizet, the Strausses and Arthur Sullivan among its elders. What he had was what they all had, the gift of song. His music bubbled and sparkled and charmed,

and he brought the precious gift of gayety to an art that often suffers from pretentiousness and self-consciousness of its practitioners." A few days later (June 1, 1924), in the New York *World*,
Mr. Taylor returned to his theme:

"Herbert was a far more important figure in American music
than he has ever had the credit for being. His chosen field was
operetta, and though his achievements in that field made him world
famous, the fact that his medium was primarily a form of entertainment caused self-styled serious musicians to regard him with
a certain measure of condescension. He felt this keenly. He was
a talented composer and a serious one and he knew it. But he knew
that the musical public whose opinion he respected most did not
bother to appraise his work at its true merits, and the knowledge
embittered him at times."

Taylor was right, of course, in condemning the musical culture
of Herbert's day for being so timid as to confuse seriousness with
solemnity. He went on:

"They compare him with Sullivan, but I think he was a far
more gifted man than Sullivan. Do not forget that Sullivan had
Gilbert. Herbert never had a librettist who was completely worthy
of him. . . . His tunes were neither glorified rhythmic patterns
nor harmonic paraphrases. They were pure song, capable of being
sung without accompaniment if need be, as pure in outline as the
melodies of Schubert or Mozart. . . . There is more harmonic
complication in a score like *Algeria* or *Mlle. Modiste* than there
is in the entire output of Donizetti, Rossini and Offenbach combined."

Henry T. Finck, in *My Adventures in the Golden Age of Music*,
written two years after the death of Herbert, was quite as fulsome.

"On the whole," he declared, "I consider Herbert the greatest musician of all time with Irish blood in his veins; greater not only than Balfe and Wallace, but than John Field, Sullivan and Stanford."

It is not a well-tempered clavichord that sounds such strains as these; Taylor's enthronement of Herbert above Sullivan did not pass without protest from New York to San Francisco. It is a subtle disservice to Herbert for his admirers to pitch their appraisals in such a key. Or to write, as the reviser of *The History of American Music* has done, that Herbert's second concerto for violoncello "is probably his finest work, and is one of the best existing works of this school." To maximize the man's achievements is quite as easy as to minimize them.

The truth is that Herbert, like most men of his nature, was too easily satisfied with the day's toil. Certainly half his bitterness at not being accepted by those who stood in his eyes for the musical élite was at himself for never quite measuring up to his own highest standards. He was thwarted by the taste of the day, by the exigencies of his circumstances, by his very fertility, which made compliance and compromise all the easier. It would have been better if some of that bitterness had been transformed into a more determined self-criticism. But the man was hurried; his public was forever waiting for his next; he signed four contracts at a time, and lived up to them; he wrote in haste—if with uncanny skill—and repented at leisure. How are we to blame too severely those of his musical friends who improperly evaluated his light operas, when he himself showed them the way by his over-valuation of opera called "grand," and by his unquenchable faith in *Natoma?*

[195]

Herbert was right when he was wont to assure Ziegfeld that it would all come out well in the orchestration. His music frequently sounds much better than it is because of his dexterity with the instruments of the band. Such a tune as "Ah, Sweet Mystery of Life!" for example, is really banal; and if, as Mr. Taylor has said, there is not a vulgar line in all of Herbert, surely there are numerous instances of banality, which is a step lower than vulgarism. I do not mean to imply any denigration of his melodic powers; at his best he was, for his genre, a gushing spring of tunefulness. I mean to suggest, however, that he was—at times as all of us so frequently are—the victim of his finer qualities, and that his orchestration could cover a multitude of sins. After all, who would not gladly surrender a few piquant harmonic combinations —a few complexities that satisfied rather the technician than the dramatic situation—for another *Barber of Seville* or even another *Grande Duchesse?* Sullivan's orchestration is a model of simplicity, of fragility, on occasion; yet this fine-spun commentary will doubtless stand the wear of time far more successfully than the torrential flow of Herbert's harmonies.

Herbert enriched the tonal palette of his countrymen; he refined the humors of musical commentary: he added robustness and ebullience to the light opera of his day. He made no contribution, however, to the form. He left it little different from what he found it, and this, despite a certain intuitive feeling for dramatic touch. He did not begin an era; he ended one.

8. Ballyhoo

Or, the Ungentle Art of Plugging.

IT was in November, 1898, that Theodore Dreiser set down for the *Metropolitan Magazine* a brief account of how a popular song was made. The account was as naïve as the street-pianos that still rumbled melodiously along the pavements of Gotham, one of the chief publicity mediums of the growing Alley. When Dreiser wrote this, both he and Tin Pan Alley were young. It is, in its way, a document, and merits generous quotation as a picture from one who was to become a novelist of international reputation.

"The history of the popularization of the average song begins with the aspiring author, who, having written what he is sure must eventually be an international song hit, sends his song to the publisher of whose business ability and general success he has heard the best report, or, if he lives convenient to New York, he takes it about in person. Usually the publisher controlling the latest song hit is the most popular victim of aspiring writers. To him they proceed, determined of course that their song shall not fail of proper recognition of its merits, if their personality counts for anything. As a rule, however, the publisher has not time to hear a new writer play over his own piece. When he appears he is courteously informed that of course a great many songs are brought in every day, and consequently each one must be left a

[197]

few days for consideration. Almost invariably he will also volunteer the information that there is always a demand for good songs and that royalties are paid on all sales, usually from four to seven per cent.

"This being satisfactory, the manuscript is left; or if not, and the author insists on being allowed to be present at the hearing of the piece or to play it for the publisher, he is invited to bring it in again. If he does so it is barely possible that some day he will bring in his manuscript at an opportunely dull time, and lo! the publisher will really allow him to play it over and receive judgment at once.

"This, of course, is the new author, for the old one who has written one or many successes has no such trouble. For him everything is published. He goes to dinner with the publisher, has the freedom of the office, can even get the average songs of his friends a hearing, and is generally smiled upon and attended to, as beseems and befits the great in every field.

"Granted, for the sake of forwardness, that the song is a good one and possesses that indefinable shade of sentiment in melody and words which make for popularity, and that it appeals to the very commercial judgment of the publisher, and that it is accepted. The next thing is to bind the author or authors by a contract, which reads that in consideration of, let us say, four per cent of the net price of every copy sold, he or they relinquish all claim to right, title, or interest, etc. The manuscript is then sent to a professional arranger of music, who looks it over and rearranges the accompaniment to what is, in his judgment, the best for general piano purposes, and the song is printed.

"Usually the first copies of the song printed are what are called 'professional copies,' for which the thinnest kind of newspaper is used. Probably five thousand of these are struck off, all intended for free distribution among the singing profession on the stage. The giving of professional copies and orchestra parts to all singers of some standing is considered a very effective method of pushing a new song before the public.

"If professional people, on hearing the song played for them in the publisher's parlors, think well of it, the publisher's hopes rise. It is then his policy to print possibly a thousand regular copies of the song, and these are sent out to 'the trade,' which is the mercantile term for all the small stores throughout the country which handle sheet music. A clever plan followed by some publishers is to enter into a contract with all the small dealers whereby the latter agree to take two copies of each of the publisher's new songs issued during the month, at, of course, a reduced rate. These copies being sold to the dealer at a cheaper rate than the older music, it is naturally to his advantage to sell them, since he makes a larger profit than on the copies of older songs regularly ordered. Thus the new song, being sent out at once under this contract, comes into the hands of singers and dealers throughout the country in very short order.

"If, after a few months' standing, the song shows signs of the public's interest in it, if dealers occasionally order a copy, singers occasionally mention it as 'going well' with their audiences, and the publisher likes the melody himself, he will endeavor to 'push it' by advertising it on the backs and the inside margins of all his good selling pieces. Furthermore, if some able singer announces that he is going to 'feature' the song in his tour, or if the sales of the song increase any after it has been well advertised

[199]

upon the good selling pieces, a large advertisement will be placed
in one of the papers which all the 'professional' singers are known
to take, in which the merits of the song are dilated upon and where
it is announced as a coming success. Where a publisher has a
reputation for good judgment and has already published a number
of successes, the professional singers throughout the country are
quite apt to take him at his word, or his advertisement, and write
in for professional copies of the song. These are sent gratuitously,
and the singers, finding it good, give it possibly an early trial
before their audience. If the latter show any appreciation of its
merits, it is very likely to be retained or 'kept on' throughout the
entire theatrical season by the keen vocalist.

"In New York the work of booming the song is followed with
the most careful attention, for it is well known among music publishers that if a song can be made popular around New York City
it is sure to be popular throughout the country. Consequently
canvassers are often sent about to the music halls where a song is
being sung for the week, to distribute little hand-bills upon which
the words are printed, to the end that the music-hall frequenters
may become familiar with it and the sooner hum and whistle it
on the streets. Boy singers are often hired to sit in the gallery and
take up the chorus with the singer, thus exciting attention. Friends
and hirelings are sent to applaud uproariously, and other small
tricks common to every trade are employed to foster any early
indication of public interest in the piece.

"While the above tactics are more or less familiar to those who
have essayed ballad-writing, very few know of the important part
played by the hand and street organ and by the phonograph in
familiarizing the masses with the merits of a song. Nearly all the

piano-organs so numerously dragged about the city are controlled
by an Italian padrone, who leases them to immigrant Greeks and
Italians at so much a day. This business is quite an extensive one,
involving as it does hundreds of organs and organ grinders, a
large repair shop, and a factory where the barrels, upon which
the melodies are indicated by steel pins, are prepared. The organs
are quite intricate affairs, and their manufacture and control require no little knowledge and business skill, albeit they are of
such humble pretensions.

"With the organ-master-general the up-to-date publisher is in
close communication, and between them the song is made a mutual
beneficiary arrangement."

Such were the simplicities of the song business in the lusty
infancy of Tin Pan Alley. . . . And the next year Theodore
Dreiser would write *Sister Càrrie* . . .

Song-Factory.

New York of the *fin de siècle*, then, found the new era of music-
publishing rapidly organizing into a well-defined pattern. "We
were dropping the hand-made," writes Mark Sullivan in *Our
Times,* and "taking up the machine-made." The observation applies perfectly to our popular music. The period in which Tin
Pan Alley starts the song racket is the hey-day of the safety bicycle, of the Gibson girl, of Ade's fables, of the dime novel—the
dime novel, which by now had become a nickel product, and which,
despite all the moral invective launched against its innocuous
pages, was as "pure" as the popular "ballads" of the day.

What was this pattern? It was, in essence, a song-factory. The multifarious duties of the publisher were being split up, by necessity, into a division of labor. There must be the songs to begin with. Under the new conditions it was becoming more and more imperative that there should be a steady supply. Less and less could the publisher sit around waiting for manuscripts to be brought in by the mails. Whenever he could, he grappled to himself by hoops of steel the composer and the lyrist whose work had found popular favor. Thus were born the staff writers who, to-day, are looked to for the staple products of their respective houses. The staff men of old also did yeomen service as pluggers and as instructors of the performers who were to make the songs popular all over the circuit. Out of this aspect of the business grew the "professional parlors" of the firm. The first "parlors," as we have seen, were the sidewalks of New York, the hotel-rooms of the actors (you paid their board-bill and they sang your song), the green-rooms of the theaters. With the growth of the industry, however, this peripatetic method was largely abandoned. The professional rooms of the leading publishers became the logical hangout for performers in search of new material. The order of things had been reversed; the mountains came to Mahomet.

As contact man between song and singer stood the plugger, earlier known as the boomer. He was—he still remains—a high-pressure salesman who sold not the song but the idea of the song —its value as a number on the program of the self-styled artist. At first he, too, pursued the performer like an evil spirit. Gradually, however, his function would become more subtle, if no less commercial and insistent. It would devolve upon him to bring his prey into the offices of his employer. There the performer would be handed over to the tender mercies of the inside staff, and

Mr. Plugger's good deed for the day was done. "Miss Beautiful Singer," his report of the night before might have run, "has promised to be here at 11:30 to-morrow morning to look over those new numbers I was telling her about last night." At eleven-thirty next morning the arrival of Miss Beautiful Singer was checked up; if she failed to appear, Mr. Plugger was sent out to get his woman, or bring back a good reason why she wasn't with him.

The Plugger is one of the darlings of Tin Pan Alley. He is a man of many aspects with the eyes of Argus and the arms of a Hindu image—a composite photograph of anybody and every-body who can help in establishing a song in the public favor. After a hit has been made, any fool can tell why. The Plugger is—he hopes—the man who can tell why *before* the hit is made, because it is his business to make it. He is the liaison-officer between Pub-lisher and Public. He is the publisher's lobbyist wherever music is played. He it is who, by all the arts of persuasion, intrigue, bribery, mayhem, malfeasance, cajolery, entreaty, threat, insinua-tion, persistence and whatever else he has, sees to it that his em-ployer's music shall be heard.

There is the plugger ordinary and the plugger extraordinary. The plugger ordinary is nothing more dignified than a musical fugleman, a drillmaster who, generally in the professional studios of his firm, puts the singers through their paces and shows them how the new song is to be sung. Now he is a singer, now a pianist. Scorn not the humble plugger, for in his modest quarters once labored a Max Dreyfus, a Jerome Kern, a George Gershwin, a Dick Rodgers, a Vincent Youmans. It is a valuable experience—this learning the business from the ground up.

[203]

Between the plugger ordinary and the plugger extraordinary was—in pre-radio days—the fleet of singers and accompanists who used to be dispatched nightly to music halls and cabarets, there to sing and play the new numbers into profitable popularity. (Ask any publisher whether popularity can ever be unprofitable; the red ink will make mute reply). They were supplied free. So were the vocalists of the movie houses, especially the smaller ones, in the days before the talkie. Once upon a time, before plugging became an art, vaudevillians used to pay for copies of the music they sang. Modern sales methods have done away with that. Vaudevillians of consequence, and many of no consequence whatsoever, get their music free. Not only this, but "big time" artists who push a favorite title of a publishing firm are often on the pay roll of the company for anything from five to fifty dollars per week, and more. Sometimes the job is done handsomely, with a flourish. For plugging a certain number, Al Jolson, who is fond of the turf, was presented with a race horse.

The plugger extraordinary is the grand contact-man of Racket Row. He takes out his song and he must land his prey. He can "make" a bad song—he has done it time and again—and without him the best of songs may remain unmade. He knows how sweet are the uses of publicity, and the size of the precious jewel that—like Shakespeare's ugly, venomous toad—it weareth in its head. The plugger is a man of business and a man of legend. He is an account-sheet and a poem. To-day, with the coming of the radio and its magic powers of annihilating Time and Space, the plugger has been bereft of much of his glory. He is like the horse confronted by the automobile—or the auto topped by the airplane. He was a giant in his time, and always we shall have him with us in one guise or another. His palmy days, however, are over. Already we see him through the colored mists of romance, the singing publicity sheet of Tin Pan Alley—the wandering advertiser of music wares, with a song in his heart and a "swindle-sheet" (*read* expense account) in his pocket.

The "bicycle built for two" gave way to the automobile; the Gibson girl, with that strange plasticity of fashions even in bodies, yielded to sisters no less beautiful in their ever-changing array; the dime novel achieved a resurrection in the first dawn of the motion pictures. With these the popular song kept undiminished pace; yet, essentially, its organization to-day is what it was when, as kids, we sang

> Spain, Spain, Spain!
> You ought to be ashame'
> Of blowing up
> Our battleship the Maine.

to the tune of "A Hot Time in the Old Town To-night."

Tin Pan Alley may change its sky—Fourteenth Street to Forty-Fifth—but not its soul.

J. Aldrich Libbey.

Plugging through prominent singers had reached a surprising degree of development as early as 1893. One of the first of these professional popularizers, whether in point of time or in power of vocal persuasion, was J. Aldrich Libbey, who frankly abandoned an artistic career for the greater profits of the Alley. In the days of the World's Fair and the national panic one singer of wide popularity was offered as much as $1000 from the first sales of a song, together with a half interest in the well-known firm that published it. Libbey, for booming "After the Ball," received a royalty on the sales of the song, as well as $500, within three months of the agreement.

At the height of his popularity it took—according to figures furnished by him in an interview—some $1300 to launch a song. Of this, $50 went for lithographing the singer's photograph on the title page; for publishing 10,000 copies, $250; for a year's advertising in a theatrical journal, $500; and for cash advanced to the singer who introduced the song, together with accrued royalties, another $500.

"Not more than one in two hundred published songs," said Libbey, "pay a large profit to the publisher. In other words, there are one hundred and ninety-nine songs out of every two hundred issued every year in America that do not any more than pay their cost of publication. Hence it will be seen that publishing popular songs is a veritable 200 to 1 shot."

There was a time, after the middle Nineties, when the publishers, in self-protection, banded together and agreed to give up the practice of buying singers to plug their wares. It was too good to last. Publishers began to make secret arrangements with headliners; the duplicity was discovered, and the lid blew off. Leo Feist, exploding one day to Harry Von Tilzer, vented his resentment in a classic phrase: "If it's spending money," he exclaimed, "I'll show them how to spend it. I'll give them the bellyache!" And he showed them, much to their gastric discomfort.

This spending continued until the formation, in 1916, of the Music Publishers Protective Association ostensibly put a stop to it. Vaudeville singers of good drawing power have received anything from five to a hundred dollars per week for carrying a song in their repertory over the Keith and Proctor, Pantages, Sullivan and Considine circuits. It is optimistic to believe that the practice has been eliminated.

The old "boomer" earned his money. Sometimes he almost endangered his skin, not to mention so inconsiderable a thing as his reputation. Here, from the early 1900's, is an anonymous confession:

"I'm a song promoter. I'm the man who makes the popular songs popular. I earn big money and I've grown into a necessity to the music publishing house that employs me.

"The company works one big town at a time. It sends on, by freight, a stack of the music of the song to be made popular. It is not put on sale until I give the word.

"I get to a town after the music has been placed in the hands of the leading music houses. I arrange with two or three theaters to aid me in introducing the song.

"Maybe I go to the swellest theater in town Monday night and sit in a lower box, in my evening clothes, like an ordinary patron. During the daytime I will have fixed the orchestra and had the music run over. Between the first and second act, perhaps, I stand up in my box and begin singing.

"The audience is startled. Ushers run through the aisles. A policeman comes in and walks toward the box. About the time the policeman is where he can be seen by all the audience I step out on to the stage in front of the curtain and begin the chorus, with the orchestra playing and the audience, that is now onto the game, clapping so hard it almost blisters its hands.

[207]

"I have, maybe, a good whistler in the gallery, whom I have taught during the day. He helps me when I begin teaching the gallery to whistle the chorus. He leads the gods and before I have done they and the whole house have caught the air.

"Please Go 'Way an' Let Me Sleep."

"I usually get the orchestra to play the chorus as the audience is going out. Everybody goes home humming or whistling it. But long before the home-going, probably, I have walked singing down the aisle of another theater between the second and third act, have been led out by an usher and have then come back and stood in front of the orchestra and taught that theater's audience to sing and whistle the song.

"The best thing I ever did to popularize a song was done right here in little old New York, in a roof garden theater. My wife knew a girl who was making a hit at the garden, so we had to go and see the girl in her act. I put the thing off for a night or two and planned a little surprise.

"I met the girl, who did a singing part, and fixed the thing up with her. The orchestra and the manager, an old friend of mine, readily fell into line. I was engaged in promoting popularity for 'Please Go 'Way an' Let Me Sleep,' about this time, and I saw a chance to do some noble work.

"My wife wanted to sit away up in front so her friend would see her, but I insisted on taking chairs in the rear of the garden, near the elevator landing. The crowd was large. The night was hot and the bill was good.

" 'I don't know what makes me so drowsy,' I said to my wife as

[208]

her friend came on. 'I guess they must have put knock-out drops in that last glass of lemonade.'

"I leaned back in my chair with one elbow on the table. As the girl sang I began to snore. I snored so loud that it disturbed those listening to the singing. They looked around in disgust. My wife gave me a kick under the table.

" 'Wake up, Charlie,' she said. 'You are attracting attention.' I snored harder than ever. A waiter came over and shook me by the arm. My wife became alarmed and stood up.

"Most of the folks in our part of the garden thought I was drunk. One man started toward the manager's office to complain, just as a policeman was brought my way by a second waiter.

"The entire audience turned our way. Some persons stood on chairs and others moved out into the aisles. Just as the policeman and the waiter raised me out of my chair I stretched and yawned like a man dead for slumber and began singing:

" 'Please go 'way an' let me sleep. Ah would rather sleep than eat.'

"Out of one corner of my eye I noticed a great light spread over my wife's face. I kept on singing as I was being carried and led to the elevator. I sang going down and I sang coming up.

"As the elevator reached the landing the girl on the stage struck into the chorus along with the orchestra, and the audience tumbled.

"I never saw an audience go so nearly crazy over anything in my life. Men laughed until the tears came and women became hysterical. My wife was the happiest woman in all the town. She admitted for the first time that I was a sure enough actor, which I had made up my mind she should do if I had to scare her half to death to bring about the conviction."

The plugger's not to reason why; his is but to sing and sigh. He megaphones his songs from airplanes; he climbs up into organ lofts and croons them from the upper mysteries; he organizes quartets for picnics; he haunts the honkey-tonks; he invades clubs; he fills palatial movie vestibules with melody, the while herded customers stand in their pens awaiting from liveried minions the signal to enter the main auditorium; he revels in radio studios. Wherever there are ears to listen, he has a song to sing, O.

The old plugger did not die; he advanced into a new avatar. Plugging methods have simply followed the transformation of the mechanical agencies for publicity. Once upon a time it was Libbey's face—and figure—that shone from the sheets on the piano racks. Now it is Rudy Vallée's. Nor is it an accident that Libbey was a singer, while Vallée is a band-leader. We have become band-minded. The big names of a later age are no longer May Irwin, Lizzie B. Raymond, Lottie Collins, Sophie Tucker, Belle Baker—purely singers all. They are Paul Whiteman, Ted Lewis, Ben Bernie, Vincent Lopez, Paul Ash. For plugging certain numbers these leaders collect—"cut in"—on payments and royalties, even as did the Libbeys of 1893. There is little philanthropy in Tin Pan Alley. If you scratch my back, I must scratch yours— or your palm.

About this arrangement there is nothing unethical. When a fellow like Vallée, through the power of his vast popularity—a phenomenon that I cannot pretend to understand—can resurrect a "Stein Song" and shoot it up within a short time to a sales figure of 350,000, he deserves a generous portion of the earnings. . . . There is here, incidentally, an oblique comment upon the supposed danger of radio to popular music. The "Stein Song" was written originally in 1901 by E. A. Fenstad, a bandmaster of the United States Army, as a march. In 1910 a student at the University of Maine, A. W. Sprague, rewrote the tune and had his room-mate, Lincoln Colcord, add a set of "lyrics." So few copies were sold during the next twenty years that the University, when the song was offered to it, refused to purchase the rights. The National Broadcasting Company, desiring to test the radio as a song plugger, bought the piece—and the rest is history.

If Eddie Cantor—as report had it—received $7,000 for a single evening on the radio, during which, prior to the release of the talkie *Whoopee* he whooped it up for the picture by broadcasting songs from that revue, it was because he was worth that much in advertising to the sponsors of the picture and the program.

What you sing and whistle, then, is hardly an accident. It is the result of a huge plot—involving thousands of dollars and thousands of organized agents—to make you hear, remember and purchase. The efforts of organized pluggery (I present that word to Webster) assail our ears wherever we go, because it is the business of this gentry to fill the air with music.

In the end, perhaps, he will plug himself out of a job. In one professional parlor, recently, I saw a singer being drilled in the technique of a song by means of a phonograph record. The machine age has invaded the territory of the plugger, too.

Song Types.

It is said that the furniture industry of the country is operated upon the technique of forcing changes in style at least once in six years. The tendency in the other trades has been in the same direction. Once upon a time fashions used to evolve; now, in everything from handbags to songs, they are created and, when they have run their profitable course, they are destroyed that other fashions—and profits—may arise. There have been natural cycles in the sheet-music trade—the waltz-vogue, ragtime, jazz; for the greater part, however, the song-types that are recognized by the Alley are so many commercial labels.

The precedence of the love song is so obvious as to require little comment. Most song is but an oft-renewed technique of saying, "I Love You." "Button up your overcoat, you belong to me" . . . "Don't be like that" . . . "You're the cream in my coffee" . . . The phrasing is all the more effective for its indirection, and he who sings it most cleverly wins the reward of all who speak for the speechless.

In the broader category there are The Ballads, Novelties, Rags and Blues, and the Production Numbers. The last named, to the hard-boiled Tin Panner, are the least interesting. They are, in a double sense, show-pieces. They are intended for stage production, and while they may win great applause they do not attract purchasers in vast multitudes. Generally they are, as music, of a higher standard than the typical Broadway tune. Formerly, a sale of 200,000 copies was considered large; now, a stage number is regarded as a hit if it reaches 75,000. There are lyrists and composers who fight shy of musical comedy work because it demands more conscientious application than the regular product and brings lower practical returns. The critics praise your work, but the buyer keeps away.

Production numbers themselves are divided into types. The "ice-breaker" is the first number after the opening chorus; it starts things going. Not every song in a big show is meant to be a hit. The hit—in so far as such things can be foreordained—is deliberately planted. It must not occur too soon, else it does not achieve its maximum effect. If it occurs too late, it falls upon an audience too weary, psychologically, to give it fresh attention. The comic song sacrifices music to audibility and effect of lines.

Fifteen years ago Billy Jerome—author of that classic, "Mr. Dooley," and of "Rip Van Winkle Was a Lucky Man," "I'm Tired," "Bedelia" and a host of other well-remembered ditties— was considered among the chief writers of stage songs. He had been going strong since the early Nineties, into which he had been graduated from the minstrel stage. With his natural feeling for a visible audience he wrote easily for the "boards." He still preserves the congenial temperament that made him a favorite forty years ago; at sixty-five he is one of the most beloved characters in the profession.

Ballads, as a rubric, cover on Broadway a multitude of sins. Originally they told a long winded story, with several different choruses. Though the tempo of a ballad may vary from a slow waltz to a vigorous march, the type now favors a more leisurely pace; the words, rather than the music, determine the classification. Ballads center about the home (mother, dad, children) cabins, shacks, cottages for two . . . and later, more. They may be racial (especially Irish); they may be rustic. Von Tilzer and Sterling began it with "My Old New Hampshire Home"; Braisted and Carter ran a close second with "The Girl I Loved in Sunny Tennessee" and "She Was Bred in Old Kentucky." Many of the State songs—"On the Banks of the Wabash," for early example,

[213]

and "My Old Kentucky Home" for an earlier—partake of this bucolic nature. The modern popular song is a Northern city product; hence its wail for green pastures and Southern languors. The ballad of the Ernest Ball type that was so popular some twenty years ago is the eternal love call in one of its thousand incarnations: "Love Me and the World Is Mine," "Last Night Was the End of the World," Frederick V. Bowers's "Because" and "Always." (Singleword titles were used long before Dodge Brothers spread them across twenty feet of signboard.) Anything that is not obviously fast and gay becomes, in Tin Pan Alley, a "semi-classic." It is usually printed between sober covers, as befits a labor of such dignity; hence its designation as a "black and white."

The Rags and Blues—the former are but historical forerunners of the jazz technique—run, as we have seen, through a riot of titles. Their form, however, is more limited than that of the ballads. There is no reason why many "blues" should not be "ballads," too. They are more easily grouped by their mood of melancholy. (Melancholy: Greek for *black* mood or humor. How these blacks became blues is a problem for some psychologist of color associations).

Novelty songs range as far afield as do the ballads. They lend themselves to action, to mimicry, to histrionic effect. They are, unlike the ballads, songs that we listen to rather than sing ourselves, and usually the emphasis is comic.

Under these various rubrics the variety of trade songs is almost infinite. Indeed, the music business plays an endless series of variations upon a surprisingly limited number of themes. And its constant prayer is for a "natural" in any category—a song that is such sure-fire stuff that it sings—and sells—itself, without benefit of plugger. .

Songs built around the name of a girl . . . "Elsie from Chelsea," "Henrietta," "Isabella"—you may name your own favorite. Songs dedicated to the seasons, with love always in season . . . Songs to current games . . . Recall the baseball and football tunes of yesteryear; I find one publisher, in 1901, complaining that "within the last six weeks I have rejected almost three ping-pong songs a day, and still they come." . . . With the revival of ping-pong, we may yet hear these resurrected manuscripts! . . . News songs . . . On the blowing up of the Maine; on the deaths of Caruso and Valentino; on the birth of Baby Lindy; on the Iroquois Theatre conflagration; on railroad wrecks; on the Arabian-Jewish clash at the Wailing Wall in Jerusalem— on anything that may bring curious purchasers to the counters . . . "Torch" songs—a graphic, and a Graphic?—designation for lovers burning up with the expression of unrequited passions. Or freezing? . . . Geographical songs, glorifying states and rivers . . . Exotic songs, of Indians, Hawaiians, South Sea Islanders, Mexicans, Alaskans, Japanese Sandmen, Queens of Never-never Lands . . . Motto Songs, embodying more advice than Polonius ever gave to Hamlet . . . Smile Songs . . .

We are especially rich in smile songs perhaps because we are especially poor in happiness. Tin Pan Alley acknowledges allegiance to Pollyanna. It smiles until it hurts; at least, until it pays, however much it may hurt the sensitive listener. The popular singer, especially the vaudeville "artist," has a Pagliacci complex. What though his heart be breaking, he must keep you in good humor and, for the nonce, chase your troubles away. He has you, coming and going. If he makes you smile, he has lightened your burden. If he has made you cry, he has eased your soul.

The significance of the song-type to the Alley lies in its commercial productiveness. These word-and-tune boys course with the hares and run with the hounds. Is war declared? Then overnight, as Rosenfeld did for Metz, they can transform "When the Roses Are in Bloom" into a martial call. For pacifist sentiment they pen "I Didn't Raise My Boy to Be a Soldier" and when popular opinion is shunted in the opposite direction they blast an "Over There." Tin Pan Alley is in the thickest of the fray, to the last drop of printer's ink. It has the soul—and the callousness—of a professional propagandist.

The publisher always keeps a number of each type on hand in his safe. He must not be caught napping. He must be ready, at the slightest shift in popular taste, to flood the market with a song of the new model. A sudden hit from another publisher's office means orders to the staff writers to follow it up and, if possible, to better it. As in the garment industry, so in the music business, styles are imitated over night. Day after next may be too late. "Valencia" reintroduced the 6-8 tempo and an extra allotment of measures. At once "Constantinople" was heard, clicking to the same time signature. This, by half, is the history of song "cycles" (*read* "trade imitations"). A hit is not an esthetic triumph; it is something that sells. The theater exists for box-office appeal. Tin Pan Alley hears its answers rung up on the cash register.

The songs that have made history in the Alley are the songs that have "clicked" over the counters. As often as not, they have deserved their success.

Prices of sheet music have fluctuated during the past forty

years. In the first days of Tin Pan Alley songs were still being sold at forty cents per copy, retail. In the early years of the new century the price had come down to twenty-five cents. The jobbers were charged about fifty percent of the retail figure; the publishers, moreover, paid out a royalty of five cents per song. (The royalty is split between author and composer; in case several hands have worked upon the piece, the division is on a pro-rata basis.) In 1916 sheet music was selling as low as ten cents per copy, with royalty reduced to a cent. Since then the price has tended to rise, until now we are paying on an average of thirty cents. There are those, however, who believe that the increase from ten cents was a commercial error, and that high prices, rather than the movie, the phonograph and the radio—which undoubtedly played their part—have damaged the sheet-music market. Indeed, a movement is already under way to restore the ten-cent price. Meantime, too, records have dropped to a new low of fifteen cents; the experiment is not yet wholly a commercial success, but it is being watched anxiously by the music trades.

Perhaps the days of vast sales are over. Music in the home, made by the family, rather than listened to, seems for the nonce to have been ousted by mechanical devices. We do not need the printed page. This state of affairs does not represent a total loss. The income of publisher and writer is added to by percentages from the sales of what the trade knows as "mechanicals"—royalties from phonograph records, piano rolls, and other types of reproduction. Radio now pays tribute to Tin Pan Alley. The showhouses, too, whose orchestras make generous use of popular tunes, are taxed for this privilege, on the basis of their seating capacity . . . something like ten cents per seat per year.

TIN PAN ALLEY

The spectacular sales get into the papers; the humble statistics die in the dark. "Till We Meet Again," by Richard Whiting (his "Japanese Sandman" has one of the best choruses that ever rose from the Alley) hit the 3,500,000 mark. ("The Rosary" by Nevin, has done little better in its thirty-two years of existence). Brockman's "I'm Forever Blowing Bubbles" sold 2,600,000. Al Bryan's "Joan of Arc" crossed well beyond 2,000,000. And to prove that they can follow the public taste, they repeat, respectively, with "Louise," "I Faw Down and Go Boom" and "Song of the Nile" . . . "Swanee," the song that made Gershwin famous, sold, in phonographic form alone, over 2,250,000 . . . Mr. Woolcott, in his urbane *Story of Irving Berlin*, gives, as samples of sales the following figures from the Berlin catalogue:

Title	Duration of Sale	Sheet Music	Piano Rolls	Phonograph Records
"You'd Be Surprised"	50 weeks	783,982	145,505	888,790
"Say It with Music"	75 "	374,408	102,127	1,239,050
"Nobody Knows"	70 "	1,143,690	62,204	843,062
"All By Myself"	75 "	1,053,493	161,650	1,225,083

Let me select, almost at random, a few additional data:

"Am I Blue?," 500,000 . . . "Dinah," 1,000,000 . . . "Baby Face," 800,000. (All by Harry Akst) . . . "Was It a Dream?," "Bebe," "Grieving for You"—each close to 1,000,000. (All by Sam Coslow) . . . "Sonny Boy" (De Sylva, Brown and Henderson), 1,250,000 . . . "Among My Souvenirs" (Leslie and Nichols) the same . . . "Me and My Shadow," 1,000,000; "I've Got a Rainbow Round My Shoulder," 900,000 (Dreyer). "Pagan Love Song," 1,000,000; "The Wedding of the Painted Doll," 1,000,000. (By Freed and Brown) . . . "Ramona," in

[218]

IRVING BERLIN

The Last of the Troubadours

sheet music and records, went to 2,000,000 . . . "Smiles,"
1,500,000 . . . "Over There," 2,000,000 . . . "Carolina
Moon," 1,000,000. "My Blue Heaven," ditto . . .

Twenty years ago the total sales of popular songs, in sheet form,
reached to more than 2,000,000,000 for a single year. In 1907,
it was computed by one statistician that, during the period from
1902 to 1907, about one hundred songs had reached a sale of
100,000 each; 50 had gone beyond 200,000; 30 had reached
250,000. Four had been "knockouts," with Harry H. Williams'
and Egbert Van Alstyne's "In the Shade of the Old Apple Tree"
topping the list at 700,000. This, in its day, was regarded as the
world's record.

The figures, to the layman, mean little except big business.
With all the massed effort put behind the sale of a song, there is
an element of accident that helps to determine the rise and fall
of the sales. Publishers may, as individuals, have their favorite
pieces. As business men, they push a good seller for all it is worth,
though personally they may dislike it; and no matter how highly
they may value the sluggish seller, they drop it unceremoniously
the moment it fails to "click."

Plagiarism.

There is a popular notion that stolen tunes are sweetest. If it
sounds good, it must have been lifted from the classics. Frank
Tinney once had an act in which, by dissecting "Narcissus" and
sewing up the gaps he managed to confect a popular song out of
the seams. Bud De Sylva, one of the cleverest fellows in the business, demonstrated some five years ago, in the columns of *Vanity*

Fair, how a song might be assembled from snatches of this, that and the other, not excluding Dvořák's "Humoresque." That stalking-horse of the amateur fiddler, indeed, is always ghosting through the bars of popular melody; the estate of the Bohemian composer should be collecting part-royalties on more than one hit of recent manufacture. Nor do I refer to such devices as direct quotation, to which Tin Pan Alley does not hesitate to stoop if there are no copyright involvements.

In this notion the populace is encouraged by the Alley itself. "We depend largely on tricks, we writers of songs," wrote Irving Berlin some fourteen years ago, in *The Green Book Magazine.* "There's no such thing as a new melody. There has been a standing offer in Vienna, holding a large prize, to anyone who can write eight bars of original music. The offer has been up for more than twenty-five years. Thousands of compositions have been submitted, but all of them have been traced back to some other melody.

"Our work is to connect the old phrases in a new way, so that they will sound like a new tune. Did you know that the public, when it hears a new song, anticipates the next passage? Well, the writers who do *not* give them *something they are expecting* are those who are successful." [1] And more to the same purpose.

Paul Whiteman, too, in his book, *Jazz,* is equally misleading. "For the truth is that, when you are listening to your favorite jazz tune, you are most likely absorbing strains that are most classic of all the classics. Do you not know that more than half the modern art of composing a popular song comes in knowing what to steal

[1] April, 1916. "Love Interest as a Commodity," in collaboration with Justus Dickinson, p. 695.

and how to adapt it—also, that at least nine-tenths of modern jazz music turned out by Tin Pan Alley is frankly stolen from the masters?"

No, I do not know. And nine-tenths is even for the Alley, a libelous figure. Why smugly overstate the case? Originality, especially in the lower or higher reaches of tonal art, lies not in one's raw material but in the personal treatment to which it is subjected. Most jazz "adaptation," as we shall see shortly, is really denaturization—the application, to noble material, of a sterilizing formula. I am not defending the frank purloiners of Tin Pan Alley. "Marcheta" *is* from Nicolai's Overture to *The Merry Wives of Windsor*: the "Russian Lullaby" *has* helped itself to a waltz by Joyce; "Avalon" *was* stolen from *La Tosca* and Ricordi settled out of court; "Yes, We Have No Bananas"—an abominable song—*was* a stew of Handel's "Hallelujah Chorus," Balfe's "I Dreamt That I Dwelt in Marble Halls," "An Old Fashioned Garden," and "I Was Seeing Nellie Home"; Beethoven's "Minuet in G" was lifted bodily for a most wretched sob-song, "If You See That Girl of Mine, Send Her Home"; "Horses!" *does* come from Tschaikovsky's "Troika," and the same composer has done valiant service for the panny pilferers, even to an instrumental effect from his "Overture, 1812" that has been widely imitated by bands and vocal harmonizers . . . But why go on? In fact, why have started? The process is patent, undeniable and undenied.

On the other hand, it is easy to suggest the appearance of "lifting" where, in truth, it does not exist. Remember that—as Sullivan answered when he was accused of having stolen "Love's Own Sweet Song" for his "When a Merry Maiden Marries" (in

The Gondoliers)—composers have only twelve notes between them. A chance similarity of melodic line is, musically, insignificant; it is also a commonplace among the classics themselves. It is hardly fair to accuse Theodore Morse—as has been done—of encroaching upon "Nearer, My God, to Thee" just because the chorus of his "Good-bye, My Bluebell" begins, as does the hymn, with a descent of three notes.

The vocabulary of music being the limited dictionary that it is, the wonder is that there are not more resemblances, fortuitous and intentional. The true composer is known by what he does to his material as well as by what he invents.

The legal proof of tune-stealing is not so easy as the reader would gather from the loose statements by Messrs. Berlin and Whiteman. Rather than repeat the commonplaces of Tin Pan Alley talk, let me recall to you a long-forgotten attack upon the integrity of Victor Herbert. It is good to record, even now, that the *Musical Courier* of thirty years ago was compelled to disgorge $15,000 for having so crudely impugned the man's musical ethics.

"Everything written by Herbert is copied," announced that organ, editorially, on July 17, 1901, after gloating over the failure of *The Fortune Teller* at the Shaftesbury Theatre in London, and using the cablegram as a peg upon which to hang its denunciation of Herbert as conductor of the Pittsburgh Symphony Orchestra. "There is not one original strain in anything he has done, and all his copies are from sources that are comic or seriocomic. He became popular suddenly by attaining command of a brass band and joining a rollicking club of actors and Bohemians known as the Lambs, who, removed entirely from any musical comprehension, accepted the good-natured band leader as their musical dictator, and, American-fashion, immediately paralleled him with serious-minded composers. It was never a serious matter in itself."

There was more of this twaddle. The editorial writer, priding himself on his prescience, reminded his readers that the *Musical Courier* had long ago put *The Fortune Teller* in its place, which was exactly nowhere. That operetta "had no merit whatever." Not this alone, but "all of Victor Herbert's written-to-order comic operas are pure and simple plagiarisms. There is not one single aria, waltz movement, polka, gallop or march in those operas that has touched the public ear"—shades (and wave-lengths!) of Marconi, Hertz, de Forest and Pupin!—"and the street pianos and organs have ignored them . . . The whole Sousa repertory is alive and pulsating; the whole Herbert repertory is stone dead . . ."

This, of course, was animus, not criticism, as the trial was to bring out. Herbert, by no means as dead as his repertory was supposed to be, retaliated with a suit. The record of the trial reads to-day almost like a libretto that he overlooked. On his side appeared Walter Damrosch, Henry K. Hadley, Julian Edwardes and Herman Perlet; for the *Courier*, Platon Brounoff, a Signor Viennesi, a Signor Buzzi-Peccia, W. C. Carl and W. J. Goodrich. Herbert's plagiarisms were alleged to have reached even into Beethoven's "Ninth Symphony," but Mr. Goodrich was hard put to it to substantiate the allegation.

Fortunately for Jim Huneker—and for the defendant—he had left the employ of the *Courier* shortly before. Huneker had a fine appreciation of Herbert's qualities and had written of them with his characteristic gusto. He would have been a prickly thorn in the side of his erstwhile employers. Their lawyer, Mr. Howes, in a lame attempt to save his clients, pretended to believe that there was no intent in the article to accuse Herbert of actually stealing music from other writers. "We have the kindest and best feelings toward Mr. Herbert personally. We would like him for a friend. But we detest his music and say that it is rot. And we earnestly say that the Pittsburgh Art Society disgraced itself when it took him as its musical director." A very winning offer of friendship, no doubt, but there is no record of Howes and Herbert embracing after the trial. It lasted, by the way, four and a half days; and the jury brought in its verdict after deliberating an hour and forty minutes.

Now, Herbert was frequently reminiscent; this his accusers could easily have shown. If such reminiscences constituted thefts, the jails would not be large enough to house the criminals, and the judges would sit on the cots of the condemned. Sometimes—more often than the listener may believe—the reminiscence is unconscious. Harris once composed a song that came bodily from *Pinafore,* and was as amazed as he was convinced when the truth was called to his attention. Fortunately the piece had not yet been printed. The Tin Pan Alleyite, in his cheaper moments, recognizes the value of a familiar line in impressing the song upon the hearer's memory, and often resorts to this lesser dishonesty of deliberate veiled borrowing. Yet the trade does not depend—as one would infer from our gifted melodist and our most original band-leader—upon "steals." They are an incident, not an essential. Let us not gild the lily; let us not, on the other hand, blacken the chimney-flue. We could dismiss the element of "lifting," "adapting" and "quotation" and still have left a considerable body of song, at once honest and viable.

This is especially true of our newer word-and-song men—and women—who have begun to feel in their work a pride that extends to its creative and technical aspects alike.

How It's Done.

Even Tin Pan Alley has its Aristotles. Since the earliest days there have appeared alluring pamphlets, and at least one full-sized book, on the Ars Poetica and the Ars Musica of Racket Row.[2] These have been invariably an attempt to codify the needs and the practices of the popular music business. Most of them, however, have consisted of stale platitudes. If they have ever had a large circulation it must have been, to speak without burrs upon one's tongue, among gullible hopefuls and ignoramuses. It gets into the newspapers that a chauffeur has written a tune which has made thousands of dollars; or that a widowed mother, turning to ballad writing as a last resort, composes a song that all the orthodox houses reject and that she is compelled to publish herself, founding a wealthy firm upon the proceeds; or that Charles K. Harris can't distinguish a note of music from a cuckoo's egg; or that Irving Berlin requires the services of a musical stenographer in order to get his inspirations down upon paper; or that George

[2] Here is a fairly complete list: *How to Write a Popular Song*, by Chas. K. Harris, 1906; *How to Write a Popular Song*, by F. B. Haviland, 1910; *Writing the Popular Song*, by E. M. Wickes, 1916; *How to Write and Make a Success Publishing Music*, by Harry J. Lincoln, 1919; *How to Publish Your Own Music Successfully*, by Jack Gordon, 1925, revised edition, 1930; *Inside Stuff on How to Write Popular Songs*, by Abel Green, 1927; *Hints on Popular Song Writing*, Anonymous, 1928. Of these, the best are the manuals of Wickes, Green and the anonymous pamphlet. Wickes and Green are full of sound trade information and practical advice.

M. Cohan jots down the words of "Over There" in an odd moment between business appointments, steals an army bugle call for the music and collects for the rights of publication $25,000 from Leo Feist.

These stories may all be true. It is upon such sensational material that the various fake publishers in the business thrive. The shark is not limited to the field of music publishing. He exists among the book firms; not only this, but many book firms of high reputation indulge in shark practices which they are loud to condemn in the case of publishers who make a regular trade of it. The musical shark operates more successfully because he deals in a product that requires only a small outlay. He advertises for words and music; his return letters invariably encourage the worst of material, as they may specify who have sent him specially concocted stuff as test cases. He has stock covers, stock music, stock advertising, all prepared to carry out in the letter, if not in the spirit, the glamorous promises that his "literature" holds out.

There have been, in the music business as in the book business, numerous cases in which the author who pays for the printing and the marketing of his own composition made a lucky strike. This was true especially in the earlier stages of the racket. As the publishing of popular music became more intricately organized the chances for such happy exceptions naturally grew fewer. Today, even when one has in hand a "natural," one requires a vast organization to put it over. Good material is probably ten times as plentiful as it was fifteen years ago—and it was fifteen times as plentiful then as it was at the turn of the century.

The writing of popular songs moreover has become something of a closed corporation. Publishers will tell you—and they mean it—that they are constantly on the lookout for fresh material. They will tell you—and it is perfectly true—that profound musical knowledge or a versatile acquaintance with English prosody are not essential to the making of a hit. Even a casual study of the average hit bears them out only too well. Harmonically the popular song has made vast strides. Although the words have improved, they remain, for the greater part, as restricted in range as the vocabulary (said to be a few hundred words) of the Italian opera libretto.

The making of a hit, in so far as hits may be predicted, has been pretty well standardized. The hit has interchangeable parts. The Alley Aristotles will tell you, for example, how many measures long the verse shall be, and how many measures the chorus. Verse in Alley parlance means the stanzas; chorus applies only to the refrain. The words of a song as a whole are dignified by the term "lyric"; this, of course, is a standing joke and somebody with a sense of humor should find another word. Meantime, every once in a while, somebody with an overgrown sense of dignity revives the debate whether word writers should be called lyrists or lyricists. The melody men have thus far been content to be called composers. For the average specimens, word-smiths and tune-smiths would do best of all.

D. M. Winkler, high in the councils of De Sylva, Brown & Henderson, has said that 80 percent of our really popular hits have been written by a group of writers that do not total over fifteen. This is not an accident of inspiration. Hits are no longer merely written; they are made by a vast system of exploitation.

Let us, then, at the beginning dismiss the amateur and the outsider. If he wishes to bite at the bait held out by the sharks his blood is on his own head and his money is out of his own pocket.

Long experience has developed an almost unchangeable method of procedure among the experienced versifiers and melody makers. They do not begin at the beginning; rather, they begin at the end. More likely than not the word man has thought of a catchy phrase or even of a title. The title, in fact, is for many non-artistic reasons of supreme importance. It is the name by which people will remember the song and ask for it at the counter. It is the name by which the baby will be known. It serves at once to classify the song, to denote its character. It piques curiosity. As one commentator has put it, the song is an expan-sion of the title. There are men in the Alley who have picked up a comfortable living on furnishing titles alone.

The vital spot of the chorus is in the final lines; this holds true likewise of the verse. In the good old Nineties a song might have seven or eight verses; time is too precious to-day, and there are many in the business who grudge even the extra minute or two that is given to a second verse. Second verses are not considered of great importance. There have been tentative efforts to abolish them; their main function is to lead back to a repetition of the chorus. Charles K. Harris, in one of his newest songs, "Dancing in a Dream," uses a verse only four measures long, to a refrain of the traditional sixteen. The chorus is the thing. Freed and Brown's "Singing in the Rain" frankly adopts, for its vocal version, the band practice of *beginning* with the chorus. Then follow the verse —there is only one—and a second chorus. All that is needed now is a song that is all chorus. The words of a song, then, point in the

[228]

direction of the punch at the end of the verse and the harder punch at the end of the chorus.

Contrary to the general belief it is the music that is written first. For the music, except in topical or comic songs, is of primary importance. It is the music that we hum, long after we have forgotten the words. If we know the tune of the "Star Spangled Banner" and "America," while we are embarrassed when we need to recollect the words, it is simply because music is by nature the more easily remembered.

Many, for some reason, see in this priority of music but added evidence of the commercialism that taints Tin Pan Alley. The orthodox procedure is for a composer to set words to music, not for a poet to set music to words. Yet there is no valid esthetic objection to the reversal of the usual practice. The Alley composer, once he has thought up a striking tune, writes it down or dictates it, and then prepares a special sheet, known as a "lead sheet," upon which only the melody appears. This is for the word man, who usually knows enough about notation to make out the general rhythm and the important accents. The sheet serves as his lead or guide; hence the name.

I should not be surprised if it is this practice that has helped lead to the much greater plasticity of our contemporary lyrics. A glance at the old type of verse that used to be written for musical setting—and here I do not refer to Tin Pan Alley alone—was usually sufficient to suggest the nature of the music. The lines were regular, even stereotyped, and unless the genius of a Sullivan were brought to bear upon them, they would receive a stereotyped setting. In this connection it is interesting to recall that Gilbert himself—the patron saint of the modern Alley lyrists—received his training by providing words to preëxistent operatic melodies, and that before he made opera out of burlesque he was making burlesque out of opera. Once, when Sullivan was asked which came first, the words or the music, he replied, "Don't be a ——— fool; the words, of course." It was not always so; and those who are curious about such matters may discover in the pre-Sullivanian lyrics of Gilbert that he was already an accomplished metrician.

Ask Rodgers & Hart about the music and words and they will tell you that in their case it's a fifty-fifty affair as to which precedes which. In the case of the Gershwin brothers the music is written first in some nine-tenths of the cases. With De Sylva, Brown & Henderson the matter is more complicated. Henderson, whose real name is Brost, is the composer of the trio; but these three phenomenal non-flop Alleyites always stand ready to pinch-hit for one another. There are rumors, for example, that the melody of "Sonny Boy" is not Henderson's, but Brown's. Each on occasion tries his skill at writing words. They seem bound, however, by a solemn oath to divulge nothing. In the case of Kay Swift and Paul James (they are, in private life, Mrs. and Mr. Paul Warburg, related to the well-known banker family) the association of words and music takes on the nature of the marriage of true minds.

In general, however, it is safe to assume that in Tin Pan Alley music comes first in the order of writing as in the order of importance. F. P. A., recollecting his association with O. Henry as the lyrist of their musical comedy, *Lo!* wrote that "most of our songs were constructed to fit tunes the composer had already written. I am not saying that this method is absolutely wrong, but it is infinitely harder for the lyrist." Infinitely harder, and, as I have said, productive of a new variety in our popular lyrics.

The contemporary tune, in the hands of a gifted musician— and one may be a gifted musician without a conservatory education—is often an ingenious production. I should say that the general improvement in the words of popular songs began with the introduction of ragtime and the coon song. The words became more alive; slang, with its revivifying influence, entered and lyrists wrote as they spoke. The verses of the Harris-Dresser era were stilted, in degenerate English, and as far from the true vernacular as they could be without relapsing into the thee-and-thou-ism that they replaced. The "coon" song was written in "American."

With the new rhythms of the jazz age came an increased complexity of melodic rhythm, and this complexity the lyric writer was forced to match with a corresponding ingenuity of phrase. Naturally, the verses were thus betrayed into an allegiance to rhyme at the cost of reason. To-day, with our undiscriminating cult of sophistication we have reached a stage where the lyrics are sometimes distressingly self-conscious. One rhyme grins or smirks as it looks obviously to the other. This has both its good and its bad effects. Bad, because the words stick out of the music like ill-fitted limbs. Good, because in our musical comedy, especially, they have restored the words to something like the importance that they had in the flourishing period of our higher class musical show. This self-conscious syllabification, indeed, is practically limited to our reviews and musical comedy. They may yet help to improve dialogue, and so lead to plot and to a more organic conception of what we loosely call comic opera.

The best verse writers of the old era were fellows like Andrew

TIN PAN ALLEY

B. Sterling, Vincent Bryan, Billy Jerome, George M. Cohan, Edgar Smith. Cleverness in verse is by no means anything new. Cohan had it in a crude way; the various Smiths had it in more consciously Gilbertian fashion. Our modernists—Cole Porter, Howard Dietz, Lorenz Hart, Ira Gershwin, Paul James, Dorothy Fields —have not created anything new; they have tried to recapture something old. So doing, they endanger their popularity, as truly good words always endanger a song in Tin Pan Alley. They make, as truly good music makes, for smaller and better audiences. This' may be art, after a fashion, but as business it is no fashion at all. Wherever we find a pronounced quality in words or music we may be sure that we have begun the ascent from Tin Pan Alley.

In between the old and the new stands, whether as lyrist or composer, Irving Berlin. His words, however clever, yet maintain contact with *hoi polloi*. His music, however much disguised by the skill of his arrangers, retains a healthy vulgarism. Years ago, he expressed the intention of writing some day an opera in syncopation. That he refrained from doing so may be an excellent example of self-criticism. Tin Pan Alley is not interested in high flights, nor could Berlin remain for long on the wing.

What is it that makes a hit? It is relatively simple to explain a hit after it has been made. For the man who can unerringly pick one before the fact a desk stands ready in every publisher's office, with a salary double that of the national president. Is it the words? Is it the tune? Is it the mood? Does the public prefer sad sentiment to happy? Theories have been advanced by every important figure in the business, but the answer remains as much in doubt as ever. Popular taste is at the mercy of whim. Songs that

[232]

sold into the millions years ago would be rejected by every contemporary firm. A song must happen at the right time. We smile at the songs as well as the styles of yesterday, yet in their own day they had the beauty of the vogue. Skillful song writing, likewise song publishing, is a matter of adjustment to the times.

> Born just to live for a short space of time,
> Often without any reason or rhyme,
> Hated by highbrows who call it a crime;
>   Loved by the masses who buy it;
> Made by the fellows who stay up at night,
> Sweating and fretting while getting it right—
> Publisher pleading with all of his might
>   With some performer to try it;
> Heard by the critic without any heart—
> One of those fellows who pick it apart,
> Cares for the finish, but don't like the start—
>   Makes many worthless suggestions;
> Sold to the public—that is, if they buy—
> Sometimes they do, and the royalty's high—
> Most times the statement brings tears to your eye—
>   Take it without any questions:
> Popular song, you will never be missed,
> Once your composer has ceased to exist,
> While Chopin and Verdi, Beethoven and Liszt
>   Live on with each generation.
> Still, though you die after having your sway,
> To be forgotten the very next day,
> A rose lives and dies in the very same way—
>   Let that be your consolation.

So sang Irving Berlin to the popular song in 1916. It was as true in the Nineties as it is in the Nineteen-thirties.

9. Transition

BETWEEN the wars that made Cuba safe from Spain and the world safe—in a manner of speaking—for democracy, ragtime developed so insidiously into jazz that the change was not noticed until long after it had taken place. Jazz had come in, definitely, before the Great War; our leading musicians and critics were still speaking of ragtime as late as 1917. There was a period of some five years when the two terms were, for all practical purposes, interchangeable.

The campaign against the intruder from the South had never truly abated. Early in the new century it had been pronounced a menace. In June of 1901 the American Federation of Musicians at its annual convention in Denver passed a resolution condemning ragtime and recommending that its members cease from playing it. (The ghost of King Canute must have smiled at such an invitation to commercial suicide.) The Dancing Teachers' Association of America and the National Music Teachers' Association joined the crusade. The Chicago Federation of Musicians was threatened with internecine warfare, and was dividing into opposing camps. Thomas Preston Brooke, leader of the Chicago Marine Band, rushed to the defense with a statement that, however exaggerated, looked in the right direction. Notice how easily one might substitute, for the word "ragtime," the word "jazz," even to the dubious allegation about the incomparable Richard:

[234]

TRANSITION

"Ragtime was not discovered or invented by anyone. Darwin says 'music was known and understood before words were spoken,' and I believe that ragtime existed in the lower animals long before the advent of man. It is simply rhythm, or intensified rhythm, and I have frequently observed animals keeping time to music having a strong, marked rhythm. Rhythm is the skeleton on which all music is hung, and if you will strip the so-called modern ragtime of its melodies you will have the music that has been in vogue since the beginning of time and that still is the only music of many of the heathen races. It is the 'juba,' buck and wing dance of the old plantation darkey, and no more inspiring ragtime was ever played than that which he patted with his hands, shuffled with his feet, or plunked on his rudely constructed banjo. All the old-time fiddlers were ragtime performers. The backwoods player who sat perched on a barrel in a corner at a 'corn-husking bee,' who held his fiddle at his elbow, and his bow at half-mast, played the 'Arkansaw Traveler' and 'Up Duck Creek' in a style that would put to shame many of the fellows who claim to have originated what they are pleased to call 'ragtime.'

"Drummers have played nothing but ragtime since the invention of the drum. The bass-drum is now used only to punctuate or emphasize the heavy beats or pulse of the music, but in the original 'sheepskin band' that has furnished martial music for our soldiers in times of war for centuries, the bass-drummer used a stick in each hand and helped out the ragtime rhythm of the snare-drum.

"I have often been asked, 'Why do you play so much ragtime at your concerts?' and I always reply that ragtime music is what is most demanded, and that my mission is to please—not to educate—the masses. It is not a crime to acknowledge that you enjoy ragtime. All the old masters wrote ragtime, and that great poet and wizard of harmony, Richard Wagner, was

[235]

a past-master at it. It is a well-known fact that the themes for many of our most popular ragtime songs were taken bodily from his operas. . . .

"Ragtime is not a fad, as many have declared, and it will not die out. It pleases the God-given sense of rhythm and will endure as long as the warm blood flows in human veins—as long as the world shall stand. Call it what you will—ragtime is as good as any other name—it existed centuries before our time and it will go on for centuries to come after we have been forgotten."

The controversy was to continue—*allegro ostinato*—for years. In 1908 it was again confidently proclaimed that ragtime had played itself to death, and that we were ripe for a return of the good old ballads. Then, a few years later the trumpet of "Alexander's Ragtime Band" summoned it to resurrection. There is no death. . . .

Cohanic Dynamics.

To this transitional era belongs George M. Cohan, a fellow full of whimsies and idiosyncrasies. More in spirit than in accomplishment, as one may gather from his amusingly frank narrative, *Twenty Years on Broadway*, and from numerous articles distributed in the magazines and newspapers during those twenty years and after. He is one of the greatest and most successful pluggers in our history. And the great theme song he plugged from the first, in frank jubilation, is George M. Cohan.

What was it that gave him his flag-waving technique? The date of his birth?

TRANSITION

I'm a Yankee Doodle dandy,
Yankee Doodle do or die.
Real live nephew of my Uncle Sam,
Born on the Fourth of July . . .

Or Loie Fuller? Cohan, barely landed on Broadway as a kid of fifteen, had passed the dancer as she was chatting to a group of newspaper men on the way to her hotel. It was time, he heard her say, that someone introduced the American flag to American audiences. "I intend," she went on "to wear a stars and stripes costume for my opening at the Gayety Theatre." A seed was planted.

Arrogance, impatience, bad temper, ambition, adaptiveness, torrential speech, swell-headedness . . . these are a few of the traits with which Cohan endows himself in the first of his auto-biographical narratives. As a child hoofer he had already made a name with his coon songs, after an unsuccessful apprenticeship at ballads, writing half a dozen of them a week. To receive from $10 to $25 per song at a time when royalty arrangements were limited to the few big guns of the Alley was no mean accomplishment. When, in 1897, he wrote "I Guess I'll Have to Telegraph My Baby," the publishers in their omniscience were sure that the coon song was already dead; it hadn't yet begun.

Cohan's policy of speed in production seems to have been rooted in his temperament. It fell in with the rhythm of the age. To him, in stage management rather than in song, we owe a "peppiness" that has by no means been outdistanced since the Cohanic zenith that arched from 1901 to 1906, from *The Governor's Son* and *Little Johnny Jones* to *45 Minutes from Broadway* and *George*

Washington, Jr. Ragtime marriage ceremonies, ragtime court trials . . . these were, in their day, refreshing sights and equally refreshing commentaries. They still are, when properly done.

We all sang Cohan's . . . "Give My Regards to Broadway" . . . "I'm a Yankee Doodle Dandy" . . . "Mary Is a Grand Old Name" . . . "So Long, Mary" . . . "It's a Grand Old Flag." We were still singing him, as the producer of Harbach and Hirsch's *Mary* in 1919; and as the author-composer of *The O'Brien Girl, Little Nelly Kelly* and *The Merry Malones.* An acquaintance with four chords in the black key of F-sharp was enough to equip him for a quarter-century of song.

His earliest songs are as good as his latest—indeed, better. For all the newness of his productions, his own words and music tended to become older in style as he himself grew older. He began to hark back to the Harrigan and Hart Hibernianisms. He could not write a long melodic line. He was full of remembrances of good tunes past.

Yet, by the magnetism of his personality, and by the power that attracts cultists to worship at the shrine of commercial or artistic success, he created an era in popular amusement and gave us an adjective from his name. He remained almost untouched by the incursion of the Viennese school of operetta, content with his rough-and-ready Americanism. From ragtime to riches. . . .

The argument about "rags" and "blues" lasted through the Great War, nor was it perceived at first that, even as the contenders fumed hotly about it and about, the music was changing before their very ears. However, let us not anticipate. A summons rings through the air. We are bidden to "the leader man, the ragged-meter man"—to "Alexander's Ragtime Band."

Irving Berlin.

The song is generally considered as one of the milestones of our popular music. Berlin himself, in an article written in 1915,[1] modestly throws himself a bouquet. "Now just one boast: I believe that such songs of mine as 'Alexander's Ragtime Band,' 'That Mysterious Rag,' 'Ragtime Violin,' 'I Want to be in Dixie,' and 'Take a Little Tip from Father,' virtually started the ragtime mania in America. Now that craze has gone all over the world. . . ."

What Berlin achieved, and it was a historic service, was not the creation of the ragtime craze—Cohan had something to say about that, too—but the revival of it. He improved upon the words in particular, and added a fillip to the tunes. He built, as he could not help building, upon predecessors who should not be forgotten. What is more, Berlin helped to inaugurate, not a ragtime era but one of jazz. He is the great transition figure of his day, a remarkable intuitive artist who combines the old and the new, the ballad style and the pseudo-Negro comic strain,—both elements of the minstrel show.

As for "Alexander's Ragtime Band," that epochal aggregation . . . if you care to hear the Swanee River played in ragtime you'll have to go elsewhere, for these men of Alexander do not play ragtime.

[1] "Words and Music." By Irving Berlin, in collaboration with Justus Dickinson. *The Green Book Magazine*, July, 1915. Pp. 104-105.

Sing over, play over, the now famous chorus:

Come on and hear, Come on and hear,
Alexander's ragtime band.
Come on and hear, Come on and hear,
It's the best band in the land.
They can play a bugle call like you never heard before,
So natural that you want to go to war;
That's just the bestest band what am, honey lamb.
Come on along, Come on along,
Let me take you by the hand,
Up to the man, up to the man,
Who's the leader of the band.
And if you care to hear the Swanee River
              played in ragtime,
Come on and hear, Come on and hear,
Alexander's Ragtime band.

The words have spirit, vigor; the one blemish is the forced accent on the *al* of natur*al*. (The music of that line, by the way, is almost the starting point of Cohan's "Over There.") But where is the ragtime? There are but two syncopations in the music to the chorus: on "That's *just* the" and on the word "rag*time*" in the reference to Swanee River. Otherwise, as more than one musician has expressed it to me, it's as "straight as Sousa." I am not attempting to diminish Mr. Berlin's importance in the history of our newer popular music. As a matter of fact, if you take the trouble to go through the songs of George Gershwin, king of the jazzers, you will come upon a surprising number of tunes that are straight composition, containing neither the elements of ragtime nor the elements of jazz. This is, whether in the case of Berlin or of Gershwin, a tribute to their creative powers rather than an indication of deficiency. There is nothing duller than ragtime or jazz when they are employed unvaryingly as formulas . . . The song, then, that revived ragtime just before the outbreak of the war was, by paradox, all but devoid of ragtime.

"It is not entirely an accident," writes Gilbert Seldes, in his pioneer volume, *The Seven Lively Arts,* "that a consideration of the effect of ragtime on popular song begins and ends with Irving Berlin. For as surely as 'Alexander's Ragtime Band' started something, 'Pack Up Your Sins' is a sign that it is coming to an end." By end Mr. Seldes means that whereas formerly songs were written to be sung, thereafter they were written to be danced. But song has always glorified the dance, and has always been danced to. Jazz, with its faster tempos, was essentially instrumental and terpsichorean, and in this deed the true heroes were the harmonists and the arrangers.

Meanwhile, jazz as we know it to-day had been born in Memphis, Tennessee, and Alexander knew nothing about it.

Where the "Blues" Came From.

William Christopher Handy, "the father of the blues," is not the inventor of the genre; he is its Moses, not its Jehovah. It was he who, first of musicians, codified the new spirit in African music and sent it forth upon its conquest of the North. The "rag" had sung and danced the joyous aspects of Negro life; the "blues," new only in their emergence, sang the sorrows of secular existence.

Handy was born in Florence, Alabama, on November 16, 1873, of a pioneer family. His father and his paternal grandfather were Methodist Episcopal ministers. In the same year and in the same

[241]

town was born Oscar de Priest, destined to achieve a notable career in statesmanship and leadership of his people. At the close of the Civil War Handy's grandfather had purchased a homestead on the west side of Florence; it is still known as Handy's Hill. It was this same ancestor who built the first Negro church in Florence, of which Handy's father in time became the Pastor.

Prejudice against a musical career, then, was deeply rooted in the Handy family. Not in William Christopher, however. The singing of the laborers on the locks fascinated him as a child. At ten he was uncommonly good as a sight-reader. His teacher, Wallace, encouraged his tenor voice, but was as hopeful of his success in politics as was Handy senior of his future eminence in religion. Why could not William rise to a bishopric? While his elders were thus planning, Handy himself was acquiring, by hook or crook, the fundamentals of a musical training. He bought a rotary-valve cornet and stole his lessons by peeking through the open door while the paying pupils inside blew their hour through the notes on the blackboard. He added his tenor to a local quartette. He sang at white entertainments. He bummed his way to Birmingham. He taught school. He discovered that he could make more than twice the amount at the Bessemer pipe works, twelve miles out of town, that he could as a teacher. And he made it—$1.85 a day—until the election of Grover Cleveland brought with it a depression in employment and sent him back to his music for its uncertain income.

He reached Birmingham with twenty cents in his pockets. In a saloon there he heard a quartette and was suddenly struck with an idea. Why not pilot these men to the World's Fair, shortly to open, and burn up Chicago with their strumming and crooning, and his

WILLIAM CHRISTOPHER HANDY

The Father of the Blues

antic cornet? Still under age, he undertook to freight the gang to the Windy City. The signs augured well; for, discovered by a brakeman in one of the empties they were able to soothe his savage breast with music from their cornet and guitar, not to speak of tender crooning. So, instead of being red-lighted, they were shown to the palatial quarters of the caboose.

Hard times, however, despite the assurance of Foster's song, came again some more. St. Louis, and a bed, in company with hundreds of others, on the cobblestones of the levee . . . Brick-laying at Evansville, at $1.50 a day . . . A job in the Hampton band, and a meeting with one Taylor, who took him to Kentucky, and to a job in the Henderson band. Henderson was, for Handy, doubly auspicious: he found there his future wife; the town, a steamboat landing, was melodious with the songs of the roustabouts and the stevedores on the levee.

On the 4th of August, 1896, he joined the Mahara Colored Minstrels in Chicago as bandmaster and soloist on the cornet. It was a strange repertory that he played: Beethoven to Ballads à la Dresser and Harris, and always in the white tradition. It was the gallery, with its unmistakable signs of pleasure and displeasure, that taught him the potency of an uncouth, but national and racial, music. The gallery wanted short, sharp rhythms, even to the tapping of the soloist's foot as he played the "Georgia Camp Meeting" . . . There were travels in Mexico, Cuba, Canada . . .

Back to Alabama and to teaching vocal and band music at the A. & M. College in Huntsville. From 1900 to 1903 he lingered here, absorbing the songs, sacred and profane, of his people. Thence to Clarksdale, Mississippi, where he organized his first orchestra. It was a nine-piece, uniformed troupe, black in color

[243]

but white in program. Curiously enough, it was the whites who taught him the esthetic values of his racial song, and who, at a momentous subscription dance, after he had served up the regular Broadway fare, cried out for him to "play some of your own music." Just what they wanted he was made to gather from the introduction of "three seedy Negroes equipped respectively with guitar, mandolin and bass viol, who sat themselves down in their uncultured way to commence—and continue—a backyard over-and-over wail that brought in more in tips than the uniforms bore home in pay." [2]

Handy, without knowing it, had begun his anthology of the "blues." Here was a new field to exploit. Two years later, in Memphis, he organized a new band that was to make history. Three colored bands divided the leadership of a city in which everything was said with music; so that, when election day came around —a three-cornered battle—Handy's men were hired by Jim Mulcahy to blare a certain E. H. Crump into office. Fortunately, Crump, who was running on a highly moral platform, did not hear the words. Handy's election-themes were founded upon the "blues" that he had picked up in Clarksdale; the central section of his piece, however, was based upon a verse that was already being sung in colored circles, *against* Mr. Crump's put-on-the-lid campaign:

> Mister Crump won't 'low no easy riders here,
> Mister Crump won't 'low no easy riders here.
> I don't care what Mister Crump don't 'low,

[2] *Blues.* An Anthology, edited by W. C. Handy. With an Introduction by Abbe Niles. New York, 1926. P. 12. This promises to be the standard volume upon the subject.

TRANSITION

I'm gwine to bar'l-house anyhow—
Mr. Crump can go an' catch hisself some air!

Which, being translated into English, is not exactly nice.

Handy's band outplayed his competitors; Crump was elected. The furore created by the new music raised the leader sky-high; he was deluged with engagements; he organized a chain of Handy bands. And, more to our purpose, after having failed with his first composition, a "Roosevelt Triumphant March," and his second, "In the Cotton Fields of Dixie" (strange, this imitation by Negroes of an insincere white imitation) he set down his "blues" à la Crump. What was this? Only twelve bars in the chorus, instead of the obligatory sixteen? That would never do. It was rejected in rapid succession by one firm after another. In 1912 Handy published it himself as an instrumental piece, and renamed it after the city of its origin: "The Memphis Blues." He had unsuspectingly enriched the national music, but he was to gain nothing from his gift. He sold the composition to T. C. Bennet, a white from Memphis, for one hundred dollars; words were added to it; it was republished and made money as well as history. But no money for Handy. *Sic vos, non vobis.*

Handy later went into business with Harry H. Pace, with whom he had written his second published piece. He was able, in a way, to establish his historical importance and to write other "blues," notably the "Beale Street" and "The St. Louis" blues. The year 1918 found Pace and Handy on Broadway, but Pace was to drop out and take with him most of the Handy organization for his new venture of the Pace Phonograph Company. (He must have got the idea for a Negro phonograph company from the Columbia

[245]

organization, which in 1917 had hired Handy's band for the making of a dozen records).

The war depression nearly annihilated Handy. Rather than go into bankruptcy and evade moral obligations that might easily have found legal relief, he slaved away to pay up notes on Northern and Southern banks. Woolworth's discontinued some six hundred music counters, thus leaving the Negro publisher with a half million unsold copies on his hands. No matter. He sold a beautiful residence on 139th Street, and ruined both his health and his sight in the unremitting labor of meeting his debts.

To-day, happily, he has regained both. He is still the undaunted "daddy" of the "blues," carrying on in his humbler Broadway quarters. It may well be, when the full history of our new American music is written, that the services of Handy will appear in the light of their true, germinal importance.

His early bands had been made up of intuitive, rather than trained, musicians. They were naturally gifted improvisers who would not resist the temptation to fly off upon a tonal rampage. There were consecrated spots in the blues, the pauses at the end of each line, where the players, as if by instinct, broke loose. Abhorring, by nature, this vacuum, they filled it with all manner of extemporaneous noises. It was in this vacuum—opportunity here for acrid comment upon the part of the miso-jazzians—that jazz, as it came to be known, was born.

Handy was the first to set jazz down upon paper—to fix the quality of the various "breaks," as these wildly filled in pauses were named. With a succession of "blues" he fixed the genre. What Paul Whiteman was soon to do for the vagrant polyphony of jazz, tethering it to the lines of the staff so as to ensure the same performance twice running, Handy had done for the stigmatic break of the blues.

The new style was shortly to be developed to a degree of truly creative splendor by a small coterie of white composers. The era of ragtime had been ushered in by a galaxy of Negroes. Jazz, after the initial impulse given by Handy, is delivered into the hands of the whites.

A Forgotten Pioneer.

Among the forgotten leaders of the transitional period is Lewis F. Muir, who flourished—as the history volumes have it—between 1910 and 1912. His "Play That Barbershop Chord" antedates "Alexander's Ragtime Band" by a year. Like Berlin and George M. Cohan, he was a one-key player. In the days when F. A. Mills was a power in the publishing business, Muir and his most constant lyrist, L. Wolfe Gilbert, with whom in 1912 he was to write "Waiting for the Robert E. Lee," were often to be seen in the Mills studio singing and playing their ditties for Irving Berlin, Ray Goetz and other notables of the period. Mills, in those days, as Gilbert recalls them, "had a transposing piano. 'Robert E. Lee' was written in two keys: the verse in C and the chorus in F. If Muir played for you, when you got to the end of the verse you would have to hold the note until Muir moved the handle under the piano and the entire keyboard moved to the key of F. Then you sang the chorus."

Muir's playing, despite his enforced allegiance to a single key, was so much in the semi-virtuosic style of the F-sharp Negroes that they always gathered about him to listen. He quickly caught

[247]

the manner of Ernest Hogan and Irving Jones, in such earlier tunes as "When Ragtime Rosy Ragged the Rosary," "Barber Shop Chord," "Mammy Jinny's Jubilee," "Here Comes My Daddy," "Camp Meeting Band."

It is asserted that "Waiting for the Robert E. Lee" was in-directly responsible for starting the ragtime craze in England. After their first hits, L. Wolfe Gilbert was employed in a Coney Island Café called the *College Inn*, where many stage stars were wont to foregather. One night William Morris, Eddie Foy, and Albert Decourville, the London producer, heard Gilbert's crew sing the "Robert E. Lee," "Hitchy Koo," "Ragging the Baby to Sleep," and other tunes of Muir's manufacture and invited Gilbert, then and there, to come to London with his songsters. They would be billed as The American Ragtime Octet. Mills, the publisher, would not hear of Gilbert's leaving the country, but the boys did go, and soon had London town ragtime-crazy.

Muir himself later accepted an engagement at the Oxford, in London. Together with Leoncavallo—it is not only politics that makes strange bed-fellows—he wrote a revue.

Abroad, the musical phenomenon was being considered with mingled approbation and scorn—the well-known condescension of the foreigner. Composers and players who could very well endure the trashy output of the French or the Italian hacks discovered, along in 1913, that ragtime was cabaret music, that it expressed "the purposeless energy of never-tiring and always alert minds, but with our best will we could find no traces of any art, new or old, in it." . . . "I found that ragtime is music meant for the tired and materially bored mind. It shows the same stirring qualities as a sensational newspaper story does. . . . Like a criminal

novel, it is full of bangs and explosions devised in order to shake
up the overworked mind. Often there is a strain of affected sentimentality and what may be termed as the melodramatic element.
But I have found no genuine emotion in a ragtime composition." . . . "Ragtime is the real thing for America, because it
pays. And as long as money is the ideal of the country ragtime
will be its national music." [3]

In England a writer in the *London Times* was singing a duet
with Arnold Bennett. Americans, Bennett had written, were "imita-
tive, with no real opinions of their own. They associate art with
Florentine frames, matinée hats, distant museums and clever talk
full of allusions to the dead. It would not occur to them to search
for American art in the architecture of railway stations and
draughtsmanship and in the sketch-writing of newspapers, because
they have not the wit to learn that genuine art flourishes best in
an atmosphere of genuine public demand."

The anonymous contributor [4] of the *London Times* applied the
argument to ragtime.

"Character and vigor earn respect all the world over, even
when the character is unpleasant and the vigor misdirected.
Now of ragtime, there can be no doubt that it is absolutely
characteristic of its inventors. From nowhere but from the
United States could such spring. It is the music of the hustler
and of the feverishly active speculator.

"If a national art is to spring from ragtime, much dross will
have to be cleared away in the process; much vulgarity and
senselessness will have to give place to a finer ideal.

[3] *The Birth Processes of Ragtime.* By Ivan Narodny. Musical America, March 29,
1913. P. 27.
[4] *Ragtime as Source of National Music.* (Report.) Ibid. February 15, 1913. P. 37.

"We look to the future for an American composer, not, indeed, to the Parkers and the MacDowells of the present, who are taking over foreign art ready made, imitating it with more or less success, and with a complete absence of vital force, but to some one as yet unknown, perhaps, unborn, who will sing the songs of his own nation in his own time and his own character.

"It is not suggested that ragtime as such will develop into a great art, but that ragtime represents the American nation. Will it not be possible to suggest to some composer of the future to follow a greater and more developed means, which will also represent the American nation, out of which will grow up an art which will be really vital, because it has roots in its own soil?

"America has waited too long for her own music. Her serious musicians must cease to look abroad for inspiration and turn their faces homeward."

It is characteristic of the general uncertainty prevailing at this time in Tin Pan Alley that before a year had passed we should be reading—again!—that "Ragtime is dead—kicked to death by popularity." [5] And what was to succeed it? The selfsame ballad that, in 1908, was announced as the regenerator of national popular song. Now, it is surer that the ballad will die than that ragtime, or its emotional equivalent, will pass from the lips and the hearts of the people. The ballad, in a verbal sense, is long dead. I Cannot Sing the Old Songs. Not because they stir memories of the dear departed, but because the life in which one could have taken the words seriously has gone forever. Music does not die so easily. It is not so definite as words, and it is a peculiarity of our psy-

[5] "Back to the Ballads." By David Moore. *The Green Book Magazine*, January, 1914. Pp. 149-153.

chology that we will accept—*as music*—a simplicity, an ingenu-
ousness, that we could not countenance when stated in the plain
terms of our daily speech—that is, in their verbal equivalents.

The old ballads, "After the Ball," "The Lost Child," "Take
Back Your Gold," "My Mother Was a Lady," and such immortal
lines as

> Somewhere a soul is drifting
> Further and far apart

from the ancient catalogue of Charlie Harris . . . these will
never return, any more than one's first set of teeth returns, or the
infant's cradle-cap.

What will return is the slower, softer mood of these songs. The
rhythm of the alternation is as sure as that between asceticism
and abandon. In reality, of course, neither of the chief moods in
popular music ever disappears. As often as not, the phenomenon
belongs rather to the song-market than to the heart of the singer.
Fast, peppy music for the moment gluts the counters. The wily
publishers sniff the change in the wind and ruffle their catalogues
accordingly.

In the columns of *The New Music Review,* in *The New Repub-
lic,* in *The Seven Arts,* the ragtime controversy still raged upon
an intellectual plane. Daniel Gregory Mason and Hiram K. Motherwell were at the negative and positive poles, respectively, of the
controversy. That was in 1915-1917. Now that ragtime has definitely become jazz—ragtime never died, it grew up—Mason and
Motherwell still defend their respective posts.

TIN PAN ALLEY

A Bold Proposal.

Ragtime was the name employed by Mason and Motherwell; jazz was the thing they were discussing. Motherwell, unabashedly, was demanding for his protégé the honors of a concert appearance on the sacrosanct stage of Æolian Hall. Here is the program that in *The Seven Arts* for July, 1917, he suggested to the singer who would be courageous enough to use it:

I

Roll Dem Cotton Bales...............	Johnson
Waiting for the Robert E. Lee	Muir
The Tennessee Blues................	Warner
The Memphis Blues.................	Handy

II

You May Bury Me in the East..........	Traditional
Bendin' Knees a-Achin'..............	Traditional
These Dead Bones Shall Rise Again.....	Traditional
Play on Your Harp, Little David........	Traditional

III

Nobody's Lookin' But the Owl an' the Moon	Johnson
Exhortation	Cook
Rain Song	Cook

IV

Everybody's Doing It	Berlin
I Love a Piano	Berlin
When I Get Back to the U. S. A.	Berlin
On the Beach at Wai-ki-ki	Kern
Ragtime Cowboy Joe................	Muir

Mason cried "Sacrilege!" . . . "To me," wrote Motherwell, "ragtime brings a type of musical experience which I can find in no other music. I find something Nietzschean in its implicit philosophy that all the world's a dance. I love the delicacy of its inner rhythms and the largeness of its rhythmic sweeps. I like to think that it is the perfect expression of the American city, with its restless bustle and motion, its multitude of unrelated details, and its underlying rhythmic progress toward a vague Somewhere. Its technical resourcefulness continually surprises me, and its melodies, at their best, delight me . . . I firmly believe that a ragtime program, well organized and well sung, would be delightful and stimulating to the best audience the community could muster. . . ." [6]

Mr. Mason, answering this and other writings of his opponent in *The New Music Review*,[7] begins urbanely enough with a tabloid technical disquisition, in which Mr. Motherwell's hyperbolic appraisal of "The Memphis Blues" is torn to snippets. The mask of dignity soon cracks, however, and Mr. Mason becomes his true self, mincing neither words nor music. Ragtime, tracked to its lair, is discovered to be "no creative process, like the syncopation of the masters, by which are struck forth new, vigorous and self-sufficing forms. It is a rule of thumb for putting a 'kink' into a tune that without such specious rehabilitation would be unbearable. It is not a new flavor, but a kind of curry or catsup strong enough to make the stale old dishes palatable to unfastidious appetites. . . . To these it can give no new musical lineaments, but

[6] "Two Views of Ragtime." *I. A Modest Proposal.* Pp. 368-376.
[7] The unlaid ghost of jazz haunts Mr. Mason still. In *The New Freeman* of September 10, 1930, in an article optimistically entitled "The Jazz Fiasco," he returns to the assault upon Motherwell. He adds nothing new, however.

only distorts the old ones as with St. Vitus's dance. . . . Ragtime is the musical expression of an attitude toward life only too familiar to us all—an attitude shallow, restless, avid of excitement, incapable of sustained attention, skimming the surface of everything, finding nowhere satisfaction, realization, or repose. It is a meaningless stirabout, a commotion without purpose, an epilepsy simulating controlled muscular action. It is the musical counterpart of the sterile cleverness we find in so much of our contemporary conversation, as well as in our theater and our books." [8]

The debate is no longer exciting. One was not, after all, compelled to choose between the classics and the jazzics, as so many sober musicians assumed. Why might not one, why may not one, have both? How far removed from the spirit of a classic scherzo is a good "rag"? How far, in spirit, is a good "blues" from the germ-material of a symphonic andante? Something in addition to a merely epileptic fit there must have been in this music of the big cities—adopted, not created by the metropolis—for it struck the imagination of every European country, and was soon inspiring not only the antic fellows of the dance halls, but the whiteheaded boys of conservatory and symphony hall. The superiority of the "Volga Boatman Song" to "The Memphis Blues" was largely an illusion of distance. So, too, in Soviet Russia, a youthful symphonist, in quest of fresh material, would weave into his tonal fabric the strains of Youmans' far-traveled "Tea for Two." Ragtime-Jazz, in origin, may have been downright indecent (read "unashamedly sexual"). This is the secret, too, of much of the resentment expressed against it in terms of technical objurgations.

Later history has smiled upon Motherwell rather than upon

[8] *The New Music Review.* "Concerning Ragtime." Pp. 112-116.

Mason. Not only, as we shall shortly see, did jazz evolve into a form that enriched the people's appreciation of music in general and that enlisted the technical, esthetic and creative interest of many youthful and independent spirits; the concert that Mother-well so dubiously suggested in 1917 became, within six years, an amazing reality, when Eva Gauthier, on the evening of November 1, 1923, included as Part III of her program a section devoted to American music, with George Gershwin as special accompanist for this division. She sang Berlin's "Alexander's Ragtime Band," Kern's "Siren Song" from *Leave It to Jane* (words by Wode-house), Walter Donaldson's "Carolina in the Morning" (words by Gus Kahn), Gershwin's "I'll Build a Stairway to Paradise" (from White's *Scandals,* words by De Sylva and Arthur Francis, the latter being an early pseudonym of Ira Gershwin), Gershwin and Daly's "Innocent Ingenue Baby" (from *Our Nell,* words by Brian Hooker), and, finally, Gershwin's "Swanee" (words by Irving Cæsar). . . . Within three months jazz, after this vocal victory, was to win an instrumental triumph with Gershwin's *Rhapsody in Blue.*

The now historic concert by Paul Whiteman and his band took place in Æolian Hall on the afternoon of February 12, 1924. It included orthodox selections, afterward presented in jazzified form; it listed, among the composers, Baer, Kern, Confrey, Grofé, Berlin, Herbert, Friml and Gershwin. It tried to justify the ways of jazz to man, and it succeeded far better than Whiteman had hoped for in his most optimistic moments.[9] The *Rhapsody in Blue* lifted jazz definitely from the status of simple dance-rhythm to something

[9] For a most interesting account of this pioneer venture, read the chapter entitled "An Experiment," in Whiteman's *Jazz.* (New York, 1926.)

[255]

above and beyond the dance. It conferred upon the form a certain symphonic dignity, which the composer himself would develop in the too-little heard *Concerto in F* and in *An American in Paris*.

Some three years after the Gauthier concert, Gershwin repeated the vocal experiment in company of Mme. Marguerite D'Alvarez. She sang, as Part V of a program, Gershwin's "The Nashville Nightingale," "The Man I Love" and "Clap Yo' Hands"; also, Kern's "Babes in the Wood." It was for this program that Gershwin composed six Preludes founded upon jazz motifs, thus proving, especially in the second, that jazz was adaptable to the consecrated forms of the classics.[10]

Popular composers do not argue their cause. They are hardly aware of a cause. They write away, if not for bread and butter, then for bootleg and penthouses.

The era from 1911 to the end of the Great War may be roughly considered as the Berlin epoch of our popular song. Berlin, at first considered as a man with one string to his harp, like his predecessor Harry Von Tilzer, displayed a surprising power of adaptation to changing circumstances. He revived ragtime and sent it blaring toward jazz. He actually restored the sentimental ballad of the Harris-Dresser decade, fitting it out with a new kind of lyric and a smoother line of melody. He brought new life to the music revue, setting it into a background of varied verse and tune, and building, as home for it, the dainty Music Box.

From now on, the connection between the musical comedy and the popular song becomes more intimate. One-finger composers still ply their trade, but they begin slowly to be replaced by true

[10] Only three of the Preludes have been printed. They are dedicated to Bill Daly.

creative spirits with a broader and deeper knowledge of their craft. It is not only a coincidence that men such as Friml, Romberg, Kern and Gershwin are thorough musicians as well as tune men.

Friml and Romberg, however delightful the songs that they have written for the pleasure of multitudes, are from a historical standpoint relatively unimportant. They add nothing to the few forms current in popular music. They follow in the path of Victor Herbert; or in the path of the Viennese school. They are capable eclectics, displaying a certain intuitive skill in more or less conscious adaptation from numerous sources. From any valid national standpoint they stand below, rather than above, such forgotten favorites as Gustav Kerker, Pixley and Luders. For the advancement of our peculiarly national forms we must look, in musical comedy, to Jerome Kern and to George Gershwin, who started his musical life as a frank imitator of Berlin and especially of Kern.

Kern and Gershwin.

Kern, in a succession of productions that were once identified with the Princess Theatre, New York, and whose latest representatives are *Show Boat* and *Sweet Adeline,* introduced into our music a new suavity and a new modulatory process. He struck away from the expected turns of the tune, from the expected harmonies of the phrase. In him, the uncouthness of the ragtime-jazz melody was planed down; the jagged edges were rounded off. Flash became flow. Recall the "Magic Melody" from *Oh, Boy!* There is, early in the chorus, a sudden surprise in the accompaniment that may be said to have inaugurated a harmonic school and provided what was to become a cliché of our piano scores. It was *The Girl from Utah*, with its "You're Here and I'm Here" and "They Didn't Believe Me" that was to waken the juvenile Gershwin into a realization of new possibilities in the popular tune.

Berlin, in 1911, had won his spurs with Alexander's playing of the "Swanee River." Gershwin, with his song named "Swanee," in 1919 was to be lifted over night into fame and fortune by Jolson's singing of the piece in the extravaganza, *Sinbad*. The shade of Foster haunts Tin Pan Alley still.

Gershwin, in his early musical comedies, was to carry on to a personal and to a logical conclusion the melodic and harmonic methods of Kern. Berlin had nothing to teach in the way of harmonies. George, by nature a demonic experimentalist, felt the need of more subtlety, greater variety. Ragtime was in abeyance; jazz was coming in, as ragtime had first come in, through instrumental music. The after-war spirit demanded a new sensitivity, a new hysteria, a new release. Drown the cares of the world in noise: hot jazz. Soothe the wounds of the world in soft insinuation: sweet jazz. Hot jazz for the cave man and the cave woman; sweet jazz for the sophisticate. And both in the service of the great God-Goddess, Aphrodisia.

What is—or what was—Jazz?

10. King Jazz

Jazz is all things to all ears. To the theological dogmatist it is a new guise of the ancient devil, to be fought as a satanic agency. To the pagan, if he is minded to interpret novelties in the language of social ethics, it is the symptom of a glorious release from the bonds of moral restraint. The musician, if he is one of the old school, looks upon it with mingled amusement and disgust; if he is of the modernist persuasion, he beholds in it rich possibilities of a new style. The conductor of the Boston Symphony Orchestra, Serge Koussevitsky, during the season of 1925-26, received more than one letter from indignant subscribers to the New York concerts of his famous band, in which the blame for the "crime wave" of that year was laid to his introduction of so much modernistic music.

The theme seems predestined to violent variations, as well as to strange confusions. The discussion begins as one in musical esthetics, and before we know it we are listening to a moral diatribe. This deviation from the path of pure music is by no means limited to the non-musical. Players, composers, critics, teachers—these have all contributed to the discussion of jazz their quota of irrelevances. Jazz was a fad that wouldn't last. Jazz was the salvation of the art. Jazz was the intrusion of the cheap dance-hall into the sacred precincts of the symphonic concert auditorium. Jazz wasn't so young as it pretended to be; it could be found in the classics, used to better advantage than it was used by the pounders and pluggers of Tin Pan Alley. Jazz came from the slums of music; it corrupted taste and manners. Jazz brought to classical music a new, if vulgar, blood that would rejuvenate the art through this necessary alliance. Jazz was, literally and figuratively, a mésalliance, an example of miscegenation that worked to the detriment of the superior race. It was a subtle triumph of black over white.

We are dealing with music, not morals. Jazz has its moral connotations, beyond a doubt, as has everything else; it has its sociological aspect, too, and a most interesting aspect it is. We are interested, however, primarily in musical values. Musically considered, a good piece of jazz is good, and a bad symphony is an abomination, far inferior to the good jazz.

There is a species of musical snobbery, for example, that pretends to deride the waltzes of Johann Strauss. The waltz, in its day, came in for the selfsame condemnation that the foxtrot, the Charleston and the Black Bottom have lately sustained.

> Endearing Waltz! to thy more tender tune
> Bow Irish jig and ancient rigadoon.
> Scotch reels avaunt! and country dance forego
> Your future claim to each fantastic toe.
> Waltz, waltz alone both legs and arms demands,
> Liberal of feet and lavish of her hands.

So Byron had written. Were he alive to-day—so thought the English critic, W. J. Turner, in a parodic mood of 1926—he would write:

KING JAZZ

Ear-splitting Jazz, thy brazen syncopation
Has routed Waltz from every modern nation;
No more frail maids to dreamy violins
In languor move their unrevealèd shins;
Athletic Jazz leaps liberally and shocks not.
Lavish of knees in one-step, tango, fox-trot.

My point is that this condemnation has little or nothing to do with the music as music, any more than has the refusal of the academicians to accept Franck's *Symphony in D,* because—forsooth—it employed an English horn. Yet consider the contemporary attitude toward the saxophone in the symphony orchestra. This is not musical criticism; it is merely the expression of caste feeling. When a squeamish lady objects to the digestive sportiveness of the slide trombone, to the leering cachinnation of the clarinet, to the slap-tonguing of the saxophone, she is not necessarily expressing a musical opinion; she is exhibiting a dislike of the manners suggested by noises that violate the books of etiquette. This is within her rights; but I must insist that it is not vitally related to criticism of jazz as music, as art. If art were only good manners and fine company, we should be able to do without it. Art, indeed, has a strange habit of appearing in bad company with questionable manners. Can it be because art, being allied to the fundamental emotions, is not too much at home with that excellent company and those fine manners which secretly fear those emotions?

In any case, we now dismiss the moral consideration.

What has jazz brought to music? Is it the new blood that its devotees proclaim it? Has it, as others maintain, already run its course?

[261]

TIN PAN ALLEY

There can be little question that, on the technical side—forgetting for the moment the artistic aspect—it has educated the people in the essentials of music. It has brought music closer to the life and thought of the untutored public; it has given that public a new appreciation of rhythm, harmony, counterpoint, instrumental timbre. It has accomplished these things, of course, quite unintentionally; it has insinuated these factors into the consciousness of the national listener. Jack may not know a chord of the ninth from a cord of wood; Jill may not know the difference between timbre and timber. Yet Jack takes a new delight in the interweaving of one melody with another, especially when he knows them both, as in the case of Dvořák's "Humoresque" and "Swanee River"; and Jill feels a new warmth when paired saxophones softly croon a duet against the E string obligato of the violin and the gentle tapping of the sticks on the snare drum. They have been educated away from—I should say *up* from—the blaring cornet, the adenoidal clarinet, the banging piano, the unoriginal fiddle and the sad trombone of the pre-war dance hall. They instinctively ask, now, for something more than a dull, unadorned melody with a dull, unadorned accompaniment.

Jazz has trained the ear of Jack and Jill to follow almost a maximum variety of rhythmic differentiation within the confines of a single musical bar; it has familiarized them with a new world of chords and makes the old-time dependence upon tonic, subdominant and dominant seem trite and vapid indeed; it has given them new instruments and a new sense of tone-color. It may very well be true that the words of the popular song have remained as empty as ever they were in the heyday of the "ballad." The music, however, has progressed amazingly. On this side there can

[262]

be no question that there has been little but gain. Since I am, for the present, concerned with technical advancement, I shall ask you simply to compare the accompaniment of the average popular song printed between 1898 and 1905 with that printed between 1914 and 1930. The notes presuppose a long stride in the direction of a richer rhythmic, harmonic and contrapuntal life.

Does such a technical advancement inevitably spell improvement in taste? No, not inevitably. It does, however, provide the elements upon which a better taste may be founded. And it has, in my opinion, raised the level of musical taste. The improvement has been, so to speak, democratic rather than aristocratic. The essentials of a good musical background have been brought to a vast audience, by means of the phonograph and the radio. For the art of music these inventions have played a part somewhat analogous to that of the printing press in literature. Just as the printing press was not an unqualified boon, so the phonograph and radio have inevitably pandered to the lowest tastes. This is an unavoidable phase of our industrial age and of democracy. It need not, however, from our standpoint, be a permanent drawback. Once we have reconciled ourselves to the circumstance that a majority must, under present conditions, be excluded from the best in life and art, we may find solace in the consideration that for an ever-increasing number that best is being made accessible. The probabilities are against the lowering of good taste to the popular level; the lover of the symphony, for all his enjoyment of jazz—and the better musician he is, the greater will be his pleasure in the better products of jazz—is not likely to desert the classics for the "jazzics." The jazz lover, on the other hand, either remains still or moves upward. If he is a jazz-hound, his interest in all likelihood is merely in jazz as a dance background; he and his flapper belong to the eternal majority and do not enter into our discussion of music. If he is attracted by music for its own sake, the chances are that he will seek, sooner or later, a more skilled, a more significant exemplification of those musical elements that he has learned to appreciate in jazz. He will seek them, or they will find him; it is almost the same thing.

Ernest Newman, himself once so angrily inhospitable to jazz, has written a delightful epigram to the effect that this difference separates the good composer from the bad: the good composer is slowly discovered; the bad composer is slowly found out. The same holds true of good music and bad. Repetition is an ordeal that only the best music can endure; it is repetition that has killed off, even for the musically untutored public, the more futile concoctions of jazz. The classics are, in fact, being discovered; the "jazzics" are being found out.

Jazz, for the most part, is still-born; so, for that matter, is music of the more standard cast. The creative spark, the kick of the unborn child that tells the mother there is life within her—these do not occur too frequently in the Tin Pan Alley of the jazz slums, or in the academic groves. If jazz, as I am convinced, has brought to the common ear a new sensitivity and therefore a new vitality, it has also cluttered the market-place with much lumber, with inert substance, with—by your leave—so much rubbish. Jazz, so arrogantly hailed as the music of the future, so soon ran out of essential material that it had to lay its hands—its dirty paws, as Newman, not entirely without justice, would say—on the classics and "jazz them up." The radio made us all too early, and all too often, acquainted with special arrangements—derangements, rather—of Chopin, Chaikovsky, Gounod, Verdi, Beethoven, Rimsky-Korsakoff. Nothing was sacred in its sight. It was said, in defense of this practice, that composers like MacDowell benefited by this process. This by Whiteman, apropos of jazzifying "To a Wild Rose." Regardless of how true this might be in a specific instance, on the whole it is none the less an open confession of sterility. If the minor jazzists had been possessed of true musical invention they would not so soon have been compelled to practice their dubious arts and sciences upon their betters.

We have, at this point, to notice a peculiar exchange of influences between the music of the concert hall and that of the cabaret. Jazz, on its everlasting lookout for novelties, has not hesitated to appropriate the chords and even the progressions of the latest modernists. The modernists themselves, returning the compliment, have, without surrendering to the process, sought inspiration in what they conceive to be its underlying spirit.

Ragtime-Jazz in Europe.

Afro-American syncopation, though on paper it looked much like the ancient European structure, in reality was something novel to trained European ears. Else why should a symphonist like Brahms be writing, as early as 1896, to his American friend, Arthur M. Abell, that he had been hearing an example of ragtime and that, greatly attracted by its novel rhythmic effects, he was thinking of introducing them into a composition? [1] A decade later, before ragtime had evolved into jazz, it had the French Six by the ears; in opera, ballet and chamber music it was beginning

[1] See the *Boston Evening Transcript*, Music and Drama Section, March 22, 1930.

to insinuate itself. Debussy wrote his "Golliwog's Cake-Walk" more than twenty years ago, long after the cake-walk had danced out of popularity. Stravinsky, with his epochal ballet, *Petrushka*, had made himself in 1911 the European pioneer of jazz. So, at least, he has been called, although his first conscious imitation of the Afro-American rhythm was in his "Piano Ragtime," and was neither ragtime fish nor jazz flesh. What need, indeed, had the Stravinsky of *Le Sacre du Printemps, Les Noces,* and *L'Histoire du Soldat* for imported poly-rhythms?

Erik Satie, in 1918, ragged music for Cocteau's ballet, *Parade.* Hindemith, in 1922, inserted a ragtime section in his *Suite 1922,* and also in his *1923.* In 1924 Frank Martin wrote a fox trot for Julia Sazonova's Marionette Theater in Paris. Honneger, in 1924 —the year in which Darius Milhaud discovered jazz in the Hotel Brunswick, Boston—jazzed up his *Concertino.* And how about certain passages in his oratorio, *King David?* The second movement of Ravel's *Violin Sonata* is frankly called "blues."

As for the Germans, consider Kurt Weil's *Royal Palace,* and his *Dreigroschenoper;* and Krenek's *Sprung Ueber den Schatten* and the famous *Jonny Spielt Auf.* The Polish-Jew, Alexandre Tansman, has jazz in his *Concertino.* It was the Russian, Shostakovich, who used Youmans' "Tea for Two" as a theme in a symphony, in just the manner that Stravinsky helped himself to current Italian airs in the Russia of his day. . . . And latterly, in England, the youngster, Constant Lambert, made a setting of Sacheverell Sitwell's "Rio Grande," for chorus and orchestra, that displays an astonishing assimilation of the fundamental esthetics of jazz.

"European jazz, the jazz of the printed sheet, is perforce stationary. At the best, a foreigner can learn argot, but he will never be able to enrich it with new words, having no living source to draw upon. But the new material thus absorbed may influence the further development of European music, eventually emerging in a shape conditioned by the peculiar European environment.

"We can note certain peculiarities of European jazz upon a brief survey. European jazz is humorous, it is often an intended caricature, it is always mischievous. As it should be, we may add, for, having no roots in the soil, it must be mannered. European jazz is lavishly incrustated with counterpoint, usually atonal, rarely polytonal. And so it should be, for atonality is European for 'blues.' European jazz is mildly insinuating, but always polite. Small wonder, for insinuation rather than plain talk is the European way. European jazz is expertly orchestrated. It was to be expected, for Europeans excel in musical salads and macedoines. The blend is always perfect whatever the ingredients may be. European jazz conceals a unifying rhythmical figure behind it, deviations are expressly pointed out, to be complemented by a counter design. Well it may be, for the sense of balance in European music governs the intangible itself." [2]

To return to Americans: George Antheil, after the windy indecision of his *Ballet Méchanique*, this year flabbergasted Germany with his jazz-film opera, *Transatlantik*.[3]

Jazz is essentially an American development of Afro-American thematic material. Its fundamental rhythm and its characteristic

[2] Nicolas Slonimsky, in the *Boston Evening Transcript*, April 20, 1929. For additional notes on ragtime-jazz among the Europeans, see the monograph, *Syncopating Saxophones*, by A. V. Frankenstein, Chicago, 1926. Among foreign works are *The Appeal of Jazz*, by R. S. Mendl, London, 1927; *Le Jazz*, by A. Coeuroy and A. Schaeffner, Paris, 1926; *Jazz*, by Paul Bernhard, Munich, 1927.
[3] It should be recorded that on the evening of April 10, 1927, at Carnegie Hall, when Eugene Goosens conducted the mechanical ballet, W. C. Handy also led his men through Antheil's *Jazz Symphony*.

melody derive from the Negro; its commercialization belongs largely to the popular-song industry of the New York white.

So that jazz, if not absolutely an autochthonous product, is really all the more American for not being purely, unadulteratedly of the soil. It is a musical symbol of the melting-pot. It traces its origin back to the African jungle; it becomes transformed in the hearts and on the lips of the American Negro; it travels North and is taken up by the white, by Gentile and Jew. At the hands of such Jews as Irving Berlin, George Gershwin, Jerome Kern and—in the symphonic realm—Gershwin, Gruenberg and Aaron Copland, it acquires international recognition. The African Negro has dwelt in other countries, without producing a characteristic music; only in America did jazz arise and could jazz have arisen. We must accept it, then, as a phenomenon peculiarly American. Psychologically, esthetically, it is, however poor a thing, our own.

Where did the name come from? What, strictly speaking, is the thing? How has it affected the constitution of our orchestras and the composition of our music? Who are its chief exponents in interpretation, who its chief composers? And what will be its probable contribution to pure music, music-for-its-own-sake, as distinguished from music as an auxiliary of dancing?

Where Does the Word Come From?

Though jazz is one of the youngest words in the language, its origin is already a matter of debate and confusion. Everybody knows what it means and nobody is certain where it comes from. Etymologies advanced by various writers somehow fail to carry conviction. Mr. J. A. Rogers, for example, writing on "Jazz at

Home" in that excellent anthology entitled *The New Negro* (edited very ably by Alain Locke), has this to offer:

"The origin of the present jazz craze is interesting. More cities claim its birthplace than claimed Homer dead. New Orleans, San Francisco, Memphis, Chicago, all assert the honor is theirs. Jazz, as it is to-day, seems to have come into being this way, however: W. C. Handy, a Negro, having digested the airs of the itinerant musicians referred to, evolved the first classic, 'Memphis Blues.' Then came Jasbo Brown, a reckless musician of a Negro cabaret in Chicago, who played this and other blues, blowing his own extravagant moods and risqué interpretations into them, while hilarious with gin. To give further meanings to his veiled allusions he would make the trombone 'talk' by putting a derby hat and later a tin can at its mouth. The delighted patrons would shout, 'More, Jasbo. More, Jas, more.' And so the name originated."

Paul Whiteman, with the aid of Mary Margaret McBride, in his chatty book, *Jazz*, has tried to add to the dictionary definition of the term. The definition quoted by him is, as he himself declares, "obviously uninspired." What are we to make, really, of jazz defined as "a form of syncopated music played in discordant tone on various instruments, as the banjo, saxophone, trombone, flageolet, drum and piano"? The word "discordant" smacks of Johnsonian rancor, and the appearance of the flageolet suggests a humorous anachronism. The question of origin is evaded. According to Sousa, the term jazz derives from a practice of the vaudeville stage, where, at the end, the entire bill of players joined in a grand *finale* called a "jazzbo." Whiteman refers also to the legend "that a particularly jazzy dark player, named James Brown and called 'Jas' from the abbreviation of his name, was the source of the peppy little word that has now gone all over the world."

Mr. Osgood, in *So This Is Jazz!* adds a number of competing etymologies. He reminds us that Lafcadio Hearn found the word jazz in the "creole patois and idiom of New Orleans (presumably in the late Seventies or early Eighties of the last century). He wrote that it had been taken by the creoles from the Negroes, that it meant to 'speed things up,' and that it was 'applied to music of a rudimentary syncopated type.' " Walter Kingsley, writing in the *New York Sun* in 1917, and quoted by the *Literary Digest*, August 25 of that year, listed such variant spellings as jas, jass, jaz, jazz, jasz and jascz. Kingsley referred the term to the plantation days, when the cry, "Jaz her up!" would be the cue for a general crescendo of the merriment. The usage found its way into vaudeville, where the advice from the wings to "put in jazz" means to pep up the performance. The name has been referred to a New Orleans band of the early 1900's—Razz's Band. But how did Razz become Jazz? Vincent Lopez, in the Jazz number of the *Etude* (summer, 1924), traced the word to Vicksburg, Mississippi, as a corruption of the name Charles. This Chaz, for short, was an illiterate drummer who, at the cry of "Now, Chaz!" from the leader, would make things lively at the end of the first chorus. The etymology reminds us of Jas. Brown. Jazz also had a very naughty meaning which is expressed by a word of four letters that does not appear in the dictionary. It is a derived meaning, however, and as such does not concern us. And, now, to wind up the discussion, let me suggest that the French word *jaser*, meaning to prattle, to blab, was undoubtedly much in use among the creoles. Could it have played any part in the etymological transformations of the word Jazz?

[270]

Jazz is chiefly a noun and a verb—a method, and a process—a spirit and a structure. It begins in darkest Africa as a rhythm; it ends in lightest America as an abandoned counterpoint. And beneath it all is a mode, so that Mr. Seldes may write against the existence of such a thing as jazz *music*, asserting that jazz is a *method of playing* music. That is at once too simple and too confusing. For our purpose we had better distinguish some five phases of jazz and proceed to analyze it on such a basis; we must bear in mind, however, that these are five phases of an organic unit that has been broken up arbitrarily for the sake of analysis. We shall consider jazz, then, succinctly as Rhythm, Harmony, Counterpoint, Color and Mood.

The Rhythm of Jazz.

When you whistle a jazz tune, you are more or less unconsciously carrying an accompaniment in your mind; when you used to whistle a ragtime tune, such a sense of the harmonic and rhythmic sub-structure was by no means so strong. "We learned syncopation," wrote Virgil Thomson in *The American Mercury* for August, 1924, "from three different teachers: the Indians, the Negroes and our neighbors in Mexico. It had become firmly established before the Civil War. It is the characteristic twist of nearly every familiar old tune. The dance craze of the last twenty-five years has simply exaggerated it. Because the way to make a strong pulse on 3 is by tying it to 2, thus,

♩ ♩♩ ♩ ♩ 𝅝

A silent accent is the strongest of all accents. It forces the body to replace it with a motion. But a syncopated tune is not jazz unless it is supported by a monotonous, accentless rhythm underneath. Alone it may confuse the listener. But with the rhythm definitely expressed, syncopation intensifies the anticipated beat into an imperative bodily motion. The shorter the anticipation the stronger the effect. The systematic striking of melodic notes an instant before the beat is the most powerful device of motor music yet discovered. But a fluent melody with a syncopated accompaniment is an inversion of the fundamental jazz process, and its effect is sedative."

Mr. Aaron Copland, in an article on "Jazz Structure and Influence," in *Modern Music* for January-February, 1927, carries Mr. Thomson's speculations a step further, incidentally making an even more concise distinction between ragtime and jazz. The reason why, when whistling a ragtime melody, we thought less of the bass part, may lie in the fact that the rhythmic foundation of ragtime—as Copland points out—was accentually regular. It was an *oom*-pah, *oom*-pah in quick tempo, with the accent on the first and third beat, just where you would expect it. Over this bass there was "invariably one of two rhythms, sometimes both: either the dotted eighth followed by a sixteenth:

or this most ordinary syncopation:

The former of these produced the characteristic ragtime jerk which is perhaps remembered from 'Everbody's Doin' It.' Ragtime is much inferior to jazz and musically uninteresting; it consists of old formulas familiar in the classics which were rediscovered one day and overworked."

The jazz that we know, it is now generally agreed, began with the fox trot. Copland was among the first to point out that with the coming of the fox trot, the regularly accented bass of ragtime underwent a most important alteration. Instead of *oom*-pah *oom*-pah, we got a slower tempo and an oom-*pah* oom-*pah*, with the accents on the second and fourth beats instead of the first and third. "With this," he goes on to indicate, "was combined another rhythmic element, sometimes in the melody but by no means always there, which is generally supposed to be a kind of 1–2–3–4 and is always written:

This notation, however, is deceptive, as Mr. Knowlton has pointed out." (The writer is referring to an article by Don Knowlton, in *Harper's* for April, 1926.) "His article reveals the practice followed by popular music publishers of writing extremely complex jazz compositions very simply so as to sell them more easily to the musically uneducated. He was the first to show that this jazz rhythm is in reality much subtler than its printed form and is properly expressed thus:

Therefore it contains no syncopation; it is instead a rhythm of four quarters split into eight eighths and is arranged thus: 1–2–3:

1–2–3–4–5, or even more precisely: 1–2–3: 1–2–3: 1–2. Put this over the four-quarter bass:

and you have the play of two independent rhythms within the space of one measure. It is the beginning, it is a molecule of jazz."

This is, however puzzling to the untrained jazz addict, of extreme importance. It means that we may have jazz without any syncopation; the divorce between ragtime and jazz is complete.

"Whatever melody is subjected to this procedure comes out jazzed," continues Copland. "This explains the widespread facile reincarnation of classic tunes as song and dance hits. It also explains Mr. Whiteman's remark: 'Jazz is not yet the thing said, it is the manner of saying it.'" Compare this quotation from Whiteman with what I quoted from Mr. Seldes some paragraphs back. It is Copland's further contention that jazz is not the melody, nor even a single well-pronounced rhythm, but the interplay of rhythms around, above and under the melody.

We are thus brought to what is called poly-rhythm, which might be called a counterpoint of rhythms: the simultaneous occurrence of well-differentiated patterns of accent. The thing itself is not quite so difficult as it sounds. To-day, even the casual listener is familiar with the simultaneous playing of two tunes, as, for common example, Dvořák's "Humoresque" and "Swanee River." The tunes happen to be in double time, so that there is no strong accentual differentiation. Imagine now two different *tempos* being played conjointly; triple time against double. Chopin, in his waltzes, obtains the effect by indicating a special accentuation of the melody as it proceeds against the 1–2–3 of the bass. In Sullivan's *The Gondoliers* occurs a pretty number in which the singer has a two-four melody against a waltz (three-four) accompaniment; the effect is that of a hidden lilt, caused by the impact of the triple-time against the double. Such jazz experts as Zez Confrey and George Gershwin—especially Gershwin, who has a vivid sense of contrasting rhythms—employ this device to lend a peculiar vitality to the jazz measure. Though their pieces, as written, seem to be in simple time, they conceal—and a good jazz player brings out—interesting samples of rhythmic counterpoint, of polyrhythm. Zez Confrey, in such pieces as "Stumbling" and "Kitten on the Keys," offers excellent illustrations of what is virtually a triple rhythm in the right hand against a double in the left: 3–4 against 4–4. You will note that in setting the words of the first of these, the composer has, three times in succession, set the same syllable—*stumbling*—to the same note (the fifth of the scale). This emphasis further helps to accentuate the melody at precisely that point which brings out its true triple character. If you will examine, or listen closely to, "Kitten on the Keys," you will notice that the right-hand part, at the beginning, does this same thing: it repeats, three times, the sixth note of the scale on which the piece opens, at just the point where the triple character of the melody will be accentuated.

Copland, in the same article to which I have referred, shows how Gershwin, taking a cue from Confrey's "Stumbling," adapted it to more complicated procedure. Gershwin's "Fascinating Rhythm" (from the musical comedy, *Lady Be Good*) has a melody that against the regular four-four bass, consists virtually of a 4–4 bar followed by a 3–4 bar, which in turn is followed by another 4–4 bar, a 2–4 bar and a 3–4 bar. This helps explain why the average mediocre pianist of the family parlor, having purchased the piano sheet after hearing the number on the stage, wonders what has become of that "fascinating rhythm" in the title. In "Clap Yo' Hands," one of the hits of Gershwin's *Oh, Kay!* the young composer has advanced another step in poly-rhythm. Instead of adhering to the pattern of an undifferentiated 4–4 bass against subtle triple time in the melody, he indulges—at the words "Hallelujah, Hallelujah," of the chorus—in two measures that are frankly 3–4 in both melody and bass. Though these are not printed as 3–4, the harmonies and the bass notes clearly indicate the intention of the composer.

"But the poly-rhythms of jazz are different in quality and effect not only from those of the madrigals but from all others as well. The peculiar excitement they produce by clashing two definitely and regularly marked rhythms is unprecedented in occidental music. Its poly-rhythm is the real contribution of jazz."

The "Blue" Harmony.

We have gone, then, a long way from a definition of jazz as a spirit rather than as a structure. Copland's article, in fact, seems to have been born of opposition to the statement, in Henry O. Osgood's book, *So This Is Jazz,* that "it is the spirit of the music, not the mechanics of its frame . . . that determines whether or not it is jazz." But if jazz is not all spirit, neither is it all rhythm. It has, as we have hinted, among other things, its harmonic connotations. It is all very well to apply to classical music the jazz formula, according to Copland's prescription, and to contemplate the jazzed product. Yet the very presence of the orthodox harmonies and progressions leaves something to be desired; the result may be something that the jazz addict can dance to with satisfaction to his motor centers, but a foreign flavor will cling none the less to the music. Jazz without its "blue" notes is a sort of denatured article.

The "blues" arose "probably within the last quarter-century, among illiterates and more or less despised classes of Southern Negroes: barroom pianists, careless nomadic laborers, watchers of incoming trains and steamboats, street-corner guitar players, strumpets and outcasts. A spiritual is a matter for choral treatment; a blues was a one-man affair, originating typically as the expression of the singer's feelings, and complete in a single verse. It might start as little more than an interjection, a single line: sung, because singing was as natural a method as speaking. But while the idea might be developed, if at all, in any one of many forms of songs, there was one which, perhaps through its very simplicity and suitability for improvisation, became very popular: the line would be sung, repeated, repeated once again; with the second repetition some inner voice would say 'Enough,' and there would have come into being a crude blues." [4]

Three lines consisting of nothing but a triplication are monotonous; unconsciously, almost, variations would creep in. The best

[4] Abbe Niles, in the anthology, *Blues*, by W. C. Handy. See Pp. 1-2.

form would be a first line repeated with a slight variation, followed by a new third line. A good example is the following:

> If I had wings, like Nora's (i.e., Noah's) faithful dove—
> Had *strong* wings, like Nora's faithful dove,
> I would fly away to the man I love.

"The blues" is, of course, an excellent colloquial term signifying depression; it is a shortened form of "blue devils"—what has become known in the later years as "the glooms." The Negro "blues" consists usually of a pure grievance, a grievance and its reason, or of a cause of depression and a plan of escape:

> Gwine to de river, take a rope an' a rock,
> Gwine to de river, take a rope an' a rock,
> Gwine to tie rope roun' my neck and jump right over de dock.

> Oh, de Mississippi River is so deep an' wide,
> Oh, de Mississippi River is so deep an' wide,
> An' my gal lives on de odder side.

There is a question whether the three-line verse is responsible for the twelve-bar melody of the typical "blues," or vice versa. In any case, that melody is twelve bars long instead of the usual eight or sixteen. As these lines are sung, there is often a long pause after the first one. The natural impulse is to fill up the wait between the first line and the second. As Niles points out, this is doubly important; it allows the singer time to improvise his following line, and it gives him a sort of free space in which to let his voice or instrument wander in by-paths. This is the reason for such interpolations as "Oh, Lawdy!" and the familiar repetitions that are introduced by some such phrase as "I said." It is to this feature of the typical "blues" that we have traced the jazz "break" —an improvisation of a single instrument or of the entire band that bridges the distance between one melodic line and the next.

The original blues did not require the complex harmony that is characteristic of jazz to-day. The humble negro composer—the tunes were not written down, nor were they ordinarily sung in parts, as are the spirituals—had a very limited scheme of chords. These were the chords based on the first note of the scale, on the fourth, and on the fifth with seventh added; in harmony they are called, respectively, the common chord, the chord of the subdominant, and the chord of the dominant seventh:

Common Chord   *Chord of the*   *Chord of*
                   Subdominant   *Dominant*
                                           Seventh

Such a harmonic basis is by no means peculiar to the Negro; it may be employed with hundreds of popular tunes, especially dance tunes. The characteristic harmony of the "blues" occurs when a seventh is added to the subdominant chord, and *flatted*; thus:

What is the origin of this flatted seventh on the subdominant chord, or, as it is called, this "blue" note? Niles' explanation is as good as any yet adduced. In the typical blues melody, the most favored note was the tonic—that is, the first note of the scale. This was natural, as each line was almost independent of the others, comprising a complete melodic unit in itself and therefore resting chiefly on the tonic (*do*). The note next favored in melodies was the third of the scale (*mi*). This was "a fact of the first importance to the blues because of the tendency of the untrained Negro voice when singing the latter tone at an important point, to *worry* it, slurring or wavering between flat and natural. Even in singing to the banjo—a cheerful instrument—the slur might be expected; if to the guitar (the strings of which are normally so arranged as to invite the use of minor chords), it might even be more prominent and would actually be duplicated on the instrument. The explanation of this peculiarity would seem to be furnished by the characteristic fondness for the flatted *seventh*—and a feeling for the key of the subdominant; of which the tonic third itself *is* the seventh. Reaching for the favorite tonic third, perhaps the Afro-American feels it as such *and* as the seventh of the subdominant, resulting in the flatting, slurring or wavering effect which has been mentioned. . . . But to the white listener, thinking in terms of a single scale, this change of key might not be apparent; instead, in view of the importance of the tonic third as an index to mode, the melody, if sung unaccompanied, might seem difficult to classify as either major or minor."

Let us elucidate this by means of a few simple illustrations.

First, we have a scale with a flatted third: (starting on the tonic)

Second, a scale on the subdominant of the same key (that is, on the fourth note as *do*), with a flatted seventh:

Notice that the flatted seventh of the subdominant scale is the same note (in this case an octave higher) as the flatted third of the tonic scale; hence the uncertainty of key.

The chord I just wrote down (that of the subdominant with seventh added), tells the same story in a different way. Write the selfsame chord with two different key signatures and its ambiguous nature at once appears; this is characteristic of chords of the seventh, and explains their value as bridges from one key to another:

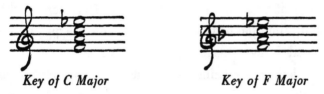

Key of C Major   *Key of F Major*

In the chord written as in the key of C, E flat is the minor third; in the chord written as in the key of F, E flat is the minor seventh.

Jazz made familiar the daring conclusion of a piece on a seventh chord. For such an ending listen to the Whiteman recording of Berlin's "Everybody Step." (This record is excellent for a number of jazz illustrations, particularly cross rhythms, tone color and spirit). I transcribe from Niles two characteristic jazz cadences, the first showing the flatted third, the second the flatted seventh:

Later developments include endings on a diminished seventh, and even on the chord of the ninth. The true significance of this is that we may be losing, in part at least, our sense of classical mode; our minors and majors become ambiguous; our tonics and octaves lose their predominance as notes on which to begin and end tunes; the chord of the tonic, especially, no longer holds undisputed position as the end of the piece. Dissonance, which has crept boldly into the body of our music, now usurps the one place that seemed forever secure against it. We no longer possess the sense of distinct beginnings and ends. Just as our dramas have assumed the right to leave problems and situations dangling in the air, unresolved, so our music—thus symbolizing the life about it—comes to an indeterminate conclusion upon unresolved dissonances.

In the late sixteenth century Monteverde sealed the triumph of the harmonic system over the polyphony of Palestrina. His introduction of what are called in harmony "unprepared dissonances" —such as chords of the seventh and the ninth—involved him in a round of controversies. What would Signor Monteverde say to-day could he hear his beloved chords of the seventh and ninth not only as unprepared dissonances but as final chords?

KING JAZZ

Jazz Counterpoint: Arrangement or Derangement?

Jazz as counterpoint we may dismiss with a few remarks, since the essence of what there is to be said has already been hinted at in the preceding pages. The very first jazz arrangements were not written down; often the musicians could not read notes. They "jazzed" their tunes by running musically amok, thus producing a counterpoint that was certainly not strict, and even freer than free; it was accidental. Mr. Newman has pointed out that this was precisely the procedure among the Englishmen of the fourteenth century. "In that epoch men were just beginning to realize dimly what a jolly effect could be made by a number of people singing different things at the same time. As yet they did not know how to combine different melodic strands, so they indulged experimentally in a sort of catch-as-catch-can descant. . . . The singers —amateurs, like the early jazzers—used to decide upon a given *canto fermo,* and then all improvise upon it simultaneously. Writers of the period have told us of the horrible results." Yet, historically, the results were anything but horrible. Those of you who have had the opportunity to listen to the English Singers during their recent tours of the United States, will have heard English polyphony at its best in the vocal works of Byrd, Gibbons, Tallis and other great composers of the Elizabethan and post-Elizabethan age.

We have, then, what I like to call counterpoint of rhythm, counterpoint of paired melodies, and, last of all—perhaps, so far as concerns results, least of all—the ordinary counterpoint specially invented to go with the main theme in hand. The importance of this counterpoint of rhythm lies in its compound character. A single rhythm in the melody could establish the character of rag-

[283]

time; for genuine jazz there must be an interplay, a contrast of rhythms. Ragtime is a monotonous type of syncopation; jazz, at its best, is an exciting blend of independent rhythms.

Counterpoint of paired melodies (sometimes more than two melodies are thus joined) is a less spontaneous procedure, since the added melodies have not been invented by the composer, but discovered in the work of others as an accidentally suitable counterpoint to the main theme. The jazz records made by the Whiteman band for dancing are full of such contrapuntal devices; it is surprising how well a number of tunes independently composed will blend in a polyphonic scheme. Sometimes the writer will take a well-known tune and jazz it up with his own counterpoint—a counterpoint that, when sung independently, is interesting jazz on its own account. The first example that occurs to me is Kern's "Blue Danube Blues," an excellent treatment that owes its origin, undoubtedly, to the occurrence of Blue in the title of the original waltz. Against the smoothly flowing strains of the waltz, which is changed to double rhythm, Kern sets a crackling, lilting melody, and the contrast of rhythms creates a new vitality that cannot possibly be present when either tune is sung or played by itself. Kern provides another example of the same process with his "Left All Alone Again Blues," in which the contrasting tune is the familiar Scotch song, "The Blue Bells of Scotland." The counterpoint, if I may say so, is here also one of ideas, for the Scotch song, like the blues of which it forms a counterpoint, concerns a missing laddie. The tunes thus contrasted are a striking illustration of a difference in epoch and national character.

Counterpoint of such melodies adds piquancy to jazz, but I do not consider it half so necessary to jazz as is counterpoint of rhythms. Such counterpoint, too, is second cousin to the "jazzing up" of the classics, which is a process that I cannot regard with the equanimity of Mr. Osgood or Mr. Whiteman. The jazzing of the classics emphasizes the essentially rhythmic nature of jazz, since it represents the application of a rhythmic formula. What emerges from the operation has rarely been to me other than an object of mild disgust. When Mr. Newman inveighs against the jazzification of Chopin and, in his righteous wrath cries "Paws Off!" I am with him to the last note. And when Mr. Osgood attempts to palliate Harry Carroll's steal from Chopin's "Fantasie-Impromptu" for the refrain of "I'm Always Chasing Rainbows," I turn positively old-fogyish. "And thus the multitude," argues Osgood, "came to know that Chopin, instead of being a classicist to be shied at, wrote catchy, whistly tunes; that he was one who might be investigated without fear of *ennui* the next time a recital-playing pianist came along."

One is tempted to profanity. To perdition with a multitude that is in danger of being bored by Chopin unadulterated. Take all the poetry out of *Hamlet* and serve it up as a cheap melodrama, and then congratulate yourself on having brought Shakespeare to the "peepul." When Carroll took the Chopin melody—and his name merely symbolizes all the other popular composers who are guilty of similar practice—he denatured it. He deprived it of its accompaniment, thus at once altering its mood; he wrenched it from its context; in a single strong word, he fouled it. When Osgood, in extenuation of such practices, argues that the old masters borrowed tunes and wrote variations upon them (Mozart from Duport, Brahms from Haydn, and so on), he is guilty of jazzing logic.

And when he writes a line further, "What was it these masters did to the tunes they borrowed? Jazzed them—nothing else," I shout "No!" through a megaphone. Such a statement is musically false and thoroughly misleading. It is a concession to popular ignorance and indifference. The borrowings of Mozart, Brahms and their compeers were made primarily to serve as the basis for an exercise in creative skill. They worked from simplicity to complexity, whereas jazz works from complexity to simplicity and even to naïveté. They sought to ennoble the borrowed material by lavishing upon it every resource of composition at their command. Jazz borrows the classics to degrade them from the level of the head to that of the feet. Liszt and Brahms took the Hungarian dances from their native surroundings and brought them to the concert hall. Jazz takes the classics from the concert hall and dances all over them on the ball-room floor. The process of the theme and variations, considered in relation to the jazzing of the classics, provides not a comparison but a clear antithesis.

What confuses Mr. Osgood and those who think as he does, is the determination to regard jazz not as a technique but as a spirit. But even regarding jazz as a spirit, it is wrong to affirm that the masters jazzed their borrowed material. When Rimsky-Korsakoff borrows the theme of a Russian dance, he creates something new, something higher than the original. When the jazz orchestra jazzes up Rimsky-Korsakoff's "Scheherazade" it destroys the beauty of what it borrows and produces only a cheap, monotonous, esthetically degraded hodge-podge. Is this to refute the claims of jazz? No. It is to point out that jazz, in such excursions as these, wanders far afield. And so doing, it leaves upon the fresh green pastures the malodorous evidence of passing cattle.

KING JAZZ

Free counterpoint, in jazz, is a matter chiefly of the clever arrangers. Much skill has gone into jazz arrangements, and the better bands have one or more men on the staff whose sole duty it is to invent new schemes of color and counterpoint. I daresay this is the phase of the work that is least appreciated by the typical jazzhound. It has its effect upon him, no doubt; it makes the music more danceable, more interesting, and lends glamor to the tune. That is all as it should be. This aspect of jazz, to me, is far more interesting than the clever carpentry of blending preëxisting melodies into a musical mosaic. It is a challenge to the inventiveness of the composer, and, by that same token, to the musical intelligence of the listener. For this reason, many have considered jazz to be first of all a style of instrumental coloration.

The Jazz Band: Color.

The special "color" of jazz comes from its preëminent use of the saxophone, an instrument that is so many years older than the boys who blow it so lustily. But not from the saxophone alone. The new fluency of this instrument is contrasted with the plank-plank of the banjo, while the piano provides for the various other elements—the demoted fiddle, the antic clarinet, the tricky trumpet, the suave trombone—a rhythmic and harmonic background. According to Mr. Osgood, the banjo preceded the saxophone as a feature of the jazz combination, and entered the new field in 1909, in San Francisco, as a means of putting life into the Texas Tommy, the dance of that year. Herman Heller was then the leader of the orchestra at the St. Francis Hotel of the Golden Gate City, and added two banjos to his assemblage. To

San Francisco, too, belongs the honor of having introduced the saxophone into popular orchestras; and it was likewise in the St. Francis Hotel, in 1914, with Art Hickman this time in charge of the players. Under Hickman was formed what Osgood calls the first complete modern jazz combination; two saxophones, cornet, trombone, violin, banjo, piano and drums. Thus, seventy-four years after its invention by Antoine Joseph Saxe, the instrument, having been experimented with by operatic and symphonic composers, found its true home and helped to initiate a minor revolution in orchestration.

It begins to appear, however, that the jazz band is, even in its contemporary make-up, much older than Hickman's group of the Golden Gate. We have already mentioned the "Memphis Students" who played at Proctor's in 1905; they had the banjos, saxophones, mandolins, guitars and singers; they had, in Buddy Gilmore, the poly-executive battery. One of their members was Jim Europe, who in 1910 organized his Clef Club on West Fifty-third Street and syndicated band-groups. As early as May of 1912 the Clef Club gave a concert in Carnegie Hall—a dozen years before the epochal concert by Whiteman. There were strings in the orchestra, but the group was truly a jazz group, with its mandolins, guitars and banjos, its saxophones and drums. Behind the bandsmen were ranged ten upright pianos; the players, in all, numbered one hundred and twenty-five, and some of them doubled in voice.[5]

The rest of Jim Europe is too brief history. He helped to bring fame and fortune to the Castles; he organized the band of the

[5] See, for these and other pertinent data, James Weldon Johnson's *Black Manhattan*, pp. 120-125.

crack Fifteenth New York (Negro) regiment, and returned un-
scathed from the war to be shot during his engagement at a Boston
theater.

The saxophone is a sort of instrumental paradox. It is a reed
instrument but, unlike the other reeds, is constructed of brass, not
wood. Moreover, as Osgood says, it is "practically both string
band and wood wind for the modern jazz orchestra,"—that is, it
replaces the violins, violas and 'cellos and does much that otherwise would go to the oboes and bassoons. There can be no doubt
that jazz "made" the saxophone, just as, for dance hall purposes,
it "unmade" the violin. In the jazz orchestra the fiddle either
doubles the melody with some other more prominent instrument,
or it provides contrapuntal filigree, usually on the E string. Here
it is no longer the combined prima donna and leading man that
it is in the symphony orchestra. That place has been usurped by
the saxophone. As a result, the saxophone player has developed
a remarkable technique; indeed, the jazz combination has been responsible for a rise of virtuosity that would, a few decades back,
have been deemed impossible. The brass section in an orchestra
like Paul Whiteman's can do things in solo or in combination that
would try the best skill of our leading symphony men. The trombone player, whom in childhood we knew as merely the blower
of sporadic bass notes, now sings melodies of his own with the
legato of a 'cello; he plays rapid passages with an uncanny con-
ciseness; he laughs, coos, glides indecently, blares majestically, at
the will of his master. The trumpet, which has ousted the less
esthetic cornet, is equally versatile. He climbs dangerous heights
until his tones thin down to an E string delicacy; he trills, slides,
cavorts during the "breaks," works wonders with the various types

of jazz mute, until the old-time cornet fails to recognize this rich relative. Verily, in more ways than one, jazz is the régime of brass.

At first, the jazz band was a crude nuisance, with the emphasis on noise. The evolution from Ted Lewis's raucous aggregation to the blandness of Lopez and the insinuations of Whiteman is one from racket to rhapsody. "Hot" jazz cools to "sweet" jazz, as the various types are tried out and the instrumental combinations are experimentally altered. Whiteman's concert orchestra has the instruments from the violin family, showing a strong tendency to reinstate the fiddle. There must be relief, after all, from brassy blowing, and it is an artistic instinct that prompts the restoration of the strings.

Jazz has, nevertheless, introduced new "colors" into music. If it has demoted the violin and the strings in general, it has actually created a new technique for the brass and, incidentally, for the piano. In so far as it has acclimated the "blue" note in music for the piano, it has added a color to the palette of that instrument. Jazz color, however, is chiefly an orchestral achievement. It is best applied to primal jazz material, where it belongs. When it is smeared over the classics, it loses its own native hue and soils what it touches. Symphonic composers have not been slow to take hints from the jazz orchestra and its home-grown virtuosity. Jazz color is an element, not an entirety. In certain types of composition it may have a logical place, but it is just as malapropos in other types. Academic composers and musicians who wish to toy with a genre that is not native to them, produce a kind of jazz music that reminds me of nothing so much as of a nice, decent white lady in her parlor trying to sing a hot jazz number that literally cries for a wild black mamma. That hypothetical white lady, in more senses than one, is simply "off color."

Residue.

Jazz as spirit is more than it seems. It is not simply "high spirits," for that we have always had with us. Nor is it intellectual playing with thematic material, in the manner that Osgood ascribed to Brahms, Mozart, Beethoven *et al.* Whiteman, in his book on *Jazz*, takes a flying leap into social psychology and returns with something that is well worth considering.

"Jazz," says Whiteman, "is not in the 'tradition' of music, according to the old sense, but is not the real tradition of music one of constant change and new developments? Jazz is the spirit of a new country. It catches up the underlying motif of a continent and period, molding it into a form which expresses the fundamental emotion of the people, the place and time so authentically that it is immediately recognizable.

"At the same time it evolves new forms, new colors, new technical methods, just as America constantly throws aside old machines for newer and more efficient ones.

"*I think it is a mistake to call jazz cheerful. The optimism of jazz is the optimism of the pessimist who says, 'Let us eat, drink and be merry, for to-morrow we die.'*

"*This cheerfulness of despair is deep in America. Our country is not the childishly jubilant nation that some people like to think it. Behind the rush of achievement is a restlessness of dissatisfaction, a vague nostalgia and yearning for something indefinable, beyond our grasp. . . . That is the thing expressed by that wail, that longing, that pain, behind all the surface clamor and rhythm and energy of jazz. The critics may call it Oriental, call it Russian, call it anything they like. It is an expression of the soul of America and America recognizes it.*"

I italicize these words because I think they express authoritatively one of the essential aspects of the so-called jazz spirit. Whiteman knows the jazz audience, listeners and dancers, as well as any man in the world, and his sensitive ear has caught the overtones that most of the jazz philosophers have missed. The race that gave us the spirituals and the blues is not a happy race, and we who have adopted and transformed these gifts have more or less unconsciously tried to drown our sorrows in the stream of rhythm and melody. Niles calls attention to an important difference between the white blues and the original. In the original, the gayety of the words is feigned; the "blues" are fundamentally sad. In the white "blues," it is the sadness that is feigned; the white "blues" are fundamentally gay. This does not invalidate the argument that they are an attempt on the part of the whites to banish worry. It helps to show, however, that what was with the Negro a conscious aim has become with the white a more or less unconscious symptom.

There is, undoubtedly, in much jazz a strain of hysteria. The rising frenzy of the Negro's "ring shout" and the voluptuous ecstasies of the jazz ball are sisters under the skin. The one accentuates the religious appeal; the other the sexual. As I showed in the beginning of these pages, our latter-day cult of the Negro has a distinct relationship to the freer sexuality of the age. The Negro is more primitive than the white; he is therefore more frankly sexual (and I imply no derogation by that remark); he is more "vital." He symbolizes, he incarnates, as I have already said, that sexual freedom and potency toward which white America is groping. The spiritual is religious; the blues are secular, and, as their words readily prove, sexual. Jazz, then, has a decidedly sexual significance. We touch now the root of the antagonism to it. That antagonism, that dour, symptomatic aversion, was largely non-musical, non-esthetic at bottom. It was the evidence of a caste, and, as we now see, a purity complex. For jazz is the sexual symbol of an inferior race.[6]

Is it merely fanciful if I find, in these selfsame observations, the reason why the Jewish composers of America have been so important in the development of jazz? Read such a novel as Carl Van Vechten's *Nigger Heaven*, and you may be struck, time and again, by certain traits of character that are quite as Jewish as they are Negro; more, the prejudices which the Harlem intellectual has to contend with have their counterpart in Jewish-American life. The Jew, racially, is also an Oriental and was originally much darker than he is to-day. He has the sad, the hysterical psychology of the oppressed race. From the cantor grandfather to the grandson who yearns "mammy" songs is no vaster a stride than from the Negro spiritual to the white "blues." The minor-major, what

[6] James E. Richardson, in an article called "Blame It on Jazz," in *The Dance* for March, 1927, discusses jazz also in terms of sex. Jazz, he writes, "is the music of adolescence, when the life of childhood begins to be colored by the obsession of sex, and where self-consciousness strives to cover up, by horse-play, the real nature of the emotions so disturbing the pleasant tenor of existence." This is a pertinent observation; all dance, of course, is to be explained upon the grounds of sex; in jazz it is the horse-play element that reveals the nature of the concealed or unconscious embarrassment. In connecting the jazz movement with the Negro's more primitive sexuality I broaden such a concept as Mr. Richardson's into its sociological counterpart. Jazz, thus considered, is the impact of an adolescent race against the adult repression of the whites.

we might call amphibious, mode of the typical blues, with its blue notes, is by no means a stranger to the Jewish ear. The ecstatic songs of the Khassidim—the pietist sect of the Polish Jews—bear striking psychological analogies to the sacred and secular tunes of the Negro. I have heard Jimmy Johnson imitate a singing colored preacher, and the cantillation could have passed—almost —for the roulades of a Jewish precentor. The simple fact is that the Jew responds naturally to the deeper implications of jazz, and that as a Jewish-American he partakes of the impulse at both its Oriental and its Occidental end. The Khassid, too, walks all over God's heaven.

Perhaps the jazz spirit is all that will remain after its limited contributions to rhythm, harmony, counterpoint and orchestration have been assimilated into the universal musical idiom. If jazz is, as some assert, primarily rhythm, then it is no more a type of music than, let us say, is the tango rhythm, or that of the polka, the mazurka, the gavotte. So, too, if jazz is chiefly a harmony (the "blue" chord), it is no more in itself music than is the Neapolitan sixth or any other chord. To counterpoint jazz has contributed a certain nonchalance that is more striking than impressive; it has made free with manners rather than with matter. To instrumental color it has added a few touches that it owes to the skill and cleverness of such arrangers as Ferdie Grofé. All of this, until very recently, has been conditioned by the fact that jazz, first of all, is music for the dance hall and ballroom. Whatever progress jazz is to make will be made largely away from its present dance hall and revue environment. Gershwin effects his escape through the *Rhapsody in Blue*, the *Concerto in F*, the *Jazz Preludes*, *An American in Paris*. The very names—Rhapsody, Concerto,

[294]

Prelude—indicate a glance upward into the realms of standard classical music.

Is jazz a technique or a mood? Is it a body or a spirit? Let us not make theology out of musical theory. Spirit cannot exist without body, and technique is an organic aspect of artistic mood. Style and substance, to repeat an esthetic platitude, are two phases of something that is an indivisible essence. Jazz, taking it for whatever it is worth, is both a technique and a mood, both a body and a spirit. You cannot, for example, subject a classical strain to the rhythmic treatment of the jazz formula without altering the mood of that strain. Reverse the process and the same holds true.

I return, then, to the proposition with which I opened this section. Though, for the sake of analysis, we consider jazz under a number of different headings, the subdivisions represent an arbitrary dissection of something that lives—when it does live—as a throbbing whole. That, eventually, jazz may disappear with the particular phase of civilization which gave birth to it, in no way invalidates its claims to recognition as a symptom of its age. That it is, on the whole, thus far a superficial product of a superficial life, does not argue against its inherent possibilities as true music. The symphonic scherzo derives from a dance-spirit that is not too far removed in origin from the spirit of jazz. The symphony as a whole has its origin in a suite of contrasted dances.

What began as Afro-American folksong became transformed into cosmopolitan culture. The commercialism of Gotham quickly denatured the article for white consumption; something of its primitivity was lost at once in the journey northward. The world seized upon it as a novelty, and, partly, as a more or less unconscious means of drowning out the madness of the war. It is, however, America's contribution to music, as Poe was one of our contributions to poetry; and in each case we began to think seriously of the gift only after it had won a measure of European imitation and approval.

Well, what is left of jazz after the fireworks have been set off? Mr. Copland, in the article from which I have quoted at the beginning of these speculations, took leave of his reader with a general statement that is even more valuable as personal illumination. Jazz may be passé in Europe, he said, but not in America. "Since jazz is not exotic here but indigenous, since it is the music an American has heard as a child, it will be traceable more and more frequently in his symphonies and concertos. Possibly the chief influence of jazz will be shown in the development of poly-rhythm. This startling new synthesis has provided the American composer with an instrument he could appreciate and utilize. It should stir his imagination; he should see it freed of its present connotations. It may be the substance not only of his fox trots and Charlestons but of his lullabies and nocturnes. He may express through it not always gayety but love, tragedy and remorse."

"Freed of its present connotations." There sounds the death-knell of jazz as its addicts know it and the fanfare of its entrance into the domain of true music.

The king is dead; long live the king!

11. Bye, Bye, Theme Song

THE motion picture had made its début in leading vaudeville houses—Keith's, Proctor's, Koster and Bial's—as early as 1896. No one, however, dreamed of its vast commercial and artistic potentialities. In the theaters, indeed, it became a "supper-chaser"— a means of clearing out the audience to make room for a fresh supply of patronage. It was used to attract the curious to department store exhibits; I recall one such exhibition in Boston that gave what pretended to be scenes from the Spanish-American war. The film was employed, likewise, for out-door advertising, at night. Upon a screen erected over a roof, or swung across the façade of a low building, were thrown, in alternation, stereopticon slides advertising various products, and brief movies of the prehistoric era: there was always a fire-engine scene, or a locomotive, or May Irwin doing her famous kiss.

The motion picture, then, in its earliest phase, was a curio. Not until 1910 would it begin to come into its own. From the beginning it was associated with music and with crude attempts to add acoustic realism. Was there a chase—and when, in the first cinema tales, was there not a chase? Then the pianist would rattle off a few bars of tremolo-staccato-agitato. A boat-ride 'neath arched bridges along a placid stream? Then a stereotyped waltz, out of a book that contained a long series of codified snatches of tune to accompany fires, races, duels, murders, robberies, and all the other stenciled minutiæ of movie life.

When the movies embarked upon a program of serials, it was natural for song-writers to seek a sales tie-up with the pictures. Thus were born such unremembered hits of their day as "Oh, Oh, Those Charlie Chaplin Feet," and "Poor Pauline." These were, in effect, *ex-post-facto* theme songs. Larger houses, on their own initiative, and in coöperation with the cinema producers, would plan a specially synchronized score to accompany the pictures. When the talkies came, such a synchronization was among the first devices to suggest itself. The movie, without the accompaniment of music, from the start was felt to be an anomaly. It is not at all improbable that the music fulfilled for the spectator an unconscious desire for sound. To behold creatures moving, even in semblance, amidst absolute silence was unnatural. Even our tight-rope walkers and jugglers on the stage must perform to the unifying influence of sympathetic or interpretative strains.

The theme-song, then, was inherent in the very technique of movie entertainment. We had it before the talkies. The first of the species to be made widely popular by association with the silent cinema was "Mickey," by Harry Williams (words) and Neil Moret. Under these circumstances Broadway and Hollywood could labor three thousand miles apart. Songs were written around plays in much the same way that Charles K. Harris, in the Nineties, had sought to build his hits around dramatic stories or situations.

Came then a new dawn . . . With sound effects.

The first Vitaphone program was presented to Broadway at the Warner Theatre on August 6, 1926. The program, however deficient it may have been from the technical and the esthetic standpoints, deserves to be recorded as a historic moment in the chronicle of universal entertainment.

Warner Bros. Pictures, Inc.
and
The Vitaphone Corporation
By Arrangement with
Western Electric Company
and
Bell Telephone Laboratories
PRESENT
VITAPHONE
with
JOHN BARRYMORE
in "DON JUAN"

VITAPHONE PRELUDE

Hon. Will H. Hays
President of Motion Picture Producers and Distributors of America welcomes
VITAPHONE.

The New York Philharmonic Orchestra
Henry Hadley, conducting; "Tannhauser," overture, Wagner.

Marion Talley
By arrangement with the Metropolitan Opera Company,
Caro Nome from "Rigoletto."
Efrem Zimbalist and Harold Bauer
Variations from "Kreutzer Sonata," Beethoven.
Roy Smeck in "His Pastimes"
Anna Case "La Fiesta,"
Supported by the Casinos and Metropolitan Opera chorus.
Accompanied by the Vitaphone Symphony Orchestra. Herman Heller conducting

Mischa Elman
Josef Bonime, accompanist; "Humoresque," Dvorak

Giovanni Martinelli
By arrangement with the Metropolitan Opera Company.
VESTI LA GIUBBA, from "I Pagliacci," Leoncavallo.
Accompanied by the New York Philharmonic Orchestra.
Incidental music to the above numbers played by members of the New York
Philharmonic Orchestra, **Herman Heller** Conducting.

JOHN BARRYMORE in "DON JUAN"
Screen story by **Bess Meredyth**
Directed by **ALAN CROSLAND**
Musical score by **Major Edward Bowes, David Mendoza** and **Dr. William Axt.**
Played on the VITAPHONE by the New York Philharmonic Orchestra
Entire Program Arranged by S. L. Warner

GENERAL PRESS REPRESENTATIVE: A. P. WAXMAN

It was a gala occasion, and Mr. Hays set the pace with a peroration that oozed sanctity and service. There was, for many in the audience, a momentary thrill that exploded into nervous tremors. It seemed, crude as it was, uncanny. Just as the early spectators of the moving-picture ducked back in their front seats when the scene showed the spraying surf at Coney Island, so the more ingenuous of the vitaphone audiences succumbed to the spookiness of the atmosphere. They would live to learn . . . even to protest ungratefully at the ill-controlled blast of sound that poured from the horns behind the screen, at the imperfect synchronization of sight and speech. Here, however, at last, was the commercially viable wedding of the screen to the phonograph. The cinema had acquired a new sense. . . .

Milady Talks.

The Screen had discovered that she had a voice, and it was music to her ears. True, she had been worshipped for her beauty, but it had been too silent a worship. Her face had been her fortune. Now she could speak. There was a revolution in Follywood; these walking dolls, overnight, must be turned into talking dolls. The voice at first was a raucous voice; she opened her lips and toads leaped forth. She cleared her throat. No; this wouldn't do. She would have to take singing lessons. And her ardent suitors— the public—would have to bear with her through the first disillusioning vocalises. The elementary ability to speak became suddenly a crowning virtue. Hear your favorite screen star talk! Hear your hitherto silent siren sing! Hollywood had found a new toy— and a new necessity.

BYE, BYE, THEME SONG

Hollywood, for a moment, was at a loss. Its entire technique had been built upon noise in the studios and on location, but silence in the projecting room and the vast auditoriums of the nation. Now the costly structure must virtually be scrapped, turned on its head. Silence in the studio and on the location; sound in the projecting room and the auditorium. No more Napoleonic directors megaphoning orders in the speech of Stentor. No more wide open spaces to reverberate to the great Voice. Faces and figures would no longer be enough.

The acoustical experimenting began; it has not yet completed its course. Sound photography brought in with it an array of technicians, who brought in turn a stern revaluation of movie values. Voices, voices, voices are what we need! You're beautiful, yes; but you're dumb! Old stars sank below the horizon; new stars appeared.

In the audiences, heads wagged sadly. We don't know how we miss them till they're gone. The silent cinema receded into history, gone but not forgotten. An art-form of brilliant promise had been slain in youth. The talkies—the squawkies? It was a screaming misalliance, and there were angry tears at the wedding. And what strange hybrids were the first offspring! Goat-glands, or pictures that had been in process when sound burst upon the silence of the screen; to give them a semblance of contemporaneousness, sound sequences were interpolated, so that at one moment Lady Screen would be inarticulate, and again she would startlingly acquire a voice, only to lose it before the picture was half over. Pictures synchronized with music and sound effects. Pictures half sound, half silence. And finally, in triumphant redundancy, the 100% All-Talkie picture.

Sound . . . It was, to Hollywood, a new dimension. Eyes had they, and had seen. Ears had they, and had heard nothing. Noises, words, music!

There had been music in the Celluloid City. Hadn't the directors employed it to enable their actors and actresses to "emote" properly amid the glare of the Kleig lights? Hadn't the cinema score, in the hands of such competent musicians as Deems Taylor and Victor Herbert, been invented to be synchronized by the orchestra of living players in the pit? Synchronized musical accompaniments had been the normal development away from expensive flesh and blood to money-saving wax and film-tracks.

The new Sound was something else again. It required to be incorporated into the action. The geniuses of the celluloid film were floundering in a sea of sound waves. They let up a lusty cry for help, and it was so loud that it was heard across the continent, on Broadway.

Go West, young song, go West. Do a Horace Greeley, young singer, go West. There's gold in them thar hills. Tin Pan Alley heard the call. California, here we come. The gold rush of '49 . . . and now the gold rush of 1929. The transcontinental trek began . . . No covered wagons, but Pullmans conveyed these conquistadores of song, these vikings of doggerel. When at long last, they landed, they were hailed by the reigning powers as veritable saviors. No Cortes ever flashed upon a Montezuma and his hordes with more glittering refulgence. Here was the White Redeemer.

Here was the sorcerer who could exorcise the new demon, Sound. There was something pathetic in the joy with which the word-men and the tune-men from the East were welcomed. Noth-

ing was too good for them. They were, indeed, semi-deities, floating somewhere between green earth and blue-heaven. Their
profession partook of the magical.

The effect upon the songsmiths and tunesmiths was commen-
surate with the whoopee of their welcome. Fat contracts . . .
Bungalows in the Maxfield Parrish hills . . . Always they had
sung about bungalows for two, but these had been mere words,
as far from reality as Dixie from the Great White Way. (And
where is Dixie?) . . . Regular meals . . . Up with the sun
and in before midnight . . . A home, not a café . . . Instead of the canyons of New York, the hills of God's own
country . . .

When, later, rumors had been spread that Hollywood was only
another prison for the melody boys—that yonder in rainless California were the time clocks, the cells and the deadlines of Broadway's steel-and-iron canyons, Bob Crawford, president of the De
Sylva, Brown and Henderson combination, and head of the First
National Pictures, swept the idle tales aside.

"Our boys at First National have it pretty nice," he cooed. "We
give them about everything they want. They have big, beautiful
rooms to work in. There's a nice quiet atmosphere; some of the
boys have windows with a view of the mountains—just the atmosphere for the composition of melodies. Why, we even let the boys
do their work at home if they want to. We don't expect too much
from them, either. When they've done two or three songs I make
them go off on a vacation and do some fishing. I usually give them
about six weeks in which to do an assignment. They don't have
to turn anything in until three or four of those six weeks have
elapsed. Then they show what they've done and I criticize it. I'm

[303]

sort of a song doctor myself, and I make suggestions to help the tunes along."

It was patriarchal; it was idyllic. It was too good to be true.

The shoutings and the murmurs died. The magnates retired to wait for these geese to lay their golden eggs.

There is nothing new under the moon. All song is theme song. The savage who has a different song for each task, for each rite, has a specialized theme for his song, and a specialized song for his theme. The sacred books of all races recognize the power of music in shaping and giving color to destiny. What else is a lullaby? In the days when campaigns were campaigns, the political ditties of the various sides—take, as pertinent example, "Tippecanoe and Tyler, Too"—were theme songs of an unmistakable order, plugging the virtues of a favorite candidate. When Ben Bernie, with the strains of "My Buddy," inaugurated the practice of radio signatures, he was using the idea of the theme song for purposes of identification. To-day the notion seems obvious; in its time, it was a happy thought. What, in a manner of speaking, are the Wagnerian leit-motifs but theme-songlets—little cards that the singers carry about likewise for purposes of identification?

The makers of the first talkies had in their mind's ear the example of the radio. More or less unconsciously they were guided, in their earliest adaptations of sound to the screen, by the technique of the radio, just as the radio, in adapting itself to sight, or television, will be guided appreciably by the cinema. Sound, even before it meant speech to Hollywood, meant music. Hence the call to the wilds of Tin Pan Alley, and hence the immediate capitulation to the Great American Din. Everything must be set to music; everything must have its song.

Who were the racketeers of melody to say them Nay? Once songs grew out of the action in a drama; now they are grafted upon that action. The latest incarnation of the Theme Song was born of the imagined need, in every picture, of music; of the need, hardly so imaginary, of large sales for popular songs. How was Sound, the Samson of Broadway, to know that Lady Screen, the Delilah of Hollywood, one day would shear his locks? For two years, however, it would be a passionate union.

Broadway to Hollywood.

Together with the boys from Broadway was imported the song-technique of Melody Lane. Every picture had its musical background, even if that background interfered with the finer audibility of the characters in the story. The directors feared a silent sequence, as if it were a confession that sound had proved inadequate to its mighty mission. The tale unrolled upon the silver screen might not bear the remotest relationship to music. No matter. Place must be found for a musical interpolation. One never knew when—certainly not why—the heroine or hero would burst into song. These lyrical effusions happened at the most incongruous moments. What of it? Had we installed this new vocalism at such great expense to have it loaf on the lots? Give us a tune!

The directors were slowly picking up a technique for the speaking voice. In the meantime, it was the most natural thing in the world to engage upon a series of musical comedies. It was no accident that the first of these—and still, in many respects, the

[305]

TIN PAN ALLEY

best—should have been called *The Broadway Melody*. Hollywood, for the moment, had surrendered to both melody and Broadway.

The theme song, too, was conditioned by the Broadway psychology and the Broadway—the Tin Pan Alley—method of exploiting popular songs. Hits are not, or at least, until recent days were not, purely fortuitous occurrences. They are, as we have seen, planned for; they are planted in the show. They are selected in advance.

The theme song, then, was meant to be the hit of the musical film, or of the drama in which music was thrust into the tale. The earliest theme songs were often ridiculous. They were manufactured by puzzled routineers whose only device seemed to be to take the title of the picture and stick on an "I Love You." Dorothy Parker, the brilliant and ironic lyrist, was lured to Hollywood in the infancy of the theme song together with everybody else the managers could ensnare. She was set to work upon the picture *Dynamite*. Now, *Dynamite* needed a theme song about as much, in the words of the homely Yiddish saying, as a bear needs an apron. Miss Parker was no Broadway hack; the directors of the picture were no poets. It was a hopeless combination, and Miss Parker, sadder and wiser, made the grand refusal, reëmbarking for the East. But not before suggesting her title for the theme song of the picture. Let it be "Dynamite, I Love You!" she swan-sang, and was seen of Follywood no more.

The ignorance of otherwise intelligent directors in matters musical is illustrated by a sad anecdote from the sound studios. In recording a certain song the familiar device of the duet was employed, wherein the juvenile sings eight bars of the chorus and is answered by eight bars from the ingenue, and so on alternately

[306]

to the end of the refrain. But the partners could not sing in the same key; the young lead was too low, the ingenue too high. Whereupon the musical advisor suggested that the ingenue sing the whole chorus in the key best adapted to her voice, and be followed by the juvenile singing the following chorus in the key best adapted to his. The director protested. This, he insisted, would be too monotonous. "Why not," he asked, "have two pianos on the set, playing the song in the two keys and let the girl stand near her accompanist and sing her eight bars in *her* key, and the boy stand near his accompanist and sing his eight bars in *his* key?"

He doesn't know yet why it couldn't be done; and can't even understand why, even if it hadn't been impossible, only one piano would have been required.

It was a short life and a merry. The theme song reached its height with "Sonny Boy." Here, at least, the song had relevancy to the plot. It was not forced into the action. It illustrates, however, another mistake of those in authority. They forced repetition of the song until it became a weariness unto the flesh. In and out of the action it came and went, unrelentingly. The purpose was clear: to drum it into our consciousness until, at the slightest touch of memory's needle, it would play back to us like a phonograph record. For a time, too, it worked. The talkies were still new. Now, they have aged rapidly. The toy-period is past, vanished as quickly as the like period in the cinema, when only its trick aspects were exploited for an open-mouthed audience.

The theme song sang itself hoarse. There was an overproduction of musical films. The effect, on the public, whether as patrons of the talkies or as consumers of sheet music, was swift and sure.

The sales of sheet music have declined considerably. It is a moot point whether even those songs that have been pushed across the million mark by the talkie would not have done quite as well if plugged in the traditional methods of the trade.

The song "Happy Days," for example, was written originally for a picture called *Chasing Rainbows*. The picture, for one of many reasons, was held back. The song, however, was released. It was plugged over the radio especially and long before the picture opened became a pronounced hit. *Chasing Rainbows*, on the other hand, when finally it did open, proved to be a definite failure. It is questioned, even by the writer of the song, whether a great majority of the purchasers knew that the song came from a picture at all. All the mechanical media—the phonograph, the piano roll, the radio, the talkie—have made sharp inroads into the sheet music business. People buy music because they desire to have it at hand when they feel like hearing and playing it. When a song is dinned into their ears around the face of the clock, they have no need of buying the printed form. They have no need of playing it. Music has become a passive pleasure; the public is not a participant, it is a spectator, an auditor.

One other factor should not be overlooked. The nation has been passing through a financial crisis that not all the Pollyanna songs of Broadway and Filmdom can smile away. One excellent reason why people are not buying books and music is that they haven't the money.

After the Theme Song?

More: the talkies and the radio especially have shortened the life of the popular song. Time was when a hit could last through a season. It was carried by a leading vaudevillian over his circuit; it was played by the bands. This took time; it traveled leisurely through space. The talkies and the radio have abolished time and space. The radio, in a single hour, can reach more people than ever any headliner of vaudeville reached in a year. The talkie, by the system of virtually simultaneous presentation, achieves a like ubiquity. A hit in New York becomes, overnight, a hit in Los Angeles.

Together with this intensification has come a speeding-up in competition. Out with the old hit; on with the new. Fifty songs struggle for recognition where formerly there were but ten. The public is caught up by the accelerating rhythm; leisureliness has departed from its musical enjoyment, simple as that is from any esthetic standpoint, and it suffers from chronic shortness of breath. Music is no longer a pleasure; it is a race.

In Hollywood a sharp reaction has set in. The Theme Song is dead; long live its successor. The production of "musicals" has been curtailed. The lyrist and the composer are no longer the sorcerers of sound. Already the retreat to the East has begun, and Little Boy "Blues" comes back to his ancient haunts, wagging his tale behind him, singing—in the rain—a different theme song.

> Wasn't it beautiful while it lasted?
> Didn't it end too soon?

The new policy of the film producers is a frank recognition that the theme song proved a boomerang. It may forecast a similar change in the habits of musical comedy production on the stage.

"Two years back," said Max Dreyfus, President of Harms,

Inc., in a recent statement, "producers would select a theme song and bank on its success. Nine times out of ten they were wrong. Occasionally they guessed correctly, as did the Warners when they picked out 'Tip Toe Through the Tulips with Me,' the popular song by Al Dubin and Joe Burke, which, though caricatured and parodied, became the outstanding song success of the year. But even in this Vitaphone picture the public was given the choice of five songs.

"The public, to give another example, will be invited to select its theme song from *Sweet Kitty Bellairs*, . . . which features eighteen songs. One is certain to captivate the fancies of the millions. Studios and prognosticators of taste have given up guessing which fortunate song the public will adopt."

The influence of sound-pictures upon popular music has been, on the whole, distinctly for the better. There is every reason to believe that the improvement will continue at an accelerated pace. The era of groping experimentation with lyrists and tune-writers is definitely over. The musical accompaniments to the screen dialogues, selected by experienced musical directors and performed by skilful players under specially trained conductors, has, without any self-proclamative didacticism, raised the taste of the millions. In this, S. T. Rothafel ("Roxy") and Hugo Riesenfeld were pioneers. "Theodore Thomas rendered no more valuable service to music in America," asserts Deems Taylor, "than have Samuel Rothafel and Hugo Riesenfeld."

The era of wild competition in musical films has come to an end. The "musicals" of the future will be written, not by ill-prepared tinkers but by the selfsame fellows who keep the capitals of the continents in tuneful humor. What Kern and Gershwin,

Friml and Romberg, Youmans and Rodgers are to Broadway, they are becoming for Los Angeles. The adaptation of reigning stage successes, in the past, has been ruined by mistaken attempts to keep the material up to date; by clumsy and obtrusive employment of the chorus; by the ill-considered iteration of special numbers—by over-plugging, in fact. The merely photographic and phonographic reproduction of stage plays is an essentially reportorial task, usually accomplished without any subtle feeling for the special qualities of the reproducing medium. It must yield to an era of plays written specially for the sound film and produced at every point with an appreciation of the sound-film's technique. Even so will the "musical" of the near future, in its finer examples, cease to be a colored graph of sound and sight based upon a production prepared for the showhouse, and take its place as an independent form, planned especially for the sounding screen.

Words and tunes will become—as they are becoming—more sophisticated. When an institution becomes self-critical, when it begins to satirize itself, it is on the way to maturity. This has already happened in our popular songs; the tear-drainers of yesterday call forth only laughter to-day. We review our first movies, we rehear our first talkies, with a most comforting sense of superiority. Snobbery is but a point in time. It consists in being, self-congratulatingly, to-day, at the spot where the crowd will be to-morrow. Let us have patience with our inferiors. They are ourselves of yesterday.

TIN PAN ALLEY

The Alley Transformed.

The industry of popular music has undergone a revolution. It is fast succumbing to centralized control. The radio and the moving picture are acquiring Tin Pan Alley by a process of benevolent assimilation. As these agencies have, with their multiple efficiency, replaced the old-time plugger, so they are replacing the old-time music publisher.

The trend of events might have been foreseen as early as 1914. Radio, in the first flush of its success, had laid light fingers upon the catalogues of Tin Pan Alley. The publishers, nightly, heard their music being broadcast without fee to the four winds. Composers and lyrists, flattered by these attentions, suddenly considered the diminution in royalty statements. It was a problem. Would radio performances so popularize a song as to create for it a vast sale, more than sufficient to offset the disadvantages of free use? If the phonograph companies and other mechanical agencies were paying for the right to reproduce words and music, why should the radio be exempt?

Accordingly, in the year that witnessed the outbreak of the European War, The American Society of Composers, Authors and Publishers was organized by nine founders: Victor Herbert, Silvio Hein, Gustave Kerker, Louis Hirsch, Glenn Macdonough, Raymond Hubbel, George Maxwell, Jay Witmark and Nathan Burkan. Within sixteen years, during which it has firmly established the property of the author and the publisher in their copyrighted compositions, it has grown to a membership of more than six hundred American writers, and of more than fifty American music publishers.

Not only radio had been guilty of appropriating, without fee, the labors of author and publisher; circuses, dance halls, amusement houses (in the persons of their orchestras or their organists) had helped themselves to the tunes and jingles of Racket Row. The purpose of the A. S. C. A. P. became at once to enforce against these appropriators the copyright law of the nation, which, in its present form, dates back to July 1, 1909. Performing rights in musical works had been covered by previous laws since 1897; the law of July 1, 1909, reënacted these provisions.

The Society has been eminently successful in prosecuting all instances of violation. Invariably, on proving its case, it has been awarded, for each infringement of copyright, the minimum damage of $250 provided by law—this, with attorney's fees frequently added. Infringement, it is pointed out by the Society, may occur through mechanical, as well as by manual, rendition of music. Naturally, the movies and the talkies were as keenly affected as was the booming business of radio broadcasting.

With the coming of the talkie and its great dependence upon music, the situation was intensified. It might prove more feasible, and cheaper in the long run, if, instead of paying tribute to the publishers, the radio and the talkie would buy not the music but the firm itself. This is precisely what is happening.

The combinations at present in force presage the policy of the immediate future. Gigantic mergers such as the Warner Brothers Company control every possible outlet of their products—the theaters in which their pictures are shown, the houses that publish their music. Of late, there has been a movement to acquire control of phonograph and even book publishing firms.

Warners control M. Witmark & Sons, the De Sylva-Brown-Henderson organization, T. B. Harms, Remick's. Radio Music (a merger of the Radio Corporation of America and the Radio-Keith-Orpheum Circuit) controls Leo Feist and Carl Fischer. The Fox Film Company owns the Red Star Publishing Company. The firm of Robbins is a subsidiary of the Metro-Goldwyn-Mayer triumvirate. Only a few independents are left: in New York, such veterans as Harry Von Tilzer, Shapiro, Bernstein and Company, Edward B. Marks; out West, Sherman, Clay and Company, Villa Moret, Inc. The smaller music publisher, like the smaller tradesman in every other field, is being pushed to the wall. They are—as, indeed, are their masters—in the grip of economic destiny.

The tie-up of the various interests is even more complicated: most of the vaudeville and motion picture theaters, and even some radio chains are owned or controlled by the picture companies. The Radio Corporation of America links up with the National Broadcasting Company and the Keith-Orpheum houses. Fox, of course, has long had his own showhouses. Paramount, ditto; it owns also the Famous Music Company. The Metro-Goldwyn-Mayer merger controls the Loew circuit. The Warner Brothers are now installing a coast-to-coast radio chain of 150 stations.

The composer, like his publisher, faces an octopod monopoly. If he expects his songs to be plugged by the new agencies of publicity he will have to join those agencies. Already, indeed, with Hollywood singing Bye, Bye, Theme Song, the unaffiliated writers are being slowly squeezed out of the popular studios. They are turning, in self-defense, to the concoction of so-called (and most humorously called) semi-classics—a bastard product that usually inherits the worst qualities of both parents. Competition in this field is low, and there is greater opportunity—so runs the theory —for the independent.

"If a non-theme writer wants exploitation," declares one of the foremost independent publishers of the West, "he will be forced to publish through Sound publishers, if these monopolies exercise their power. It is not a pretty picture for the non-theme publishers of to-day, nor the non-theme writers of to-day. . . . One thing is certain, I think. The Sound publishers that have entered the publishing field have found the returns most discouraging. They have to do something besides theming a song to make it sell. They, no doubt, were under the impression that all they had to do was put a song in a picture and it had to be a hit. Well, hits are in the writing, not alone in exploitation. To-day the Public, that merry old judge, is song-and-show-wise. People won't be knocked off the seats any longer, nor will they tear up the furniture, over any old song or any old picture. When they like a number they will buy it, as in the case of the 'Maine College Stein Song,' 'Springtime in the Rockies,' and so on, which were both absolutely made over the radio. But will this Air Route eventually be closed to competition, or will the radio companies remain neutral and fair? That's the big question now, as I see it."

Just what the radio and the talkies have done to the popular music trades remains, in its totality, to be seen. Mr. Charles B. Daniels (Neil Moret, composer of the once ubiquitous "Hiawatha") sums up in the preceding paragraph one important phase of a situation that is changing even as one writes. Radio and the talkie, it would appear, make some songs and break others. When, five years ago, radio assumed intercontinental importance, its immediate effect upon the song-publishers was such that the House of

Witmark closed up twenty-two branch offices throughout the country, and reduced its professional studios from fifteen to three. Then came the talkies as a kind Samaritan, and the Witmark offices grew to double their original number. Twelve thousand show houses with an audience of some thirty millions mean a vast potential army of buyers.

A peculiar effect of the radio has been the popularization, among the inhabitants of the hinterlands themselves, of the old hill-billy songs and of ancient Tin Pan Alley stuff in general. Several Eastern publishers have told me that orders for these numbers, once considered dead and deeply buried, are on the increase. If, on the one hand, the radio slays new songs prematurely, it restores life to the old. There is no death. . . .

Again, if the talkies have plugged the theme song almost out of existence, they have opened, nevertheless, an avenue of publicity that has by no means reached the end of its possibilities. The summer of 1930 was a sad season in Tin Pan Alley. Sales of sheet music had sunk to something like 75 percent below normal, with a slight rise beginning toward autumn. Yet one of the leading firms of to-day rose to its present fortunes through association, exclusively, with the talkies. The success of the Robbins Music Corporation rounds out, for the present, the story of Tin Pan Alley.

It is considered the foremost publisher of talking-picture music, having become affiliated, in a subsidiary capacity, with the Metro-Goldwyn-Mayer organization in 1929. It is not more than five years old, although the corporations out of which it grew have been in business for almost twenty-five years. It was about fifteen years ago that Maurice Richmond, founder of Maurice Richmond, Inc., took his nephew, Jack Robbins, into the business. A few years later, Robbins was appointed General Manager of the enterprise, and his accession to power was signalized by Lee Roberts' "Smiles"—one of the biggest hits of the war period. Other hits, "Tell Me," by Max Kortlander, recording manager of the Q. R. S. Music Roll Company, and "La Veeda," a widely popular dance tune, followed. Robbins, a born plugger, went after the bands, even as the earlier pluggers had gone after the actors. He did much to establish this method of plugging.

He is considered, indeed, as being largely responsible for the success of Paul Whiteman, Vincent Lopez and George Olsen. Whiteman he is said to have discovered in Atlantic City. By his insistence he brought Whiteman to the attention of the Victor phonograph company, compelling several executives to come to the resort and listen to the band. Olsen he knew as a drummer in California and urged him to come East. He aided him in organizing an orchestra and introduced him to influential showfolk who gave him his first opportunity. It was Robbins, again, who discovered Vincent Lopez in the old Peking Restaurant on Broadway, recognized the man's promise, and sponsored his first orchestra.

Ten years ago the firm name was changed to Richmond-Robbins, with offices at 1658 Broadway. Maurice Richmond, one of the pioneer jobbers in the business, withdrew from publishing about seven years ago to devote his time to jobbing alone; he has since become the leading distributor of music in the country.

Since its linking up with Metro-Goldwyn-Mayer, the Robbins Music Corporation has had—at a rough estimate—more than half the hits of the nation. (A few titles: "You Were Meant for Me," "Broadway Melody" and "Love Boat," from the picture, *The*

Broadway Melody; "Pagan Love Song," from *The Pagan;* "Singing in the Rain," from *The Hollywood Revue;* "Should I," from *Lord Byron on Broadway.*)

The percentage of "flops" in picture songs has been so high that the music dealer has become wary of them. He favors the "popular song," by which is meant the non-picture, free-lance publication. There are signs, indeed, that the popular song, thus interpreted, is coming back to its own. The music business, as the old-timers begin to remember, and to proclaim anew, belongs after all to the men who know the music trades.

We shall hear what we shall hear.

After Jazz.

In the meantime, elegies are being sung to jazz. It is through, we are told in the same voice that once announced the death of the ballad and of the waltz. What has happened, however, is more like this: jazz has been absorbed; the democratization of music, moreover, has resuscitated old forms; the need of contrast, within the structure of a single art-form, or among the forms themselves, is a physiological as well as a psychological necessity. "Give us something new," is the eternal cry. And when we get it, we go at it hard until the new seems old and the old, slyly returning, seems new again.

Meantime, another strange development has appeared. The movies early gave a new significance to the phrase, "in person." The visit of a star to the local theater brought a new, and but an imperfectly recognized, thrill. The closer the talkies came to producing the illusion of reality, with color effects and suggestions

[318]

of the missing dimension, the subtler yet the more certain became the desire of the public—for many of which the theater had never been a reality—to behold the actor in the flesh. With the coming of sound to sight, human presence in the pit and on the stage suffered a tremendous setback. Organists, orchestras, stage bands, vocalists, were summarily dismissed. Now, however, it seems that, through the increasing illusion perfected by the screen, it has nurtured a rising demand for the flesh and blood that it has sought to replace.

There is a return, likewise, to the old style of plugging upon the stage, through flesh-and-blood singers. It has been discovered that even the talkie "shorts" that feature old songs and new create a fresh demand for the songs thus advertised. Publishers, with the advent of the talkies, allowed stage acts to languish in neglect; now they are coming back to the methods that were in vogue at the height of the plugging era.

The world is round, and Life is a circle. . . .

12. Codetta

TIN PAN ALLEY is forty years old. Beginning as a musical zone of New York City it blazed a trail along Broadway in close pursuit of the theater. The moving picture did not destroy it; the radio poured new life into its veins; the talkies adopted it, until they found that the child was endangering its foster parents; the coming of television can have no adverse effect upon this singing fool; if anything, the contrary.

Once a lane in Gotham, the Alley now reaches across the continent from the Great White Way to Hollywood. Triumphantly it rides the air waves upon every point of the compass. Styles in music and styles in words may come and go, but the humble song of the people lives on forever.

The Alley is an industry, tainted by commercialism and insincerity. So be it. In this respect it differs not a jot or tittle from other industries the world over, and least of all from the self-styled non-commercial music publishing firms. And one thing the Alley achieves that has yet to be paralleled by the humorless "art" song of the conservatories: it manages, stammeringly yet at times inimitably, to speak the yearnings, the sorrows and the joys of a new, an emergent folk, different from any other people in the world; and it is most gratefully accepted by that folk in the one true way that song may be accepted: it is sung. Tin Pan Alley, in brief, has cradled a new folk song, a song of the city, synthetic in facture, as short-lived as a breath, yet not for these reasons any the less authentic. The ancient folk song, in the slow course of its evolution, was not sung by as many throats in a hundred years as is the urban folk song of to-day in a single week. Time and space, by modern invention, have been conquered, telescoped into the magic of an instant. The very concept of the folk has of necessity been altered by the whir of machinery and the accelerated tempo of contemporary life.

The range of Tin Pan Alley is narrow, shallow. True enough. Yet, whoever would know the real philosophy of the multitude— its aims and aspirations, its simple notions of hell, purgatory and paradise, needs but make a journey through this most undivine comedy.

The song of Tin Pan Alley, unlike our more pretentious "art" song, establishes a vital circuit with the life out of which it arises. That "art" song, it should not be necessary to insist, belongs in the selfsame category with the "commercial" song, and is often bettered by it. Here, in the Alley, is something that has a life of its own—something that speaks of and for a considerable portion of our new America, even as our hymns—most of them so inferior to the better Tin Pan Alley tunes, and even more sterile than they in a structural sense—speak for another sector of America.

The Alley did not and does not destroy good taste. It is a complement, not a competitor, of major music. For, just as there is minor poetry, so may there be minor music.

Ballads, as the Alley knows them, we still have with us and ever shall. Yet the sterile morality of the old sentimental song (and it is just as sterile in the abomination known as the "semi-classic") has perhaps been relegated for good to a secondary or tertiary place in our popular music. It was early absorbed by the Movies, which seemingly were sent into the world to rescue from merited death all the stupidities of song and stage. Vaudeville, melodrama, detective fiction . . . resurrected by celluloid.

It is all the more amazing, then, that the synthetic folk song of Tin Pan Alley, within the short period of four decades, should have produced two movements—in reality one—that rose to the status of international importance. Ragtime and jazz, for the past quarter of a century, have affected not deeply but indubitably the symphonic composers of America and Europe. While our academicians were debating about the qualities of a truly American music, the thing they scorned and unconsciously feared was rising from the musical slums of the nation, from the poundings of our Tin Bohemia. Nor was the Americanism of ragtime and jazz a self-conscious product. Seeking to capture, for profit, the ear and heart of the American public, these jongleurs were compelled to interpret that public—to speak for it, sing for it, recreate it in terms of its own lingo and tune.

So doing, they created a product that, upon its own scale, was the more vigorously esthetic for being unconsciously so. Not any individual product, so much as the movement itself, was important. Already we have a rich body of simple song that awaits incorporation into higher forms that may evolve from that selfsame material. This, indeed, is the great esthetic problem that awaits the American composer, who must be first of all not an American but a musician. Our popular music need not be, for such a pioneer, everything; it may be an element in a unity that absorbs it perhaps beyond the possibility of ready recognition. The history of symphonic music—of all music, in fact—supports such a prognosis. The true significance of George Gershwin is not that he achieved this goal, but that, originating in Tin Pan Alley, he made the great transition.

He has followers, not only in style but in aspiration. Ray Henderson, of the remarkably successful De Sylva, Brown and Henderson combination, may some day surprise his playmates with a Concerto that has been brewing in his mind for many a moon. His tunes for such hits as *Good News, Follow Thru, Hold Everything* and *Flying High* are replete with pleasant excursions from routine. In the last-named musical comedy, the song "Without Love" was an interesting experiment in liberation from the chorus-formula. Instead of the regular sixteen bars it had twenty-one. Such things as these, in Tin Pan Alley, amount to a revolution. What, at its height, was jazz, if not a mad dash for liberty from the prison of routine,—routine rhythms, routine tunes, routine harmonies, routine instrumentation, and most of all, routine living?

Kay Swift and Paul James contributed to the second edition of the *Garrick Gaieties* an admirable moment of satire in the Gilbert-and-Sullivanesque "Johnny Wanamaker." Their "Can't We Be Friends" introduced, through the first *Little Show*, a pair that in *Fine and Dandy* suggest interesting potentialities for our better musical comedy. La Swift's music has breeding. She, too, leads the double life—musically speaking—of the Gershwins and the Hendersons, one eye on the showhouse and the other on the concert hall, with string quartets burgeoning in leisure hours.

Newest of recruits to our popular music, and to the Jekyll-and-Hyde club of Tin Pan Alley, is Vladimir Dukelsky. As Vernon Duke, he writes the scores of musical plays and such tunes as "I

Am Only Human After All," evidencing a remarkable faculty of adaptation to our native musical idiom. Under his own name he creates symphonies, sonatas, ballets and operas that find their way to the sacrosanct auditoriums of Europe and America.

I do not regard the later Gershwin and the post-Gershwinians as belonging wholly to Tin Pan Alley. Such personalities as Irving Berlin and Walter Donaldson, evolving hit after hit out of a meager technical acquaintance with music and prosody, are more in the tradition. Let us not ask of the Alley what it cannot, in the nature of things, supply: sustained inspiration, the endurance to write organic scores. Yet let us rejoice when the Gershwins and Kaufman, when Rodgers and Hart, when Swift and James, or Cole Porter, suggest the emergence of a national operetta in tune with the times, and when gradually they begin the long ascent from the melodious underworld of music.

There is nothing, in the popular song of any other nation during the past forty years, that equals the vitality of Tin Pan Alley. It has made a genuine contribution to the raw material of music. What Charlie has been to the movie; what our comic strip has been to the gay arts; what the skyscraper has been to architecture —this Tin Pan Alley has been to the minor music of the continents. To the blaring pandemonium of the circus, to the crude caricature of the minstrel show, we must add as a distinctly American contribution the less and less accidental beauty—if at times a crude and uncouth beauty—of the Tin Pan Alley song.

Acknowledgments

THIS is an unpretentious pioneer work that could not have been written without the generous coöperation of those who founded Tin Pan Alley. It suffers, no doubt, from the shortcomings of all pioneer efforts; I trust, however, that it lays down at least a pattern of development that may, with further investigation and the accumulation of data, take on something like a definitive shape. For this reason I should be glad to receive from qualified readers, in care of the publishers, anything in the nature of illuminative or corrective comment: significant anecdotes, historical addenda pertaining either to important figures or to outstanding firms and their publications,—whatever, in fact, may help in a future edition to make the book more authentic and more representative.

I have not tried to write an orthodox history. Neither has it been my intention to storify songs, writers or publishers. For such purposes there are already in print a number of gay and gaudy books, led by the singing shelf of Sigmund Spaeth; more are promised. What I have attempted is to indicate strands of interest and to suggest the design into which—as warp and woof across the loom of our national background—they may be woven.

Much of the account was not to be exhumed out of books or other cemeteries of print, so that this, far from being a book made out of other books, is largely a book made of human beings. My indebtedness to the chief personages of Tin Pan Alley, old and

[326]

ACKNOWLEDGMENTS

new, is paid throughout the text. Not the least pleasant aspect of the labor was the opportunity of holding long and fascinating conversations with old-timers and new-timers. To name them all, as well as numerous correspondents on the Western coast, would be to fill several pages. May they be content with this expression of gratitude, as sincere as it must, so far as concerns individuals, remain unspecified. For matters of opinion, of course, I alone am responsible. As to matters of fact, not being among those who confuse originality with a neglect to acknowledge one's sources, I have tried scrupulously to indicate them.

Material here used has in several instances appeared before, particularly in the columns of *The American Mercury* and the Haldeman-Julius publications; it has been revised for the special purposes of the book.

I owe much to two friends: Gerald B. Guise and John McCauley. Mr. Guise gave me access to his large collection of popular music and permitted me to make use of data upon ragtime; Mr. Mc-Cauley was of invaluable assistance in interviewing and in intelligent research that here and there fairly amounted to collaboration.

ISAAC GOLDBERG.

Roxbury, Massachusetts
1930.

Index

INDEX

Evans, "Honey," 49, 120
Every Month, 121

Fagan, Barney, 48
Fall of a Nation, The, 184
Famous Music Co., 314
Feist, Leo, 131, 169, 206, 314
Ferguson and Mack, 4, 50, 52
Fields, Dorothy, 99, 232
Finck, Harry T., 194, 195
First National Pictures, 303
Firth, Son and Co., 108
Fischer, Carl, 314
Fisher, A. J., 108
Fisher, Fred, 105
Foerster, Therese, 186
Ford, James L., 62
Forrest, Edward, 36
Fortune Teller, The, 186, 187, 192, 222
Forty-five Minutes from Broadway, 237
Foster, Stephen Collins, 43-46, 139
Four Cohans, The, 103
Fox Film Co., 314
Foy, Eddie, 65, 248
Francis, DeSylva Arthur. (*See* Ira Gershwin)
Frankenthaler, 131
Freed, 218, 228
Friml, Rudolf, 119, 255, 257, 311
Fuller, Loie, 237

Garrick Theatre. (*See* Harrigan's Theatre)
Gaunt, Percy, 96
Gauthier, Eva, 255
George Washington, Jr., 237
German Brothers, 230
Gershwin, George, 119, 172, 190, 203, 218, 240, 255-258, 275, 294, 310, 323, 324
Gershwin, Ira, 232, 255
Gilbert, Henry F., 16
Gilbert, L. Wolfe, 105, 247, 248
Gilbert, Mr., 115
Gilbert & Sullivan, 66, 67, 188, 221
Gillespie, Arthur, 48
Gillespie, Marion, 99
Gilmore, Buddy, 288
Gilson, Lottie, 110, 170
Girl from Utah, The, 258
Golden, John, 119
Gondoliers, The, 221, 275
Goodrich, W. J., 223
Goodwin, Nat, 65, 91
Gottschalk, 87
Governor's Son, The, 237
Graupner, Gottlieb, 36
Gray, William, 75

Grofé, Frederick, 255, 294
Gruenberg, 268
Guise, Gerald B., 326

Hack and Anderson, 105
Hadley, Henry K., 16, 223
Hale, Philip, 56
Hall, Frank, 49
Hallan, Lewis, 35
Ham Fat, 38, 39
Handy, William C., 64, 141, 142, 146, 241-247, 269
Harbach and Hirsch, 238
Harding, 108, 110
Harley, 50, 52
Harms, T. B., Co., 108, 120, 309, 314
Harney, Ben, 147-149
Harrigan, Edward. (*See* Harrigan and Hart)
Harrigan and Hart, 59, 66-77, 110
Harrigan's Theatre, 78
Harris, Billy, 51
Harris, Charles K., 90-95, 105, 109, 176, 224, 298
Harrold, Orville, 192
Hart, 71, 72-77
Hart, Lorenz, 232
Haverley's Mastodons, 47, 48, 49, 50, 51
Haviland, Howley and, 108, 109, 112, 118-122, 175, 176
Haviland, F. B., Co., 113, 175
Hein, Silvio, 312
Heiser, F. (*See* M. H. Rosenfeld)
Heller, Hermann, 287
Henderson, Ray, 323
Henlet, Martin W., 74
Henry, O., 95, 230
Herbert, "Pig-Pie," 36
Herbert, Victor, 17, 79, 83, 124, 178, 181-196, 222-224, 302, 312
Hickman, Art, 288
Hillman, 158
Himan, Alberto. (*See* Berti)
Hindemith, 266
Hirsch, Louis A., 143, 312
Hitchcock, B. W., 108
Hoffman, Max, 146
Hogan, Ernest, 146, 150, 153, 156, 157, 248
Holland, Alfred, 52
Holmes, D. S., 113
Honneger, 266
Hooker, Bryant, 255
Hooley and Rice, 50, 51, 52
Hootchy Kootchy, 102, 103, 161
Hopkinson, Frederick, 19
Horowitz, Charles, 91
Howard, 49, 50

[331]

INDEX

McAuley, George W., 52
McBride, Mary Margaret, 269
McCauley, John, 326
McDowell, 16
McFadden, Clarence, 83
McGlennon, Felix, 136
McKinley, Mabel, 99
McPherson, 158
Memphis Students, The, 165, 288
Merry Malones, The, 238
Metro-Goldwyn-Mayer, 314-316
Metz, Theodore, 114, 159-166, 167
Milhaud, Darius, 266
Miller, Harry S., 105
Miller and Lyles, 56
Mills, F. A., 247, 248
Mills, Kerry, 149-174
Minstrelsy, 34-38
Minstrels:
  Arlington's, 72
  Backus's, 54
  Barlow, Wilson, Primrose and West, 49
  Buckley's, 58
  Callendar, 53
  Campbell's, 70
  Christy's, 41, 58, 85
  Dan Bryant's, 58
  Female, 53
  Haverly's, 85
  Mahara Colored, 243
  Manning's, 71
  Ordway, 43
  Plantation, 34
  Pony Moore's, 73
  San Francisco, 53, 58
  Taylor's, 54
  Virginia, 41
  Wood's, 58
Mlle. Modiste, 186, 192
Monaco, Jimmy, 105
Monteverde, 282
Moore, Flora, 115
Moret, Neil, 298, 315
Morris, Pell and Trowbridge, 58
Morris, William, 248
Morse, Dolly, 99
Morse, Theodore, 175, 176, 222
Morton, Richard, 115
Motherwell, Hiram K., 251-253
Motion Pictures, 297-308
Muir, Lewis F., 247
Mulcahey, Jim, 244
Mulcahey Twins, The, 71
Mulligan cycle, 73, 74-77
Mulligan Guards, The, 75
Mulligan Guards Ball, The, 74, 80
Mulligan Guards' Christmas, The, 80
Mulligan Guards Nominee, The, 76-80

Mulligans' Chowder, The, 76
Mulligans' Surprise, The, 76
Music Box, 256
Music Publishers Protective Association, 206
Musical Courier, 222-223
My Wild Irish Rose, 124

National Broadcasting Co., 314
National Music Teachers' Assn., 234
Natoma, 17, 184, 188
Naughty Marietta, 192
Negro, Influence of the, 20, 31-34, 268
Nevin, 218
New England Psalm Singer, The, 19
New York Clipper, 105, 135, 270
New York World, 97
Newman, Ernest, 264, 283, 285
Nichols, 218
Nichols, George, 37
Nicodemus Johnson, 59
Nielson, Alice, 187
Nielson, Francis, 192
Niles, Abbe, 277-278
Nonpareils, The, 72
Nugent, Maude, 98, 136

O'Brien, Alec, 71
O'Brien Girl, The, 238
Octoroons, The, 153
Oh, Boy!, 257
Oh, Kay!, 276
Olcott, Chauncey, 52, 124
Old Lavender, 77, 80
Orchestras, 53, 287-290
Oriental America, 153
Oroonoko, 36
Osgood, Henry O., 269, 276, 285
Our Nell, 255
Owen, Anita, 98

Pace, Harry H., 245
Paddock, The, 35
Palmer and Ward, 96
Parade, 266
Paramount, 314
Parin, Arthur, 124
Parker and Ring, 43
Parker, Dorothy, 306
Pastor, Tony, 51, 60-65, 125, 172
Pelham, Dick, 40
Pell and Trowbridge, 58
Perlet, Herman, 223
Perrin, 158
Peter Ibbetson, 16
Petrie, 174
Philadelphia Ledger, The, 18
Piantadosi, Al, 105, 161, 172

[333]

INDEX

[335]

TIN PAN ALLEY

INDEX

INDEX

[339]

INDEX

THE

JOHN DAY

COMPANY
INC.